Voluntarism, Planning, and the State

Recent Titles in
Contributions in American History
Series Editor: Jon L. Wakelyn

The Antislavery Rank and File: A Social Profile of the Abolitionists' Constituency
Edward Magdol

The Paradox of Professionalism: Reform and Public Service in Urban America, 1900–1940
Don S. Kirschner

American Frontier and Western Issues: A Historiographical Review
Roger L. Nichols, editor

Continuity and Change in Electoral Politics, 1893–1928
Paul Kleppner

Arms at Rest: Peacemaking and Peacekeeping in American History
Joan R. Challinor and Robert L. Beisner, editors

Close Neighbors, Distant Friends: United States–Central American Relations
John E. Findling

American Urbanism: A Historiographical Review
Howard Gillette, Jr., and Zane L. Miller, editors

The South Is Another Land: Essays on the Twentieth-Century South
Bruce L. Clayton and John A. Salmond, editors

A State Divided: Opposition in Pennsylvania to the American Revolution
Anne M. Ousterhout

The Collapse of the Middle Way: Senate Republicans and the Bipartisan Foreign Policy, 1948–1952
David R. Kepley

Developing Dixie: Modernization in a Traditional Society
Winifred B. Moore, Jr., Joseph F. Tripp, an Lyon G. Tyler, Jr., editors

Shades of the Sunbelt: Essays on Ethnicity, Race, and the Urban South
Randall M. Miller and George E. Pozzetta, editors

Keepers of Our Past: Local Historical Writing in the United States, 1820s–1930s
David J. Russo

VOLUNTARISM, PLANNING, AND THE STATE

The American Planning Experience, 1914–1946

Edited by JEROLD E. BROWN
and PATRICK D. REAGAN

Foreword by ELLIS W. HAWLEY

CONTRIBUTIONS IN AMERICAN HISTORY, NUMBER 130

GREENWOOD PRESS
New York • Westport, Connecticut • London

Library of Congress Cataloging-in-Publication Data

Voluntarism, planning, and the state : the American planning experience, 1914–1946 / edited by Jerold E. Brown and Patrick D. Reagan : foreword by Ellis W. Hawley.
p. cm.—(Contributions in American history, ISSN 0084–9219 no. 130)
Bibliography: p.
Includes index.
ISBN 0–313–26177–6
1. Political planning—United States—History—20th century.
I. Brown, Jerold E. II. Reagan, Patrick D., 1953– . III. Series.
JK421.V62 1988
350.007'2'0973—dc19 88–15462

British Library Cataloguing in Publication Data is available.

Library of Congress Catalog Card Number: 88–15462
ISBN: 0–313–26177–6
ISSN: 0084–9219

First published in 1988

Greenwood Press, Inc.
88 Post Road West, Westport, Connecticut 06881

Printed in the United States of America

The paper used in this book complies with the Permanent Paper Standard issued by the National Information Standards Organization (Z39.48–1984).

10 9 8 7 6 5 4 3 2 1

Copyright Acknowledgments

The following publishers have generously given permission to use previously published material:

From *The Crisis of the Old Order* by Arthur Schlesinger, Jr. Copyright © 1957 by Arthur M. Schlesinger, Jr. Reprinted by permission of Houghton Mifflin Company.

From *Labor and the New Deal*, ed. Milton Derber and Edwin Young (Madison: The University of Wisconsin Press; © 1957, renewed 1985 by the Board of Regents of the University of Wisconsin System), page 167. Reprinted by permission of the University of Wisconsin Press.

From *The Limits of Legitimacy: Political Contradictions of Contemporary Capitalism* by Alan Wolfe. Copyright © 1977 by the Free Press, a Division of Macmillan, Inc. Reprinted by permission of Macmillan Publishing Company.

From *The Recovery Problem in the United States*, copyright © 1936 by The Brookings Institution. Reprinted by permission of the publisher.

From *The Battle of Democracy* by Rexford Tugwell. Copyright © 1935 by Rexford Tugwell. Reprinted by permission of Columbia University Press.

From *The New Deal: Analysis and Interpretation*, ed. Alonzo Hamby, copyright © 1981; *Central Planning for the Market Economy: An Analysis of The French Theory and Experience* by Vera Lutz, copyright © 1969. Reprinted by permission of Longman, Inc.

From *The New Deal and the Problem of Monopoly* by Ellis W. Hawley. Copyright © 1965 by Princeton Univeristy Press. Reprinted by permission.

Contents

Tables

Foreword

Ellis W. Hawley

Through much of their history, the American people have sought to order their society through the workings of markets, associations, community structures, and a government of parties, courts, and subnational units. This was particularly true of the nineteenth century, and in the twentieth century much of this traditional ordering apparatus has remained intact. America has been slow to develop either a national administrative state or a formalized system of corporatist coordination; and, as a variety of recent studies have pointed out, it has ended up with a disorderly complex of administrative units functioning more as interest groups or market operators than as integral parts of a coherent system of national administration.

This is not to say, however, that the United States has been a land unaffected by bureaucratic ideals and bureaucratizing impulses. To a degree, modern America has shared in the revulsion against market-determined social outputs, partisan politics, and legalistic constitutionalism that helped bureaucratic elites to acquire power in other nations. And one of the major changes in its ordering apparatus over the last hundred years has been the addition of an administrative component operating within and sometimes at odds with the older coordinative framework. Appearing first in the large business firm, such a component subsequently became an important feature of the twentieth century's new associationalism, of reformed municipal governments, of state governments to which new coordinative duties were being entrusted, and of the enlarged national government emerging from periods of crisis, reform, and modernization. Despite the persistence of antibureaucratic attitudes and traditions, Americans have created and become enmeshed in a wide variety of modern bureaucratic structures.

As a part of this administrative component, moreover, a land reluctant to establish a central planning agency and supportive institutions has found institutional room for a variety of planning agencies engaged in making informed and presumably scientific plans for the rational exercise of administrative power. Again large business firms and new municipal governments modeled after them led the way. Each became users of a new planning expertise, founders of new planning units, fashioners of new occupational roles supporting the rise of new planning professions, and places where new planning assignments could be accommodated to existing power and value structures. And again, as in the case of administrative coordination in general, counterparts to this kind of activity subsequently appeared elsewhere, notably in the new associational, educational, military, diplomatic, resource management, and social service agencies that became parts of the nation's altered ordering apparatus. If the sphere within which a growing array of planners did their work remained limited and constrained, the demand for such work became an expanding one; and institutional formation followed patterns that gave the nation more and more planning specialists valued for their credentialed capacity to link administrative goals, knowledge, and resources in coherent designs for action.

Partly because of this development, too, twentieth-century America has not been a land entirely hostile to the idea and practice of national planning. In times of perceived national emergency or crisis, it has proceeded to erect temporary agencies charged with this task. In times of reformist agitation, it has considered reform prescriptions calling for a new administrative state with planning capabilities, particularly when these were presented as building upon and utilizing its previous accumulation of planning agencies, professions, and experience. And from the early twentieth century on, it has been the home of numerous schemes for reconciling a persisting anti-statism with the acquisition of national planning capabilities, schemes that in essence would entrust the making and implementation of national plans to enlightened forms of private power or to a system of extragovernmental councils and associations designed to give a liberal social order the capacity to plan. If the United States has yet to develop formal institutions for national planning, either of the statist or the corporatist variety, it has experienced important efforts to do this and its national record is littered with numerous instances where groups and institutions arising for other purposes have been informally entrusted with national planning assignments.

Planning in America, then, does have a history going well beyond the interest that certain planning specialists have shown in the origins and development of their professions. It is a history that encompasses both the emergence of planning specialities and agencies within the nation's administrative structures and the impulses toward, resistance to, and efforts to erect social and political machinery that would give the nation as a whole a planning capacity. It is also a history that has been intricately interwoven with the story of clashing value systems in American culture, especially the clashes between individualism and community, democracy and efficiency, entrepreneurship and managerialism, expertise and anti-intellectualism. And it is a history that has been connected in significant ways and at significant points with the political, intellectual, and societal formations generally stressed in accounts of the making of modern America.

Such a history, it would seem, might be well worth recovering. A fuller knowledge and understanding of it could presumably add important new dimensions not only to our understanding of organizational and administrative development in the American context but also to current understandings of what has taken place in the cultural sphere, political practice, and social relationships. Yet it is a history that so far has remained relatively unexplored and unstudied. In the writing of twentieth-century American history, the nation's industrial magnates, political reformers and standpatters, organization builders and resisters, and socially disadvantaged and deprived have all had their chroniclers. But only a beginning has been made toward recovering and making sense of that portion of the historical record created by the emergence and usage of planning expertise and by the accompanying search for institutional and cultural formations that would give a liberal society and polity the planning capacities regarded as necessary for continued progress.

In a 1983 application to the National Endowment for the Humanities, Professor Lawrence Gelfand and I pointed to this state of affairs in regard to the history of planning in America and proposed a Summer Seminar for College Teachers that would use materials in the Iowa City area to study aspects of planning during the period from World War I through World War II. Funding was forthcoming; and in the summer of 1984 we assembled an able group of historians and political scientists who produced a series of thoughtful papers illuminating the work of those entrusted with planning assignments or seeking to develop appropriate planning capacities, and took part in lively discussions focused on the meaning of the historical experience that had been and was being recovered. The seminar, we felt, showed that the history of planning in America was indeed worth recovering and that study of it could be exciting and fruitful.

Some of the scholarship produced or begun in the seminar has since been published elsewhere. This collection makes more of it available, as well as some of the other work done by seminar participants. The essays printed here do not and were never intended to constitute a comprehensive history of the American experience with planning between 1914 and 1946. Nor are they essays that advance or were ever intended to advance one particular thesis concerning the meaning and larger implications of that experience. What they do provide, as the title indicates, is differing perspectives on a common subject, perspectives that arise from researching particular aspects of it in depth, subjecting these to close scrutiny, and seeking to make sense of the results. The essays stand as the products of early forays into promising territory. As such they add to our knowledge and understanding of it in ways that reveal important features and suggestive detail and should stimulate further research and study.

More specifically, the essays illuminate both the workings of particular agencies and groups engaged in carrying out planning assignments or trying to develop new planning capacities and the broader structural, institutional, and cultural contexts that facilitated some types of planning, thwarted other types, and thus helped to shape a distinctively American usage of planning expertise. The collection begins with an essay on the changing efforts of the American Association for Labor Legislation to equip the nation with a capacity for employment planning. It proceeds through essays illuminating the workings and legacies of the Industrial Conferences of 1919–1920, the President's Aircraft Board in 1925, and the planning machinery set up to implement the military aviation program authorized in 1926. It then moves to essays shedding new light on the planning operations and impulses of the New Deal period, one showing the connections between organizational developments in the 1910s and 1920s and the composition and approach of the New Deal's national planning agency, the other showing how the quest for new planning capacities undertaken under the aegis of the National Recovery Administration became tied to the expansion of administrative law and shifted directions in 1934 and 1935. The collection closes with an essay illuminating and analyzing the post–World War II reaction against economic planning as manifested in the debate over extension of the Office of Price Administration.

For those interested in recovering and understanding the history of planning in twentieth-century America, a history that appears more and more worth recovering and understanding, the essays that follow are a welcome addition to a growing body of relevant literature.

Preface

Patrick D. Reagan and Jerold E. Brown

For more than half a century, scholars have recognized the importance of planning in modern states. This intellectual recognition, however, has stemmed from the historical experiences of the Soviet Union, Fascist Italy, Nazi Germany, and post–World War II experiments in Great Britain, France, and Japan. More recently scholars have paid attention to cross-national perspectives on planning. But rarely do they associate "planning" with an ongoing process inside the United States of America. Historians and most other scholars have assumed that planning has involved a process of centralized control of the economy and society from above by ruling elites acting within the realm of the public sector, that is, the state. As such planning has been viewed as antithetical to laissez-faire, free-market capitalism, and, therefore, incongruous with the American experience.

Yet planning in America does have a history. Since the publication of Otis L. Graham, Jr.'s *Toward a Planned Society: From Roosevelt to Nixon* (1976), planning in the United States increasingly has attracted the attention of historians, political scientists, economists, public policy specialists, and practicing planners. The essays in this volume attempt to clarify just how central the planning experience from the Progressive Era through the end of World War II has been in marking the emergence of modern America. The American planning experience has involved more than an attempt to impose centralized state authority in economic decision making as Marxists and practitioners of the "corporate liberal" interpretation of the American political economy often have argued. As these essays emphasize, planning in the United States took diverse forms to deal with a wide variety of issues including unemployment, labor relations, industrial and economic development, national defense, and wartime price controls. In providing detailed narrative case studies in American planning that existing literature on the subject overlooks, this volume attempts to show the widespread use of planning from an American perspective. These essays demonstrate the broad perspectives from which scholars can approach the subject and suggest their ongoing applicability to the planning process in the future.

Historians of twentieth-century America will find the essays particularly useful in understanding the emergence of the organizational society. While Marxist scholars might take issue with the interpretations presented here, the contributors of these essays hold no one brief for the secret of unraveling the complexities of the American planning experience. Scholars of the "organizational school" of modern American history such as Samuel P. Hays, Robert H. Wiebe, Alfred D. Chandler, Jr., Louis Galambos, Ellis W. Hawley, and others have begun to identify key issues and time periods which have parallels in planning history. Progressive reformers attached great significance to the ideology of efficiency and scientific management. Prewar domestic reform efforts carried over into the wartime mobilization experience of 1917–1918. Events immediately after the Great War helped in shaping the institutional life of the 1920s. Voluntary efforts in institutional life during the 1920s were central in building what Ellis W. Hawley has termed "the associative state" during the New Era. There were continuities in public policy efforts from the New Era to the New Deal. National mobilization during World War II not only effected changes in national economic policies, but also public perception of those policies.

Political scientists and economists traditionally have paid attention to the formative role of the state in developing policies that effect matters in both the public and the private sector. Recent studies such as Stephen Skowronek's *Building a New American State* (1982) address the issue of the growing importance of building national administrative capacities so as to modernize the state structure in light of political, economic, and social changes in the late nineteenth century. Whether the United States has been able to develop these sorts of capacities is a question under some debate in recent years. Due to its national tradition of voluntary association noted ever since Alexis de Tocqueville's classic *Democracy in America* (1835), the United States has had to wrestle with the contradiction of developing modern institutional structures through the state while preserving its historic resistance to centralized state authority. Voluntarist-oriented planning mechanisms seem to have played a larger role in the United States than in other countries. These case studies of American planning should spark further debate on whether the American experience has been unique or merely one variation in a continuous spectrum of planning alternatives in part dependent upon differences in the historical experience of various nations.

Practicing planners and public policy analysts often assume that a given plan is either a blueprint for perfection or an invitation to disaster. For those who have the daily responsibility to plan and to implement those plans for the future, these case studies show that planning in America has been neither perfect nor disastrous. Rather, the historical record presents a mixed picture of ambitious plans, quite human planners, some partially successful plans, and an antiplanning ideology that proved quite strongly resistant to planning in certain areas and at certain times. Nevertheless, current planners can learn from the experiences of their predecessors.

The research for these essays began under the aegis of a National Endowment for the Humanities seminar at the University of Iowa in the summer of 1984. A group of younger scholars which included historians, political scientists, public policy specialists, and planning experts, examined the nature and history of planning in twentieth-century America. Initially, codirectors Lawrence E. Gelfand and Ellis W. Hawley of the Department of History at the University of Iowa posed a series of organizing questions aimed at addressing the history of the planning process in the United States since 1914. Using the resources of the Herbert Hoover Presidential Library, the University of Iowa Library, and the Iowa State Historical Society, seminar participants identified issues and problems relating to limitations in the extant literature on the subject. The essays in this volume seek to enhance the currently available literature by providing a number of detailed narrative case studies on planning in America.

Donald J. Murphy, who has taught modern American history at Humboldt State University in Arcata, California, begins the work with an essay on the changing conceptions of unemployment planning advocated by reformers in the American Association for Labor Legislation. As conditions changed, so did the ideology and institutional mechanisms of the planners. Hence by the decade of the 1920s, these planners sought to promote a voluntarist conception of planning for future unemployment using the predominant corporate organizational forms. But when these forms came under criticism toward the end of the New Era, the reformers returned to an older statist version of planning that retained partial coloring from the voluntary associational efforts of the 1920s.

Charles E. Harvey, Professor of American History at California State University at Chico, offers a controversial thesis about the interrelationship between the post–World War I industrial conferences sponsored by President Woodrow Wilson and the institutional legacy of these efforts for labor relations in the 1920s. Harvey suggests that John D. Rockefeller's pre–World War I experiment in labor relations planning at the Colorado Fuel and Iron Company may have served as a precedent for the labor relations ideology of Herbert Hoover, who as Secretary of Commerce from 1921 through 1928, served in a central position mediating between the state and private business firms.

Stephen D. Bodayla, biographer, diplomatic historian, and chairman of the History Department at Marycrest College in Davenport, Iowa, provides a different perspective on planning in the 1920s. His study of interwar military planning examines the origins and course of the President's Aircraft Board which led up to passage of the Air Corps Act of 1926. Bodayla's emphasis on the military side of aviation planning complements the work of Ellis W. Hawley and David D. Lee who have shown that Secretary of Commerce Hoover used the Department of Commerce to promote new industries through the associational state via activity leading to the Air Commerce Act of 1926. In this sense, military air planning involved a partially successful attempt at building state administrative capacities for peacetime planning for the armed forces.

Jerold E. Brown, a military historian at the U.S. Army Command and General Staff College in Fort Leavenworth, Kansas, follows with a study of the Air Corps Five-Year Program, a central part of the Air Corps Act of 1926. He demonstrates that implementing the provisions of the Air Corps Act proved far more difficult that its proponents initially anticipated. While the Five-Year Program began with considerable expectations and hopes, it faced many obstacles including flawed legislation, inexperienced planners, and an unsupportive Congress. Brown concludes that the Five-Year Program was actually an experiment in planning and serves as an example of the institutional limits of national planning prior to the New Deal.

Patrick D. Reagan, who teaches American economic and labor history and twentieth-century American history at Tennessee Technological University in Cookeville, Tennessee, argues that the origins of national planning under the New Deal can be traced to the pre–1933 years. The planners who served on the New Deal planning agency from 1933 through 1943 acted on the basis of ideas, experience, and institutional backgrounds gained from participation in such mainstream American organizations as business corporations, professional associations, social science research groups, and organized philanthropies. Rather than relying on the European model of state-led command planning, these New Deal planners sought to narrow the gap between nineteenth-century voluntarist values and twentieth-century institutional capacities at the national level that mixed private and public activities.

Francis Perna, a political scientist at Lock Haven University in Lock Haven, Pennsylvania, provides a case study in New Deal economic planning through an examination of the National Recovery Administration and Section 7(a), the right to collective bargaining provision of the National Industrial Recovery Act. Perna argues that these New Deal industrial and labor relations planning efforts involved successful attempts to expand administrative law regulation of the economy that allowed for state-led stabilization of a troubled market economy during the Great Depression.

Gordon P. Henderson, who teaches political theory and American politics as Widener University in Chester, Pennsylvania, pays close attention to the resistance to planning efforts of the Office of Price Administration during World War II. Through analysis of newspaper editorials published in 1945 and 1946, Henderson focuses on the major arguments against planning—the lack of sufficient factual data, the lack of cooperation in continuing support for price controls, and the inherent political difficulties in enforcing continued planning. By focusing on "the knowledge problem," Henderson redirects our attention to arguments against planning emphasized in the works of Fredrich A. Hayek, Milton Friedman, and more recent neoclassical and libertarian economists.

In sum, these essays on planning in America indicate the historical diversity and range of planning efforts in the United States between 1914 and 1946. They offer historians, political scientists, economists, public policy specialists, and planners a broad context in which to understand the American experience with planning. Rather than definitively answering questions about the American variant of planning experience, these essays are intended to stimulate further debate through close attention to factual details and establishment of a chronological framework.

Acknowledgments

The contributors would like to thank Lawrence E. Gelfand and Ellis W. Hawley for their guidance at the initial stages of research as codirectors of the summer seminar at the University of Iowa. We would also like to thank the National Endowment for the Humanities and the University of Iowa for their generous assistance in providing the opportunity to engage in such stimulating scholarly exchange in the seminar format. The staffs of the Herbert Hoover Presidential Library, the Iowa State Historical Society, and the University of Iowa Library proved very helpful in assisting contributors in locating research materials.

Our colleagues at Tennessee Technological University and the U.S. Army Command and General Staff College provided invaluable support and encouragement. We would like to extend our warmest thanks to Dean Joseph Lerner of the College of Arts and Sciences, Tennessee Technological University and the Committee for Faculty Research of Tennessee Technological University for grants leading to completion of the project.

We also thank Cathy S. Hunter of Cookeville, Tennessee for her superb performance in typing, proofreading, and revising several drafts of the manuscript.

Voluntarism, Planning, and the State

1

John B. Andrews, the American Association for Labor Legislation, and Unemployment Reform, 1914–1929

Donald J. Murphy

Between the economic depression of 1914 and the Great Depression beginning in 1929, the American Association for Labor Legislation (AALL), led by its energetic Executive Secretary John B. Andrews, espoused a comprehensive mix of public and private sector reforms to deal with the persistent problem of unemployment. By the time of American entry into World War I, the AALL had established itself as the leading voluntary reform organization in the field of labor and social insurance legislation. An initial and successful AALL focus on securing passage of workmen's compensation laws gave way by 1915 to a more ambitious campaign to secure model state public health insurance laws. The troublesome economic slump of 1914, however, also raised the unemployment issue as a vital AALL concern. This crisis acted as a catalyst to Andrews and the Association as they forged *A Practical Program for the Prevention of Unemployment* by early 1915.

Although not original with Andrews, the *Practical Program* became the AALL's trademark remedy for the complex problem of unemployment that reemerged in 1920–1921 and never quite disappeared during the "prosperity decade" of the 1920s. Consistent with the ideological rejection of laissez-faire that had led to the AALL's founding in 1906, Andrews welcomed governmental intervention (mainly at the *state* level) to counter the chronic unemployment of a free labor market. Yet in agreement with his University of Wisconsin mentor and close friend, John R. Commons, Andrews looked to American business leaders as equal partners with government in the crusade against unemployment. Previous studies of John B. Andrews and the American Association for Labor Legislation have clarified their work for unemployment reform, but their typically Progressive ambivalence over "statist" and "voluntarist" strategies of reform deserves further attention.[1]

Scholars who have examined AALL's leadership in both unemployment reform and social insurance, especially Roy Lubove, argue that the Commons-Andrews wing, for complex ideological and tactical reasons, gradually compromised the effectiveness of the AALL's message and program by the

1920s. The AALL increasingly accommodated business interests at the expense of the preferred purpose of social insurance: income maintenance of the injured, the ill, and the involuntarily unemployed. Lubove suggests latent differences over the purposes and methods of social insurance existed even before 1917. A "statist" component of the AALL may have begun and ended in the person of Isaac Max Rubinow, the brilliant Russian-Jewish immigrant whom Lubove properly views as the leading theoretician of the movement. By the 1920s, however, Rubinow was no longer alone in criticizing the AALL leadership, being joined by such formidable exponents of guarantees of income maintenance for eligible workers as Abraham Epstein, Paul H. Douglas, and others within the AALL. The state, not private sector employers, Rubinow argued, must play the major role in insuring workers and their families against the hazards of industry. While Commons and Andrews assigned increasing importance over time to reducing industrial accidents, sickness, and unemployment through legislative and administrative devices offering financial incentives to employers, Rubinow and the statists considered such approaches either irrelevant or harmful to the real purpose of social insurance—income maintenance. Rubinow and his followers charged the AALL leadership with abandoning the original aim of substituting state insurance for the flawed "voluntarist" insurance schemes of companies, fraternal societies, and trade unions in order really to secure workers' incomes. To these critics, "voluntarism," the American ideology that enshrined nonstatist organizational effort in meeting social needs, severely compromised the very organization that so effectively challenged laissez-faire and voluntarist shibboleths in its first years.[2]

The unemployment reform program advanced by John B. Andrews and the AALL that crystallized in the depression of 1914–1915, including its key component of unemployment insurance legislation, reflected the ambiguous concept of "prevention" that shaped the Commons-Andrews approach to workmen's compensation and health insurance legislation. Commons played a leading role in the genesis of Wisconsin's 1911 Workmen's Compensation Act, which sought through variable insurance premiums to induce employers to reduce accidents by practicing industrial safety in their establishments. Both men regarded the Wisconsin act and parallel AALL-sponsored accident compensation laws in other states as models for a similar strategic assault on the hazard of unemployment. Unemployment insurance legislation, the cornerstone of AALL's *Practical Program for the Prevention of Unemployment in America* (1914), would offer incentives to employers to hire employment managers to regularize employment, just as safety engineers and health experts would be unleashed under accident and health insurance legislation. Income support of the unemployed was considered a less important function of such legislation.[3]

Yet despite their shared ideology of "prevention" (a concept itself influenced by the Progressive awe of sensational advances in medical science and public health techniques), the differences between Commons and Andrews need balancing against the profound similarities. Andrews managed a difficult reform enterprise in the mecca of an emerging urban liberalism, New York City. Commons' reform role receded somewhat by 1915 as he continued teaching in Madison. In the 1920s, the two combined in a quest for "unemployment prevention" through legislation, but Commons became more deferential towards business values than Andrews, who remained more exposed to competing ideas and the rising urban liberalism, both by reason of his metropolitan location and his activist role as manager of a labor reform organization. Still, both Commons and Andrews probably shared a fundamental perspective on the American business community. They divided it into a minority of "progressive" employers whose employment practices they praised, a somewhat larger group of business exploiters who fought all good legislation, and an uncommitted majority of business leaders the two hoped to evangelize with the gospel of preventive, employer-oriented unemployment insurance.[4]

The AALL's campaign against unemployment emerged slowly before 1914. Even prior to the 1914–1915 depression with its increased unemployment, AALL leaders were concentrating attention on unemployment as a perennial problem of industrial society evident in periods of general prosperity in the forms of seasonal and casual labor joblessness and, in times of depression, in the form of cyclical unemployment. John B. Andrews and Columbia University economist and AALL President Henry R. Seager used the recent analysis of unemployment by Britain's William Beveridge as a theoretical foundation for their own ideas. AALL leaders were profoundly influenced by the successful launching of Britain's national labor exchange network (1909) and compulsory national unemployment insurance system (1911), both shaped significantly by Beveridge. Prior to the adoption of its *Practical Program for the Prevention of Unemployment* in late 1914, AALL emphasized, as did Beveridge, the need for an efficient national network of public employment exchanges. Only later in 1914–1915 did it shift to making regularization work by private employers and unemployment insurance the more pressing concerns.[5]

By early 1914, John B. Andrews increasingly took charge of the AALL's nascent campaign against unemployment. In February 1914, he convened the First National Conference on Unemployment in New York City, a meeting given urgency by rising unemployment throughout the United States. Although a latecomer to the issue compared with AALL members like Charles R. Henderson and Henry R. Seager, Andrews now became the energetic leader as the AALL attempted to capitalize on public concern over joblessness that worsened again with the economic shocks caused by the start of the European war in the summer of 1914. As editor of the *American Labor Legislation Review (ALLR)*, Andrews devoted an entire issue of the AALL's quarterly journal to the papers and proceedings of the New York conference. He prefaced these papers with his own analysis of unemployment as a "problem of industry" and of a disorganized American labor market. Andrews found "the demoralizing effect of unemployment upon the individual... matched only by the wastefulness to society," a formulation that suggested a Progressive concern with both the debilitating moral results of lack of work and its economic inefficiency. More significantly, Andrews emphasized the need to mobilize American employers to achieve greater stability of employment at the firm and industry level. Without naming names, Andrews praised "a few progressive employers" who were already experimenting in this direction. By late 1914, Andrews and the AALL began to shift the mix of public and private sector initiatives they advocated to combat unemployment to the advantage of private sector efforts.[6]

The First National Conference on Unemployment revealed to AALL leaders and to the public the complexity and severity of unemployment and its potential threat to social stability. Delegates from dozens of cities, states, and labor organizations painted a composite picture of high levels of joblessness, grossly inadequate statistics on the problem, and sporadic but alarming social unrest. Jewish garment workers in Chicago mobbed city hall demanding work, hungry unemployed in Portland, Oregon, stormed restaurants, and "armies" of the jobless crisscrossed northern California. The AALL's urgency in devising a concrete program of reform during 1914 reflected these worrisome events. By the time a Second National Conference on Unemployment convened by the AALL met in December 1914 in Philadelphia, Andrews and Seager, after wide consultations, drafted and obtained the second conference's endorsement of an action program that set the AALL's unemployment agenda for the next two decades. The *Practical Program for the Prevention of Unemployment*, published under Andrews' authorship in December 1914, endorsed a variety of emergency and stopgap remedies for the unemployment crisis, such as the formation of local mayors' committees to organize relief efforts, but it decisively emphasized a long-run permanent program of unemployment "prevention." With this program, the AALL brought to fruition over two years of investigation and debate within its ranks and defined more coherently than ever before its four interrelated, long-range measures to control and greatly reduce the scourge of unemployment.[7]

The first plank of the *Practical Program* endorsed a national system of public employment exchanges coordinated by the federal government as an antidote to a disorganized labor market. Andrews contrasted the inefficiency of existing methods of labor placement—"Help Wanted" signs, newspaper ads, profiteering private employment agencies, and the like—with the need for businesslike public employment agencies run by efficient civil servants linked in a national system. The second major plank recommended countercyclical use of public works spending by all levels of government to reduce unemployment in periods of economic depression. Andrews emphasized that advanced planning of such public works was essential. He also distinguished such planned public works from "make-work" relief activities which he, like all other AALL spokesmen, deplored as demoralizing to the unemployed.[8] The third major plank of the *Practical Program* called for the "Regularization of Industry." By late 1914, Andrews considered this step more important than public employment exchanges, because he had apparently concluded that employer efforts to stabilize output, sales, and ultimately employment held more promise of cutting unemployment than any public sector program save unemployment insurance as a stimulus to regularization. Andrews and other AALL leaders conceded here to a crucial primacy of the private business sector in the fight against unemployment. The regularization plank argued the benefits to employers, workers, and consumers of a smoother production and employment curve through the efforts of individual companies and industries. If employers organized personnel departments to aid in reducing excessive labor turnover, balanced production and sales by "Forward Planning," expanded slack season demand for company products, developed new lines of products, and made similar managerial reforms, unemployment would be less likely. The proposals in the *Practical Program* paralleled the demands of the scientific management and personnel management movements that gained strength around 1914–1915.[9]

Unemployment insurance legislation served as the capstone of the *Practical Program*. This remedy primarily aimed at preventing unemployment through a combination of financial pressure and incentives to employers to "regularize" their employment of workers. In effect, unemployment insurance legislation would serve as a tool to the end of regularization of industry and employment. Adjustable insurance premiums would act as the carrot-and-stick to prod employers to reform within the framework of a state unemployment insurance system. Again, as with Commons' workmen's compensation scheme, Andrews ranked prevention above income maintenance. The *Practical Program* cited the Wisconsin Workmen's Compensation Act as a model for unemployment insurance. Just as workmen's compensation laws generated a "nation-wide movement for 'safety-first' " and just as pending AALL health insurance legislation promised "a similar movement for the conservation of the national health," so state unemployment insurance would spur businessmen to regularize employment by a mix of financial incentives and penalties. In sum, Andrews and AALL leaders viewed state unemployment insurance financed by employers, workers, and government as a synthesis of British and American approaches to the problem. The legislative framework was derived from the British model as were the joint contributory features. But the emphasis on prevention through variable employer unemployment ratings reflected Wisconsin and American experience with workmen's compensation, although Andrews and Seager would also point to an overlooked employer refund clause in the British unemployment insurance code to bolster their case.[10]

The *Practical Program* gave much less attention to other remedies to reduce unemployment. Nevertheless, it endorsed vocational guidance and training, improved distribution of immigrant workers, reduction of hours of labor, and "constructive care of the unemployable," a rubric that encompassed both humane measures such as health insurance and old age pension coverage for unemployables, but also the coercive control in penal colonies of people who refused to work and those defined as "semi-criminal."[11]

By late 1915, war orders fueled an industrial recovery from the economic depression that had energized the AALL's campaign against unemployment. Andrews could take satisfaction in some perceived net gains. Unemployment, he argued, for the first time had been grasped by many as "an *American* problem and a problem of *Industry*."[12] The AALL had greatly assisted this advance beyond laissez-faire provincialism with its continuous educational work. The AALL secretary noted tentative efforts underway to establish a national system of public employment exchanges through congressional legislation and to launch public works planning at least locally. But he was most impressed with the increasing acceptance of the view that employers held the key to the regularization of employment with unemployment insurance legislation also necessary to stimulate such efforts.

In 1915 an AALL committee proceeded to draft model unemployment insurance legislation and cooperated with local groups to introduce this bill in the Massachusetts legislature in 1916. At about the same time, the AALL published the results of its "Unemployment Survey," documenting the "economic and social wastes" of joblessness in more than 115 American cities. A series of AALL *Standard Recommendations* for dealing with unemployment by both emergency relief and long-range preventative measures were published with the results of the survey in the *ALLR*. These recommendations restated the four major planks of the *Practical Program* in a format more suitable for mass distribution to the public.[13]

The *Practical Program* marked a major stride by John B. Andrews towards a less statist approach to unemployment than the organization's pre–1914 discussions had suggested. The *Practical Program* hinted at an elastic set or priorities, alternately accenting public and private sector initiatives on unemployment that the AALL might opportunistically invoke as political and economic circumstances changed. Over the next two decades, Andrews pragmatically emphasized different mixes of these remedies for unemployment. In 1914–1915, he had shifted towards employer regularization as the goal with state unemployment insurance legislation as the means to that end.[14]

American mobilization for the world war during 1917–1918 created a perceived labor shortage, not unemployment. During the conflict, Andrews and the AALL gave priority to the defense of standards of labor legislation and an increasingly time-consuming health insurance campaign. Nevertheless, the AALL utilized the wartime crisis in labor supply for vital industries to crusade again for its first plank of 1914, an efficient national system of public employment offices. AALL lobbied hard for a federal-state public employment exchange system in 1917–1918. In January 1918, the Wilson administration, by executive order instead of legislation, created the United States Employment Service (USES) within the Department of Labor to overcome acute labor shortages. By the war's end, 832 new public employment offices had been established in less than a year and over four thousand personnel staffed the system. But despite support by unemployment reformers including Seager and Andrews, an economy-minded Congress gutted the agency in 1919 and rejected the AALL's call for a permanent system. Both Congress and Wilson viewed the USES—like so many wartime agencies—as an emergency measure rather than as a springboard to postwar economic and social "reconstruction."[15]

The immediate postwar years of 1919–1920 were confusing for the AALL as much as for the nation itself. The Massachusetts unemployment insurance bill was long dead, and the AALL suffered an even more spectacular and damaging defeat when its model health insurance bill failed in New York state amid hysterical charges that "alien" and "un-American" influences including the AALL concocted the measure. Andrews complained in April 1920 of an "extraordinary wave of reaction" in the United States that boded ill for labor legislation of any sort.[16]

Between 1920 and 1921, prospects for a revived USES and for countercyclical public works tended to fade as congressional legislation to establish these programs succumbed to the climate of retrenchment and reaction. Andrews and the AALL concentrated energies on the other major planks of the *Practical Program*, regularization and unemployment insurance. Daniel Nelson has noted that at least three variables affected any success the AALL might have had in the new decade on unemployment insurance: organized labor's attitude toward such legislation, the performance of British and European plans of compulsory unemployment insurance, and the extent of unemployment in the United States. Consistent with his version of voluntarism, American Federation of Labor (AFL) chieftain Samuel Gompers stoutly opposed state unemployment insurance legislation. He and other AFL leaders feared that the government agencies enforcing such laws would use them to subvert union strength. Many local and state AFL leaders, however, backed the AALL's position on the issue. In 1920–1921, the British unemployment insurance system entered a period of growing crisis as a postwar economic depression led to mass unemployment and tested that hitherto successful experiment to its limits. The onset of one of the sharpest business depressions in American history in late 1920 caused unemployment to peak near 12 percent and posed both a challenge and an opportunity to the AALL. While this depression was over by early 1922, continued high levels of unemployment plagued the otherwise booming American economy of the 1920s. Adding to the unfavorable environment the AALL faced in 1920–1921 was the transfer of political power to conservative Republicans in some states and in the nation's capital. The latter event was tempered somewhat by the presence of a progressive favorite, Herbert Hoover, in the Harding cabinet.[17]

In spite of this generally bleak prospect, Andrews and the AALL moved quickly to define the economic depression of 1920–1921 as an opportunity to mount a sustained drive for state-level unemployment insurance legislation. By 1920 Andrews, Commons (cooperating with his former student more closely on the issue than ever before), and the AALL increasingly looked to enlightened employers to regularize employment with unemployment insurance legislation acting as an incentive to the laggard majority of employers to imitate the employment-stabilizing behavior of the progressive few. By 1921 Andrews, Commons, and the AALL advocated a new "American" approach to unemployment insurance, although one strongly foreshadowed by the *Practical Program* of 1914. In 1922, a young economist with ties to the AALL's leadership, Herman Feldman, coined the term "New Emphasis" to refer to the emergence of a new nonstatist "American" answer to the problem of irregular employment—emphasis on prevention by the techniques of business management, not on state relief or maintenance of the unemployed as a primary aim. It proved quite compatible with the ascendancy of a business leadership searching for nonstatist solutions and concerned to extend scientific management to labor reserves as they had done to production and marketing problems. The personnel management movement and 1920–1921 *Waste in Industry* studies pushed by Herbert Hoover, his aide Edward Eyre Hunt, and the progressive Taylorite engineers were other manifestations of this search for nonstatist solutions to economic "disorganization" that came to typify the New Era. The prominence of managerial values in the 1920s made Andrews more than ever ready to accent the role of employers in achieving the AALL's regularization and state unemployment insurance planks. Sound political tactics and some ideological cooptation probably also influenced Andrews and his colleagues.[18]

In closely coordinating the AALL's unemployment insurance campaign between 1920 and 1922, Andrews and Commons continued to argue the necessity of legislation, but Commons in particular emphasized the strategic role of powerful employers in accomplishing change. In *Industrial Goodwill* (1919), Commons argued strongly for the personnel management movement and for regularization of employment by employers as critical first steps toward industrial peace and away from any revolutionary socialist challenge to capitalism. Andrews also showed a rising interest in employer initiatives to regularize by voluntary firm-level or industry-wide efforts. Again the model of efficient preventive insurance that shaped their arguments was the

Wisconsin Workmen's Compensation Act. The cooperation of Commons and Andrews culminated with the Huber bill, a cautious, preventive, employer-oriented unemployment compensation bill that Commons shaped and which almost passed the Wisconsin legislature in 1921 and was introduced unsuccessfully a number of times later in the decade. But the two men's endeavors were not limited to Wisconsin. Through the *American Labor Legislation Review*, the offices of the AALL, the speakers circuit, and correspondence with progressive employers and other groups attracted to a renewed unemployment insurance drive, Andrews and Commons tried to seize upon the unemployment crisis to achieve their program and minimally educate the newer business leadership.[19]

In a December 1920 article in the *ALLR*, Andrews chided the American public for forgetting the depression of 1914–1915 and for not demanding more implementation of the *Practical Program*. Speaking the language of scientific management, Andrews urged the "regularization of private industry," so as to achieve "the prevention of inexcusable waste" in the labor market. Yet he also found some real progress since 1914–1915 for which "too much credit cannot be given" to those industrial firms that launched regularization programs. The similar goals of progressive Taylorites and "inspirational teachers like Herbert Hoover" suggested to Andrews that the new engineers and managers might yet save America from the "captains of industry [who] periodically march us into a hopeless, wasteful unemployment muddle."[20] This somewhat Veblenian formulation suggests a crucial ambiguity in Andrews' thought on the relationship of businessmen and unemployment. The AALL secretary looked hopefully to progressive employers and the new generation of managers while still insisting that most business firms needed the rod of reform.

As part of his campaign for unemployment insurance in late 1920, Andrews focused the AALL's annual meeting on the problem of unemployment. Speaker after speaker registered concern with mounting joblessness and its social costs. Labor leader Sidney Hillman, progressive employers like Henry S. Dennison, public works champion Otto T. Mallery, and personnel management enthusiast Meyer Bloomfield, all spoke of the urgency of the problem and offered their solutions. As in 1914–1915, Andrews once again organized an "Unemployment Survey." Based on the responses to questionnaires sent to community leaders around the nation, he concluded that very little progress had been made in perfecting public employment offices and developing countercyclical public works planning. Only a few firms experimented with regularization of employment programs. No state had enacted unemployment insurance despite campaigns underway in Wisconsin and Pennsylvania. What made the 1920–1921 slump less acute for workers, argued Andrews, were their wartime savings which would no longer be available as a cushion in the approaching winter of 1921–1922.[21]

Perhaps the most revealing example of the AALL's increasing support for the employer prevention method of unemployment reform was Commons' March 1922 article in the *ALLR*. Correspondence between Andrews and Commons before this time revealed an identity of views on selling the employer prevention concept to employers. Commons' argument underlined an observation he made in his 1934 autobiography: "I was trying to save capitalism by making it good." The Wisconsin economist saw American business leaders in an unrivaled position of economic and financial power, but labor unions were much less powerful. Commons also distrusted the expansion of national governmental power. Along with other Americans, he searched for nonstatist alternatives to the danger of state interventionism that seemed to culminate, Commons suggested, in the Bolshevik tyranny in Russia. Responsibility for stabilizing employment should be assumed by employers. Workers lacked job security, but investors were secured in their investments by business management. Business leaders had the power, deserved the power, but must responsibly exercise the power to regularize employment by accepting unemployment insurance laws. These laws would spur increased efficiency in the management of labor turnover through financial incentives similar to the model workmen's compensation laws. Reduced unemployment insurance premiums and higher profits for employers would be the cooperative employer's reward. Commons believed that American bankers could be enlisted in the cause of unemployment prevention, since the pressure of unemployment insurance costs would force bankers to restrain credit when business expanded and thereby lessen the extent of cyclical downturns and unemployment.[22]

The 1921 Huber bill in Wisconsin directly reflected Commons' tilt toward voluntarism. Unlike the British plan and even the AALL's own 1916 Massachusetts bill, the Huber bill funded the unemployment insurance program exclusively through a tax on employers. The bill had other conservative features as well: short duration of benefits, low benefit amounts, and minimal administrative costs through use of an existing state agency, the Industrial Commission. Employers could even administer most of the plan themselves by creating mutual insurance companies. Despite these voluntarist provisions, Commons and Andrews labeled the Huber bill a "compulsory" unemployment insurance bill. What Commons elsewhere called "cooperative" legislation affecting business, as distinct from "repressive" measures like antitrust laws, was a more apt description of his goals in the Huber bill.[23]

In late summer 1921, Andrews and the AALL had distinguished company in their anxiety over the continuing economic depression that left somewhere between three and five million Americans jobless. Herbert Hoover, the new Secretary of Commerce, moved to convene the first national unemployment conference ever organized by a federal department. Hoover's aims stemmed from his vision of an "associative state" that could provide a "middle way" between laissez-faire, antistatist economic forumlae that would ruthlessly "liquidate" wages and jobs and statist proposals that would expand bureaucratic controls destructive to American enterprise. Hoover turned to an arrangement of "promotional conferences, expert inquiries, and cooperating committees" to achieve his goals which included increasing the productivity and efficiency of the American economy in order to provide larger shares of income for all sectors of society. Both Hoover and AALL leaders like Andrews envisioned unemployment as a tragic waste of human and economic resources. Not surprisingly, Hoover called on AALL experts for major assistance as he organized, largely through his secretary E. E. Hunt, the President's Conference on Unemployment in September 1921.[24]

Hoover displayed the respect for trained social science expertise that became his hallmark through the 1920s, assigning to an expert Economic Advisory Committee (EAC) the key tasks of preparing the conference agenda and the crafting of reports for approval by the full conference membership. The EAC reflected AALL membership in its representative delegates: Andrews, Edwin F. Gay, Otto T. Mallery, Samuel McCune Lindsay, Henry R. Seager, Sam A. Lewisohn, George Barnett, Leo Wolman, Henry S. Dennison, and Wesley C. Mitchell. A number of other members, including Mary Van Kleeck, would serve on later conference committees and play influential roles. Andrews in particular influenced the direction and content of the conference's recommendations. Invited to serve as a secretary of the Committee on Public Hearings, he accepted willingly without pay. He also served on subcommittees dealing with emergency relief and, more significantly, unemployment prevention. Cooperating closely with Hunt, Andrews fed names, ideas, and reports to Hunt and Hoover. To Hunt, Andrews sent the AALL Unemployment Survey of 1920–1921; Hunt would have this material digested by his own staff for the conference. From Commons, Andrews asked for the quick dispatch of suggestions to reinforce his effort to write Wisconsin ideas of unemployment prevention into a committee report. Commons apparently agreed and promised to forward to all conference members an article he had just completed on unemployment prevention for *The Survey*.[25]

Both preliminary and final reports of the conference suggested that the Hoover-orchestrated gathering imbibed many of the key proposals of the AALL's *Practical Program* and *Standard Recommendations* of 1914–1915. The conference recommended strengthening the United States Employment Service; public works planning for long-run economic stabilization and accelerated federal, state, and local governmental and private construction expenditures along lines Otto T. Mallery advocated; and employer efforts at regularization of production and employment. Only in the area of unemployment insurance did Andrews have cause for concern: "Any forms of unemployment insurance which would create an economic motive to regularize employment [were] . . . worthy of the most careful consideration," the final report fuzzily concluded. This disappointingly vague recommendation foreshadowed an eventual conflict separating Andrews from Hoover and Hunt in the aftermath of the conference.[26]

John Andrews' correspondence during the late months of 1921 suggested his considerable admiration for Herbert Hoover's leadership in dramatizing the issue of unemployment. The AALL secretary shared with Hoover an abhorrence of unemployment as waste and a belief that private sector employers were the strategic actors in attacking the problem. After traveling to the West Coast and personally noting the impact of unemployment, Andrews wrote one state official that amid the gloom, the "most promising thing on the horizon [was] . . . that Secretary Hoover is directly taking hold of the problem." Andrews was impressed by the efficient direction of the conference by both Hoover and Hunt through carefully coordinated committees. The AALL secretary particularly wished to exploit the conference's invitation to, and hopefully education of, leading American manufacturers in the ways of unemployment prevention. Writing to Commons, he made two crucial points about the conference's significance. First, the meeting was really a "*manufacturers*' conference on unemployment, organized by the Department of Commerce and pretty largely composed of key men in the industries . . . most affected by present unemployment." The "biggest thing" that could result from the conference would be the recognition by these "managers of private industry" that they were responsible for minimizing unemployment by better business management. Andrews' second theme was more troubling: "much depends on the make-up of the [Unemployment Conference's] continuing committee" which would implement and advance the conference recommendations for long-range preventive action. In the months that followed, Andrews realized that opponents of unemployment insurance legislation representative of the very "managers of private industry" he wished to evangelize dominated this Standing Committee of the conference.[27]

Andrews' differences with Hoover and Hunt over the issue of unemployment insurance legislation and a more forceful endorsement of unemployment prevention by employers simmered quietly until the end of 1921. The AALL secretary became aware soon after the conference that the composition of the conference's Business Cycle Committee (a subcommittee named by the Standing Committee chaired by industrialist Owen D. Young and consisting of two other businessmen, AFL leader Matthew Woll, the AALL's Mary Van Kleeck, and Hoover aide E. E. Hunt) leaned against AALL doctrine on unemployment insurance. Still, Andrews courted Hoover as late as December 1921 when he was trying to persuade the Secretary of Commerce to chair the AALL's annual meeting in Pittsburgh. In an article in the *ALLR* that month, Andrews once again cited substantial gains from the unemployment conference, since it effectively endorsed AALL's *Standard Recommendations* for combating unemployment by organized local campaigns and apparently awakened some business leaders to their responsibility in preventing joblessness. Nevertheless, Andrews insisted that the Business Cycle Committee's crucial report would decide whether the Hooverian Unemployment Conference was truly worthwhile.[28]

In a December 1921 exchange of letters, Andrews and Hoover's assistant, E. E. Hunt, jousted over their differences on a legislative or completely voluntarist route to unemployment insurance. Hunt chided Andrews with being too concerned with "social legislation" and argued that the success of the conference rested on its spur to voluntarist and nonstatist employer and local community action. The AALL secretary remained less sanguine and unconvinced by Hunt's logic. Over the next few years, editorials and articles in the *ALLR* pointed to an outright split between reformer Andrews and Department of Commerce policymakers over the issue. When the Business Cycle Committee's recommendations were publicized in early 1923, Andrews reacted by endorsing only the fact-finding section of the report authored by Wesley C. Mitchell's team of economic experts which sympathized with legislating unemployment insurance. He attacked as inadequate, however, the full committee's endorsement of only voluntary plans. Andrews happily published Mitchell's "report on a report" in the *ALLR*, while drafting a minor piece of his own in the Mitchell/National Bureau of Economic Research report that criticized American trade union "out of work" funds and strongly implied the superiority of state legislation for unemployment insurance. AALL member Leo Wolman contributed the major paper on unemployment insurance. Wolman emphatically favored unemployment insurance legislation, although he faulted the British system for neglecting preventive methods and the Huber bill for its inadequate penalties on employers.[29]

In the June 1923 *ALLR*, Andrews' assistant, Frederick MacKenzie, openly criticized the Business Cycle Committee report for its "disappointing" recommendations. There was no call for "social action" linked to announcement of the committee's recommendations, MacKenzie argued. "All emphasis," he wrote, "is on private initiative and voluntary effort." Andrews' aide did endorse the committee's call for improved statistics and other efforts, but he rejected its simple reliance on employer "good will" as the sole solvent of unemployment. The AALL strongly supported individual employer efforts to stabilize employment through company or industry-wide reserve funds, but "social compulsion" was needed to prod employers into such good will. To MacKenzie, "enlightened industrial standards" required legislation both in Great Britain and in the American states. In sum, the Business Cycle Committee had failed to recommend that "complete, constructive program of prevention" needed to combat the problem. Although it had long delayed its report on the plea for more time, what the Committee needed most was not more time "but greater social vision and more courage," concluded MacKenzie.[30]

The reluctance of the Business Cycle Committee to endorse unemployment insurance legislation owed, ultimately, to Herbert Hoover's appointments to that body and Hoover's own antipathy to a legislative framework of jobless insurance. During the President's Unemployment Conference, Hoover denounced such legislation as "relief plans" and "hallucinations imported from Europe" and referred to the "dole" as "this most vicious of solutions" the America, unlike Europe, had happily "escaped." In 1923 Hoover was still assailing the notion. Before the managers of the Metropolitan Life Insurance Company, Hoover pleaded with the company to promote the concept of voluntary, firm-level unemployment insurance. He coupled this plea for voluntarist action with a warning that compulsory state legislation on the subject would end in "the disaster of incompetent and vicious encroachment of bureaucracy into the daily lives of our people."[31] Although Hoover was not lacking in concern to combat unemployment and mitigate its harmful effects on workers, his strong ideology of voluntarism aligned him against the approaches of Andrews and the AALL.

After 1922 as the economic boom of the New Era included a public amnesia about the problem of unemployment, Andrews continued vigorously to agitate the AALL's long-range program of unemployment reform. As always, the AALL pushed other campaigns which competed for Andrews' time and energy: improvement and extension of workmen's compensation, old age pensions, coal mine safety, and similar causes. From 1922 to 1927, Andrews expressed the hope in frequent editorials and articles in the *ALLR* that the few, but growing number of company regularization plans, company unemployment insurance plans, and joint union-management unemployment insurance plans would spread more widely. He interpreted these voluntary ventures as important experiments of educational value on the road to inevitable unemployment insurance legislation. However, he felt that the latter also had to accompany and preferably precede such plans. Annual AALL conferences between 1922 and 1924 echoed this support for unemployment prevention among the AALL leaders and their progressive business allies. Henry S. Dennison documented the success of a "depression insurance" scheme at his Framingham, Massachusetts paper products firm and confidently urged other businessmen to launch similar experiments. Although company regularization plans were publicized in the *ALLR*, company and joint union-management plans for unemployment insurance received more attention, since the latter promoted regularization suggestive of the *Practical Program's* linkage of employment regularization and jobless insurance as tandem reforms. Progressive businessmen who endorsed unemployment insurance legislation, including Herbert F. Johnson, the Wisconsin wax manufacturer, Hills Brothers' Company executive Ernest R. Draper, and Henry S. Dennison were welcome contributors. Meanwhile, Andrews also gave strong journalistic support to the joint union-management plans beginning with a Cleveland Plan negotiated between a Garment Workers' local union and Cleveland garment manufacturers in 1919–1920 that emphasized refunds to individual companies which reduced unemployment. The Chicago Plan of 1923 adopted by that city's men's clothing firms and the Amalgamated Clothing Workers (ACW) was admired even more by Andrews. It covered more workers (thirty-five thousand) than any other plan of the 1920s, included incentives to employers to regularize, and had John R. Commons as head of the unemployment fund's board of trustees. Andrews' backing for this scheme suggested that his enthusiasm for the progressive "new unionism" of Sidney Hillman and the ACW matched his admiration for the minority of progressive employers.[32]

In the mid–1920s, Andrews and the AALL were at the peak of their courtship of business support. As editor of the *ALLR*, Andrews excoriated "reactionary employers" and "hard-boiled statesmen" who obstructed AALL programs in 1925, but he still praised the progressive business minority who, he hoped, would both grow in number and cooperate with public officials in attacking joblessness through unemployment insurance legislation.[33] In 1926 the *ALLR* praised two books that explained and extolled the virtues of a growing business regularization movement. Herman Feldman's *The Regularization of Employment* argued the merits of planning by individual companies to prevent unemployment. The *ALLR*'s review of his significant study, however, played up Feldman's much more limited endorsement of unemployment insurance. Likewise, the *ALLR* praised *Can Business Prevent Unemployment?*, a "dynamic little book" jointly authored by AALL members Commons, Draper, Sam A. Lewisohn, and Don D. Lescohier for its documentation of some 114 experiments in regularization by business and for its support for Wisconsin-style, preventionist unemployment insurance legislation. In March 1926, Feldman summarized his argument for a "distinctively American" approach to employment stabilization in the *ALLR*. He criticized Britain's William Beveridge for overlooking "better methods of business administration" when Beveridge analyzed remedies for unemployment in 1909. The "new emphasis" of American managers on stabilization of employment at the company level offered a superior method to Beveridge's stress on public labor exchanges, one that could greatly reduce not only seasonal but also cyclical unemployment. Feldman concluded his article by endorsing "incentive" unemployment insurance modeled on Wisconsin's Huber bill as superior to the British plan. Although this final point may have pleased Andrews, Feldman's argument placed him closer to the managerial advocates of regularization than to longtime exponents of legislative methods like Andrews.[34]

While Andrews leant AALL support to the mid–1920s regularization crusade, his commitment to this goal may well have been in part a tactical adjustment to the antistatist climate of opinion at the time. The progressive employers within the AALL and Feldman were much more enthusiastic backers of regularization techniques than Andrews. A brief item in the December 1923 *ALLR* seemed to call into question the ability of American business to achieve voluntary regularization or voluntary unemployment insurance on any significant scale. The note recounted how a leading employers' association, the National Industrial Conference Board (NICB), had confidently claimed that American business could reduce unemployment greatly through company or industry plans and without state or federal legislation. The *ALLR* sarcastically questioned whether the nation could expect three hundred thousand American employers quickly to prove the NICB correct. Andrews recalled this very brief 1923 caveat in early 1928 when be became completely disillusioned with the snail's pace progress of voluntary company plans and, by implication, the entire regularization movement. By then Andrews' doubts had been reinforced by a renewal of rising unemployment and a growing criticism of voluntary methods by unemployment experts.[35]

Andrews' residual doubts about purely voluntarist remedies for unemployment reflected his continuing concern to advance the public as well as private sector attack on the problem in the New Era. In late 1927 and early 1928, an economic recession and a sharp rise in unemployment provided occasion for John B. Andrews and the AALL to shift once again towards the public rather than private sector side of their unemployment program. Cities such as New York experienced rising claims for public and charitable assistance. Andrews used this evidence, as he had perennially in the past, to plead again for advanced planning to contain or prevent unemployment by implementation of the *Practical Program*. The AALL secretary took note of what some experts by the late 1920s called the "new unemployment": the increasing displacement of workers, especially in manufacturing, by new technology, production processes, and managerial innovations. Without fully grasping the irony, Andrews credited Secretary of Commerce Hoover with helping to lead this campaign for higher productivity which was increasing unemployment. At the same time, Andrews continued to endorse the Hooverian work of the 1921 Unemployment Conference precisely because that meeting had supported the AALL's *Practical Program* with the exception of state unemployment insurance.

As Andrews viewed the rising unemployment of 1927–1928, he clearly recognized the new crisis as a golden opportunity to demand renewed action on the AALL's agenda. Significantly, Andrews emphatically repudiated employer-led voluntary regularization and company unemployment insurance as a feasible approach. He had hinted at this in the early 1920s when he otherwise profusely publicized employer experiments in this field. What decisively changed Andrews' mind in 1928 was a remarkably exhaustive technical report focused on voluntary American unemployment plans written by Bryce M. Stewart and sponsored by a Rockefeller Foundation-funded research group, Industrial Relations Counselors, Inc. The AALL secretary cited the Stewart/IRC study's conclusion that a mere twelve companies had functioning unemployment insurance funds during the decade and that less than twelve thousand workers were eligible for benefits under the plans. To Andrews this was a "meager showing" indeed for those advocating purely voluntary effort against unemployment. It also revealed, he argued, the hollowness of the complacent optimism of the Coolidge administration and laissez-faire critics of state unemployment insurance.[36]

Andrews and the AALL proposed to meet the current unemployment crisis and plan for future crises by increased publicity of unemployment and determined support for all legislative efforts—national, state, and local—to enact the *Practical Program* into law. In particular, by 1928 Andrews revived the cry for a federal-state public employment exchange system. His vehicle would be New York Democratic Senator Robert F. Wagner's bill to rejuvenate the United States Employment Service (USES) and provide federal subsidies to states cooperating in new rules and regulations emanating from the USES. Andrews and AALL staffer Margaret D. Meyer backed Wagner's Senate resolution calling for an inquiry into the shoddy and inept statistical work of the Department of Labor—the Coolidge administration claimed that unemployment was about 1.7 million; some in the reform community believed it was more than four million. These two public sector demands were closely related. Unemployment experts argued that without an effective USES, unemployment statistics would be too inaccurate for sound policy-making; moreover, without unemployment insurance payments distributed by a public employment exchange system, the unemployed could not be induced to register for work.

A final plank of the *Practical Program*, advanced planning of public works to counter cyclical economic slumps, also received vigorous new support from Andrews and the AALL. The AALL lobbied for Washington Republican Senator Wesley Jones's "prosperity reserve" bill calling for appropriating $150 million in reserved federal public works projects when the president determined that the volume of construction contracts had fallen below a given average. This version of advanced public works planning was largely the work of Otto T. Mallery, the AALL's longtime public works missionary and colleague of Andrews.[37]

In the months before the Great Crash, a critical stocktaking by Andrews occurred with respect to the mix of private and public sector unemployment reforms the AALL needed to advance. The 1927–1928 recession, combining both a cyclical downturn with the new unemployment caused by machines and managerial techniques which eliminated jobs, disillusioned Andrews as well as other reformers with voluntary company unemployment insurance plans. As Bryce M. Stewart suggested, such plans were adopted by too few firms to matter. Despite their worth as experiments, these voluntary plans were too dependent on the insecure financial health of often small individual companies. Typically, they favored skilled workers with long service at the expense of newer and part-time workers. Companies could often simply escape any benefit payments by laying off workers permanently and thus ruling them out of the plan. A new concern for the more public sector components of the AALL's *Practical Program*—coordinated public employment exchanges and planned public works—plus improved governmental statistical capability suggested Andrews had come a considerable way from his cheerleading for employer leadership in solving the problem of unemployment that characterized the mid–1920s.

The stock market crash of October 1929 and the subsequent Great Depression profoundly altered the economic and political environment in which John B. Andrews and the AALL operated. Mass unemployment provided a new opportunity for Andrews to advance his program, especially unemployment insurance along Wisconsin preventionist lines. But a rising, somewhat younger group of statist and collectivist social insurance advocates, including Abraham Epstein and Paul H. Douglas, challenged Andrews for leadership of the unemployment insurance movement. The details of these controversies have been well discussed by Daniel Nelson and Roy Lubove, but they boil down to renewed conflict over whether employer prevention or worker income maintenance was the prime aim of unemployment insurance and the important technical means to implement either program. What seems clear from these accounts is that Andrews' ideas on unemployment insurance, if not on the other components of the *Practical Program*, were fundamentally flawed and increasingly inappropriate to the circumstances of the early Depression era. As critics to his left correctly argued, the individual American employer and even whole industries were relatively helpless to stem massive unemployment due to worldwide cyclical and market forces. Andrews' dependence on John R. Commons' economic speculations ill served him in trying to grapple intellectually with the impact of the Great Depression and devising a workable formula for unemployment reform for unemployment insurance. As an ideologue of unemployment reform, Andrews would soon be bypassed by a younger generation of social insurance advocates who wanted a stronger dose of governmental intervention, state and federal, to make unemployment insurance effective.

Yet Nelson's study suggests that Andrews, despite his increasing intellectual irrelevance and obsolescence, still performed crucial work as he searched for a working political consensus among proponents of unemployment insurance legislation between 1930 and 1935. Possibly to avoid losing all leadership in the drive for unemployment insurance, but more probably to achieve the longtime reform goal of making the program part of national public policy, Andrews compromised with his critics, revised his own proposals, and effectively rallied the "social insurance crowd" to pressure congressional committees into enactment of what became a key part of the Social Security Act of 1935.[38]

As a tireless advocate and activist for both private and public sector planning against the contingencies of unemployment from 1914 to the eve of the Great Depression, John B. Andrews deserves recognition as more than a blind practitioner of John R. Commons' flawed economic notions. As an organizational leader, he advanced a sophisticated, if partially flawed, *Practical Program* that had as its major premise the contention that it was inhumane as well as inefficient for the nation to drift unconsciously into economic depression and unemployment when advanced planning and countercyclical techniques could either prevent or mitigate these social disasters. His career suggests frequent concession to voluntarist pressures during the 1920s, but no total retreat from the public sector programs that had defined the ideology of the AALL since 1906.

NOTES

1. On the AALL's social insurance crusades, see Roy Lubove, *The Struggle for Social Security, 1900–1935* (Cambridge: Harvard University Press, 1968); Daniel Nelson, *Unemployment Insurance: The American Experience, 1915–1935* (Madison: University of Wisconsin Press, 1969); Hace Sorel Tishler, *Self-Reliance and Social Security, 1870–1917* (Port Washington, N.Y.: Kennikat Press, 1971); Irwin Yellowitz, "The Origins of Unemployment Reform in the United States," *Labor History* 9 (1968): 338–60; Clarke A. Chambers, *Seedtime of Reform: American Social Service and Social Action, 1918–1933* (Minneapolis: University of Minnesota Press, 1963), chaps. 7–8. Insightful on the AALL's mix of public and private labor market reforms is Sanford M. Jacoby, *Employing Bureaucracy: Managers, Unions, and the Transformation of Work in American Industry, 1910–1945* (New York: Columbia University Press, 1985), 105–15. A good case study of the AALL's efforts in one state is Alexander Keyssar, *Out of Work: The First Century of Unemployment in Massachusetts* (Cambridge and New York: Cambridge University Press, 1986), esp. 265–72. An assessment by a reformer close to the AALL "Wisconsin" group is John A. Fitch, "The American Association for Labor Legislation, 1907–1942," *John B. Andrews Memorial Symposium on Labor Legislation and Social Security, November 4 and 5, 1949* (Madison: University of Wisconsin Press, 1949), 81–86.

2. Lubove, *Social Security*, 34–44, 141–43, 173–74; Nelson, *Unemployment Insurance*, chaps. 7–9.

3. Lubove, *Social Security*, 42–43, 53–54; Gerd Korman, *Industrialization, Immigrants, and Americanizers: The View From Milwaukee, 1866–1921* (Madison: State Historical Society of Wisconsin, 1967), 114–20; Robert Asher, "The 1911 Wisconsin Workmen's Compensation Law: A Study in Conservative Labor Reform," *Wisconsin Magazine of History* 57 (Winter 1973–1974): 126–29; John B. Andrews, "Practical Program for the Prevention of Unemployment in America,"*American Labor Legislation Review* 5 (June 1915):189, hereafter cited as *ALLR*; John R. Commons, "Unemployment: Compensation and Prevention," *The Survey*, 1 October 1921, 8–9.

4. Commons, "Address Delivered at Fifteenth Annual Meeting, National Tuberculosis Association, June, 1919," in *Trade Unionism and Labor Problems* (Boston: Ginn and Co., 1921), 81–93; *Dictionary of American Biography*, s.v. "Commons, John Rogers"; Korman, *Industrialization*, 8–10.

5. Nelson, *Unemployment Insurance*, 10–15; William Hard, "Unemployment as a Coming Issue," *ALLR* 2 (February 1912): 93–100; Charles R. Henderson,

"Recent Advances in the Struggle Against Unemployment," ibid., 105–10; Henderson, "Insurance Against Unemployment," *ALLR* 4 (May 1914): 291–92; John B. Andrews, "Introductory Note," ibid., 209–17. Andrews used the title of Beveridge's book, *Unemployment: A Problem of Industry*, as the theme of the May 1914 issue of the *ALLR*.

6. *ALLR* 4 (March 1914): 145; Andrews to Samuel McCune Lindsay, 22 January 1914; Seager to Thomas W. Lamont, 2 February 1914; circular letter, January 1914; Seager to Frances A. Kellor, 14 February 1914; W. Jett Lauck to Andrews, 14 March 1914, Reel 11, American Association for Labor Legislation Papers, Wisconsin State Historical Society, microfilm edition, hereafter cited as AALLP; quotation from Andrews, "Introductory Note," *ALLR* 4 (May 1914): 209–17.

7. "Report of Official Delegates on the State of Unemployment," *ALLR* 4 (May 1914): 223–54; Nelson, *Unemployment Insurance*, 15–16; Seager to Frances A. Kellor, 14 February 1914, Reel 11, and Andrews to Henderson, 14 December 1914, Reel 13, AALLP.

8. Andrews, "A Practical Program," *ALLR* 5 (June 1915): 171–83; John B. Andrews, "A National System of Labor Exchanges," *New Republic*, supplement, 26 December 1914, 1–8.

9. Andrews, "Practical Program," 184–88.

10. Ibid., 189–92; Seager, "English Methods," *ALLR* 4 (May 1914): 290–91. Like Commons, Andrews believed that employers would hire experts to reduce labor turnover and other inefficiencies similar to the earlier hiring of safety and health experts to reduce industrial accidents and sickness. On Andrews' view that he and Commons held prevention as more vital than relief as the major function of unemployment insurance and his exaggeration of the British act's employer refund clause, see Andrews to Olga S. Halsey, 27 January 1915, Reel 13, AALLP; Lubove, *Social Security*, 159, 196; Yellowitz, "Unemployment Reform," 344.

11. Andrews, "Practical Program," 191–92.

12. Andrews, "Introductory Note," *ALLR* 5 (November 1915): 469–72. For assessments of the *Practical Program*, see Lubove, *Social Security*, 147–49, and Nelson, *Unemployment Insurance*, 16–17.

13. Nelson, *Unemployment Insurance*, 17–18; "Unemployment Survey: 1914–1915," *ALLR* 5 (November 1915): 475–595, esp. 494.

14. Andrews sensed in 1914–1915 the appearance of a new group of "progressive" employers and corporations that the AALL might cooperate with in combating unemployment. AALL member Ida Tarbell celebrated the new welfare capitalism in her series of articles in *American Magazine*, "The Golden Rule in Business" from November 1914 through early 1915. She praised business regularization in "Keeping Men at Work," *American Magazine* 78 (December 1914): 26–27. Tarbell was more effusive about these employers than Andrews, but Commons shared much of her perspective.

15. Nelson, *Unemployment Insurance*, 21–22; Lubove, *Social Security*, chap. 4 and pp. 156–57; Andrews, "Social Insurance," *The Annals* 69 (January 1917): 42–49; "Introductory Note," *ALLR* 8 (March 1918): 5–6; Seager, "Coordination of Federal, State, and City Systems of Employment Offices," ibid., 21–26; Andrews, "Labor Laws in the Crucible," *The Survey*, 16 February 1918, 542–44; "Introductory Note," *ALLR* 8 (December 1918): 285–86; "Report of Work, 1917," *ALLR* 8 (March 1918): 116–17; "Report of Work, 1918," *ALLR* 9 (June 1919): 161–

71; Don D. Lescohier, *The Labor Market*, (New York: Macmillan Co., 1919), chaps. 7–10.

16. Nelson, *Unemployment Insurance*, 18–20; Lubove, *Social Security*, 82–90; Andrews to E. B. Butler, Esq., 5 April 1920, Reel 22, AALLP.

17. Nelson, *Unemployment Insurance*, 21–26, 70–72; Lubove, *Social Security*, 158–59; Gompers to Andrews, n.d. [November 1921?], Reel 24, AALLP; the Amalgamated Clothing Workers also endorsed unemployment insurance at their 1920 Boston convention; Andrews to J. J. Handley, 24 September 1920, AALLP; Guy Alchon, *The Invisible Hand of Planning: Capitalism, Social Science, and the State in the 1920s* (Princeton: Princeton University Press, 1985), 71.

18. Nelson, *Unemployment Insurance*, 28–36; Herman Feldman, *The Regularization of Employment* (New York: Harper & Bros., 1925), chap. 3. Feldman's study was sponsored by the American Management Association and dedicated to Sam A. Lewisohn, a businessman very prominent in the AALL's leadership as well; on the search for alternatives to statism and laissez-faire in 1920–1921, see Ellis W. Hawley, *The Great War and the Search for a Modern Order* (New York: St. Martin's Press, 1979), 52–55.

19. John R. Commons, *Industrial Goodwill* (1919; reprint, New York: Arno Press, 1969); Andrews to Greist, Greist Mfg. Co., 28 February 1921; Andrews to John Calder, c/o Swift & Co., 30 September 1921; Andrews to N. I. Stone, c/o Hickey-Freeman Co., 4 October 1921; Andrews to Henry S. Dennison, 1 and 11 November 1921; Andrews to L. D. H. Weld, 7 November 1921, AALLP; Commons, "Unemployment," *The Survey*, 1 October 1921, 8–9 and Commons, "Unemployment Prevention," *ALLR* 12 (March 1922): 22–23; J. J. Hundley to Andrews, 20 September 1920 and Andrews to Hundley, 24 September 1920, AALLP suggest the origins of the Huber bill; Nelson, *Unemployment Insurance*, 107–16; Andrews to Commons, 9 March, 15 October, 5 and 15 November 1921 and Commons to Andrews, 11 November 1921, AALLP.

20. Andrews, "Unemployment Insurance," *ALLR* (December 1920): 233–39.

21. Andrews, "Introductory Note," *ALLR* 11 (March 1921): 5–6; papers by Hillman, H. A. Hatch (Deering, Millikin & Co., textiles), N. I. Stone (Hickey-Freeman Co., men's clothing), Bloomfield, Mallery, Whiting Williams, and Dennison, ibid., 25–59; "Unemployment Survey: 1920–1921," *ALLR* 11 (June 1921): 191–219.

22. Andrews to Commons, 9 March, 15 October, 5 and 14 November 1921; Commons to Andrews, 11 November 1921, Reel 24, AALLP; Commons, "Unemployment Prevention," *ALLR* 12 (March 1922): 15–24.

23. Commons, "Unemployment," *The Survey*, 1 October 1921, 5–9; Nelson, *Unemployment Insurance*, 109–10; John R. Commons and John B. Andrews, *Principles of Labor Legislation* (New York: Harper & Bros., 1927), 491–92; Commons, "Address . . . June, 1919" in *Trade Unionism*, 86.

24. Ellis W. Hawley, "Herbert Hoover, the Commerce Secretariat, and the Vision of an 'Associative State,' 1921–28," *Journal of American History* 61 (June 1974): 116–40.

25. Carolyn Grin, "The Unemployment Conference of 1921: An Experiment in National Cooperative Planning," *Mid-America* 55 (April 1973): 83–107; Economic Advisory Committee—Correspondence A–M, September 1921, Commerce Papers, Herbert Hoover Papers, Herbert Hoover Presidential Library, hereafter, CP, HHP,

HHPL; Nelson, *Unemployment Insurance*, 37; Andrews to Hoover, 9 September 1921, Unemployment—John B. Andrews File, Unemployment, CP, HHP, HHPL; Hunt to Andrews, 13 September 1921 and Andrews to Hunt, 15 September 1921; Andrews to Commons, 8 September 1921, and Commons to Andrews, 15 October 1921, Reel 24, AALLP.

26. Nelson, *Unemployment Insurance*, 38, and *Report of the President's Conference on Unemployment, September 26–October 12, 1921* (Washington, D.C., 1921), esp. 166–69.

27. Andrews to Frederick Almy, 2 September 1921 for quote; Andrews to Mr. and Mrs. Frederick MacKenzie, 6 September 1921; Andrews to William Rossiter, 3 October 1921, and Andrews to Royal Meeker, 14 October 1921; Andrews to Commons, 15 October 1921; Andrews to Henry P. Shattuck, 15 October 1921, AALLP.

28. Andrews to Dennison, 6 December 1921, Reel 24, AALLP; Andrews, "The President's Conference on Unemployment—Success or Failure?" *ALLR* 11 (December 1921): 307–10.

29. Andrews to Hunt, 3 December 1921; Hunt to Andrews, 5 December and 20 December 1921, Reel 24, AALLP; Andrews, "Introductory Note," *ALLR* 12 (March 1922) complained of little national action on unemployment prevention, but his target here was Congress which defeated both the Kenyon bill for long-range public works planning and a modest $400 thousand appropriation for the struggling USES. Hoover and the Unemployment Conference backed both at least nominally. Still Andrews' disenchantment extended to Hoover and the Conference report itself. See also Andrews, "Foreward," *ALLR* 13 (March 1923): 3–4. AALL leaders could take some comfort, however, from the Business Cycle Committee's endorsement of the remaining remedies of the *Practical Program*. Nelson, *Unemployment Insurance*, 40, and Alchon, *The Invisible Hand of Planning*, chaps. 5–6; for Wolman and Andrews papers, see *Business Cycles and Unemployment* (New York: McGraw-Hill, 1923), chaps. 17–18.

30. Frederick MacKenzie, "Stabilizing Employment: Official Findings," *ALLR* 13 (June 1923): 146–48.

31. Vaughan Davis Bornet, "Herbert Hoover's Planning for Unemployment and Old Age Insurance Coverage, 1921–1933," in *The Quest for Security: Papers on the Origins and the Future of the American Social Insurance System*, ed. John N. Schacht (Iowa City: The Center for the Study of the Recent History of the United States, 1982), 38–39. Hoover also proposed a voluntary unemployment insurance plan for the economically "sick," soft coal industry, for which see Ellis W. Hawley, "Secretary Hoover and the Bituminous Coal Problem," *Business History Review* 42 (Autumn 1968): 279–80.

32. [Andrews], "Gains of the Past Year in Combatting Unemployment in the United States," *ALLR* 14 (June 1924): 160–69; Henry S. Dennison, "Depression Insurance," *ALLR* 12 (March 1922): 31–36; "A Manufacturer Averts Unemployment by Intelligent Planning," *ALLR* 13 (March 1923): 23; "Unemployment Insurance in the Clothing Industry," *ALLR* 13 (September 1923): 198; "A Manufacturer Guarantees Steady Employment," ibid., 199; Herbert Johnson, "Unemployment Prevention Insurance an Aid to Stabilizing Business," *ALLR* 13 (December 1923): 241–43; Ernest G. Draper, "Laboratories of Unemployment Insurance," *ALLR* 14 (June 1924): 131; Earl Dean Howard, "Unemployment In-

surance in the Chicago Clothing Industry," ibid., 135–36; Fred C. Butler, "Guaranteed Employment in the Cleveland Garment Industry," ibid., 137–42; Nelson, *Unemployment Insurance*, chaps. 3 and 5.

33. Andrews, "Reactionary Demagogues," *ALLR* 15 (September 1925): 179–80.

34. "Can Business Prevent Unemployment?" ibid., 219–21; Herman Feldman, "Newer Methods in the Stabilization of Employment," *ALLR* 16 (March 1926): 47–56; H. Feldman, *The Regularization of Employment* (New York: Harper & Bros., 1925); Sam A. Lewisohn et al., *Can Business Prevent Unemployment?* (New York: Harper & Bros., 1925).

35. "Legislative Notes," *ALLR* 13 (December 1923): 227; Andrews, "Increasing Unemployment Calls for Adoption of Constructive Program of Relief and Prevention," *ALLR* 18 (March 1928): 73.

36. Andrews, "Significant New Developments," and "Increasing Unemployment," *ALLR* 18 (March 1928): 3–4, 65–75; Leo Wolman, "The New Unemployment," ibid., 81–84; Wolman, "The Shadows of Prosperity," *The Survey*, 1 March 1928, 677–78; Bryce M. Stewart, "American Experiments with Unemployment Insurance," *Survey Graphic* 62 (April 1929): 57–59; Stewart, *Unemployment Benefits in the United States* (New York: Industrial Relations Counselors, Inc., 1930), esp. chap. 8; Nelson, *Unemployment Insurance*, 47; Lubove, *Social Security*, 161–62.

37. Andrews, "Increasing Unemployment," *ALLR* 18 (March 1928): 74; "Need for Unemployment Facts Shown by Issue Raised at Washington," *ALLR* 18 (June 1928): 149–52; Margaret D. Meyer, "What About Unemployment?" ibid., 153–62; Otto T. Mallery, " 'Prosperity Reserve' of Public Work Needed to Combat Unemployment," *ALLR* 18 (March 1928): 77–80.

38. Lubove, *Social Security*, 163–64, 167–74; Nelson, *Unemployment Insurance*, chaps. 7–9, esp. 145–52, 216–18. For a respectful, but critical view of the leadership of John B. and Irene Osgood Andrews, see Paul H. Douglas, *In the Fullness of Time* (New York: Harcourt Brace Jovanovich, 1972), 68–69. Douglas stressed, as did Isaac M. Rubinow in the early 1930s, that the Andrews' leadership never recovered from the health insurance debacle of 1915–1920 and that he and the AALL turned cautious by the 1920s. For praise of Andrews and his wife, the AALL's assistant secretary, as courageous battlers for social justice and builders of the welfare state see *John B. Andrews Memorial Symposium.*

2

John D. Rockefeller, Jr., Herbert Hoover, and President Wilson's Industrial Conferences of 1919–1920

Charles E. Harvey

In September 1919, as Woodrow Wilson began his tour to win support for American membership in the League of Nations, he called an industrial conference to settle the impending nationwide steel strike. The ensuing tragedy of Wilson's debilitating stroke, the Senate's vote against joining the League, and labor's failure to consolidate its wartime gains amidst the "red scare" of those months is well recalled. Less well remembered is the extension of the industrial conference into the spring, its alteration from an open event led by cabinet members to a confidential gathering guided by Herbert Hoover, and its removal of industrial relations from the public to the private realm. Nor has the role of John D. Rockefeller, Jr., in this episode been illumined by historians. The purpose of this essay is to suggest how and why Rockefeller and Hoover effected the transfer of industrial relations from the public to the private arena after the famous deadlock between Elbert Gary and Samuel Gompers, the leaders of organized capital and labor, at the first conference. This sequence of events will be viewed in the context of Rockefeller's promotion of employee representation on company grievance panels as the way to avoid industrial strife and unionization.[1]

The obscurity of Rockefeller's role is partly due to his artful circumspection as heir to the world's largest industrial fortune and the controversies surrounding its formation. The oversight is also due, one suspects, to the aversion of historians to what might seem a vulgar economic determinism or even a conspiracy thesis. Yet, as with a number of other major developments in the first half of the twentieth century, to ignore Rockefeller is to miss much of the inside story. In many instances, such as the outcome of the industrial conferences, Rockefeller could well be considered the principal figure, the more visible actor, Hoover, his agent.[2]

This suggestion qualifies an influential view of modern American history which stresses the growth of managerial organization. It does so by insisting upon the centrality of great wealth in the process. For despite fundamental changes in America's economic system, it remains distinctly capitalist.

Among capitalists Rockefeller's role was commensurate with his unmatched financial resources.[3]

Previous reports of the postwar industrial conferences have failed to notice Rockefeller's pivotal action in the transition from the first to the second, not to mention his central place in the underlying evolution of industrial relations over the previous half decade. Historians have also neglected the configuration of Hoover's and Rockefeller's international activities in the postwar years, shaped as it was by their common perception of a global struggle between capitalism and socialism.[4]

Rockefeller and Hoover shared the basic assumption that social relations arise out of private agreements to which the public, through government, is a third party or only a collection of third parties. If this premise distinguishes capitalist from socialist theory, then for these men the crux of domestic and world problems after World War I was ideological. By slighting that dimension historians have veiled the significance of the second conference's removal of industrial relations from the public and political realm to the private and economic realm, from the sphere where people allocate power to that where money holds sway.[5]

Because Rockefeller's employee representation plan turned away from mere reliance on governmental protection of capital's property rights and formally respected the right of unions to recruit workers independently from the grievance system, it was acceptable to Gompers, if not to Gary. Espoused by the Wilson administration during the war, it had spread rapidly among large corporations and with it, union membership. Meanwhile, Hoover came to include it in the broader view of scientific management then emerging among engineers. To Rockefeller, Hoover—and Gompers—it provided an "American" alternative to "European" theories of industrial democracy in the postwar international tumult.[6]

But the balance of forces shifted dramatically once the second conference was under way. The red scare identification of American labor militancy with European revolutionary violence contributed strongly to the defeat of the national steel strike and to the decline of public sympathy with industrial democracy in general. These months also witnessed the quashing of revolutions in Central Europe and the confinement of the new Communist International to Russia's heartland. By the end of 1919 the postwar surge of labor power that many had hoped, or feared, would create a new world-order had crested. In its place appeared the New Era of American international business, with Rockefeller its appropriately invisible prime mover and Hoover its major spokesman. Under these circumstances, the Rockefeller labor plan, endorsed by the final report of Hoover's second industrial conference, became a basic component of the system of informal cartels that both men envisioned for modern industrial society.[7]

Rockefeller and Hoover brought considerable expertise to the situation they faced in the fall of 1919. Their experience was based upon the emergence of systematic philanthropy, welfare capitalism, and scientific management in the preceding decades. Rockefeller, in charge of his father's holdings by the time "the great coalfield war" broke out in the Colorado mines early in the Wilson administration, unexpectedly found himself at the center of action in "the age of industrial violence." He reflexively supported Colorado Fuel and Iron officials in their refusal to recognize the United Mine Workers union (UMW) as bargaining agent for the miners. On 25 April 1914, a group of women and children suffocated during a militia attack on the miners' tent colony at Ludlow, Colorado. Suddenly, the forty-year-old heir became internationally notorious as the symbol of exploitative capitalism.

As president of the newly chartered Rockefeller Foundation, he obtained the counsel of Mackenzie King, the astute Harvard trained Liberal labor minister of Canada, then out of office. Soon, however, the United States Industrial Commission subpoenaed Rockefeller's papers and exposed his direction of the struggle against the UMW, aided by King and publicity agent Ivy Lee.[8]

In the fall of 1914 the Wilson administration determined the outcome of the strike by sending federal troops into the mining area to restore order. Yet it wanted to set a more liberal trend in industrial relations for the country at large that would help form an alliance with labor and build a national majority for the Democratic Party. To this end a moderate former UMW official and Pennsylvania congressman, William B. Wilson, had been named the first Secretary of Labor. By the time the Industrial Commission held further hearings in the spring of 1915, the strike had been broken and Rockefeller's company had instituted King's shrewd and timely solution to his employer's disgrace.[9]

At the heart of King's plan lay a grievance system involving employee representation. While it actually usurped the function of an independent union and allowed the company to compete for worker loyalty, it did not discriminate against union members. So Rockefeller could claim before the Industrial Commission and the press that he supported the right of labor to organize and engage in collective bargaining, although he still refused to recognize unions as bargaining agents for his own employees.[10]

The plan also satisfied President Wilson's need to placate the AFL which accepted half a loaf. Given AFL hostility to socialism and its fear of hostile government action against its affiliates, the formal freedom to organize seemed enough especially in an economy stimulated by the war in Europe. Rockefeller's handshakes had gone a long way. The public would be provided with information by a state commission whose powers, under the Colorado law modeled on King's Canadian statute, were limited to investigation, publicity, and delay—all adverse to successful strike organization. Wilson, Rockefeller, and AFL President Samuel Gompers agreed with King on the principle of limiting governmental authority in industrial relations.[11]

Rockefeller saw King's scheme of employee representation as the best approach to the problem of class conflict in modern industrial society, and he became its leading exponent. At the same time, he set King to work installing the grievance system in all the companies under his control or influence, an important portion of the economy in those days. Encouraged by King, Rockefeller further enhanced the Colorado Plan by emphasizing its religious aspect, a congenial undertaking for him. He blended his father's personal piety with the growing penchant for science of their philanthropic adviser, former Northern Baptist educational secretary, Frederick T. Gates. He also shared the global missionary perspective of YMCA eminence John R. Mott. In contrast to the new biblical fundamentalism that saw evangelizing the world as a sign of the apocalypse, Rockefeller and Mott professed a modernism that would build the kingdom of God on earth through economic progress. This depended most of all upon harmonious industrial relations, both as an expression of Christian love and as the prerequisite for increasing economic efficiency through mechanization.[12]

Hoover would not have disagreed with Rockefeller's "practical Christianity," but his own emphasis was upon scientific management or human engineering as the main avenue of progress. Far from inheriting a Standard Oil fortune, he was a self-made man who rose from orphaned poverty to wealth and fame as a mining engineer, businessman and relief administrator. Yet his international experience and confidence in the American economic system led him to share the cultural expansionism that came to Rockefeller through his religious, business, and philanthropic interests. Both men sought social stability and rapidly increasing productivity as the basic answer to conditions that bred disruption.[13]

Between 1915 and 1919 while Rockefeller underwrote King's plan of industrial relations and Mott's form of modernizing religion, Hoover moved from heading famine relief in German-occupied Belgium to directing President Wilson's wartime Food Administration. His methods of managing market forces through voluntary cooperation in the production and conservation of food supplies made him a national byword: everyone "Hooverized." His style of operation also became the model for America's whole program of economic mobilization for the war. Its emphasis upon promotional techniques to obtain voluntary support maintained the traditional ideal of a limited state while exerting governmental authority over private interests.[14]

In the field of industrial relations, the government's creation of the National War Labor Board (NWLB) gradually made the Colorado Plan normative for the military contractors. Former President Taft and prewar Industrial Commission chairman Frank Walsh, who brought along his chief of staff, union advocate W. Jett Lauck, concurred as NWLB cochairmen in upholding both labor's right to organize and management's right to refuse to bargain with unions. The Board and the War Labor Policies Board led by Felix Frankfurter adopted King's plan of employee representation on grievance panels as official policy, and they forced many major corporations to accept this expression of Rockefeller's social theology. It provided the framework for the ongoing struggle for and against unionization.[15]

Wartime voluntarism peaked in November 1918, when the Armistice prompted President Wilson to scuttle the whole mobilization program. The NWLB floundered for several months before its demise. The week the war ended, John R. Mott, with Rockefeller's ardent backing, went ahead with the United War Work Campaign. Protestant, Catholic, and Jewish groups joined the YMCA in an appeal for funds to support morale work with servicemen. This giant publicity drive raised over $200 million to be administered by Raymond B. Fosdick, director of the War Department's Training Camp Commission.[16]

Before the war, Rockefeller had hired Fosdick, younger brother of the noted modernist preacher, Henry Emerson Fosdick, to study European and American police systems and their methods of controlling prostitution. He then sent Fosdick to help clean up border towns during General Pershing's 1916 "punitive expedition" into Mexico and next to Washington to coordinate military efforts to "keep the boys fit to fight" and come home clean after America entered the European war in 1917. While in Europe early in 1919 on this mission, Fosdick was named Associate Secretary General of the League of Nations by President Wilson, his former professor at Princeton.[17]

Hoover also went to Europe immediately after the Armistice to supervise American food relief for the devastated continent. He was soon made director of the Supreme Allied Economic Council and assumed responsibility for restoring the social stability required for economic recovery. This entailed quelling revolution and labor unrest in Central Europe while containing if not overthrowing Bolshevism in Russia itself. Hoover's undertaking overlapped that of the Rockefeller Foundation which expended over $17 million on war relief. Because Wilson's peace plans depended upon the restoration of order in Europe, Hoover kept him well-informed about his analysis of social conditions. Fosdick's concern for economic issues in his League post and growing closeness to Rockefeller (his brother served on the board of the Foundation at this time) suggests a probable sharing of ideas all around.[18]

In America, the end of hostilities brought sudden termination of war contracts, dismantling of wartime bureaus including the employment service, return of servicemen—and renewed industrial conflict punctuated by political demonstrations and radical rhetoric. Genuine revolution in Europe with nationalist uprisings in colonial lands inspired America's few sympathizers. Yet the combination of revolution abroad and labor activism laced with socialist slogans at home led to profound anxiety in the land. While those in higher circles were cautious about contact with its more paranoid manifestations, they were not immune and developed their own long term strategies to restore order.[19]

Lending apparent substance to the fear that socialism was coming, at its convention in June 1919, the AFL not only demanded full union recognition for collective bargaining in industry but also voted for the Plumb Plan to nationalize the railroads, which were still under wartime government control. Such aims, moderate by European standards, were also endorsed by a special meeting of the liberal Protestant Federal Council of Churches and by the National Catholic War Council. These bold actions marked the high point thus far in America of the dream of industrial democracy that had arisen with mass production since the Civil War.[20]

By 3 September 1919 when the President started his nearly fatal tour of the country on behalf of liberal internationalism, the spirit of conservative nationalism was solidifying. Governor Calvin Coolidge of Massachusetts had tapped nationwide enthusiasm by sending state troopers into Boston to halt a police strike for AFL affiliation. When the steelworkers went on strike on 22 September for the same purpose, public opinion had been sensitized to warnings of lawlessness and even revolution. The red scare was on, and the mood intensified when coal miners left the pits on 1 November demanding higher wages to meet inflated postwar prices.[21]

The day he set out on his speaking tour for the League of Nations, President Wilson made a vain attempt to avert the steel strike by issuing invitations to a National Industrial Conference to begin on 6 October. He did so at the behest of Secretary of Labor Wilson and Secretary of Interior Franklin K. Lane who with others in the cabinet wished to make permanent the wartime system of economic cooperation. But before the sessions could begin, the strike was called and the President suffered the stroke that left the mounting domestic crisis and a disordered world without his moderating leadership.[22]

The conference nevertheless took place. It was organized on the familiar model developed early in the century by the National Civic Federation of adding a third party, the public, to help conciliate disputes between capital and labor. Employers at the conference were represented by several organizations led by the National Industrial Conference Board, while the AFL was foremost among the union groups that spoke for labor. The public delegation—with the President's revision of the Labor Secretary's list naming fewer Democrats and more big businessmen—included reformers, academics, and notables, among them both Judge Elbert H. Gary and John D. Rockefeller, Jr. It promptly elected Bernard Baruch, former head of the War Industries Board, its chairman.[23]

President Wilson also retreated in his letter of invitation from the Secretary of Labor's draft which drew on the President's message to Congress from Paris the previous May. At that time Wilson had called for definite legislation to secure "a genuine democratization of industry based upon the full recognition of the rights of those who work in whatever rank to participate in some organic way in every decision which directly affects their welfare or the part they play in industry." He had also specified requests for an extension of the eight-hour day into the private sector and the creation of new federal agencies to replace wartime boards in the interest of "conciliation and adjustment." By September, however, the President merely questioned if "in a genuine spirit of cooperation a practicable method of association based upon a real community of interest which will redound to the welfare of all our people" could not be worked out based upon tried methods and the existing situation. From advocating federal protection of labor's rights in the spring, Wilson had fallen back to encouraging private moderation in the fall.[24]

Opening the conference a month later for the by-then-incapacitated President, Secretary Wilson brought the matter down to making the wartime compromise permanent with "machinery by which justice can be secured and by which everybody at interest has the opportunity of knowing that justice has been secured." In this way the spring's vision of democratizing industry had been reduced by fall to an appeal for perpetuating the NWLB's policy—essentially the Colorado Plan that Mackenzie King had devised for Rockefeller five years before. Yet even that modest proposal turned out to be too ambitious in the wake of postwar reaction.[25]

By the end of October, the Industrial Conference reached an impasse over the issue of union recognition. Meanwhile, the dispute was investigated by both the United States Senate and the fledgling Interchurch World Movement which had all but absorbed the Federal Council of Churches as it mobilized a massive fund drive to support global social gospel outreach. The Senate fanned the red scare by exposing the prewar radicalism of the steelworkers' chief organizer, William Z. Foster, who later, in fact, became a leading Communist. The Interchurch took the opposite tack of reporting management's violations of the workers' right to organize. Gradually, the balance of social forces, including the presence of federal troops under General Leonard D. Wood, tipped toward the companies. By the end of the year the steel strike was defeated. Over the next few years the whole labor movement was severely weakened.[26]

That ends the story of the postwar industrial crisis as it is usually told. One standard account of the steel strike even views the outcome as a setback for Rockefeller's employee representation plan, but it focuses on the loss of labor's wartime gains after the strike rather than on the advance of management's aim of preempting unionism through the plan. A more general study of American labor in the postwar era more accurately stresses the plan's emergence in this period as the centerpiece of welfare capitalism in big business. The end of 1919 marked Rockefeller's great opportunity to make his style of labor management normative for modern industry.[27]

How did this come about? In late October Samuel Gompers, in a move little noticed then or since, reversed his original resolution at the conference which demanded union recognition by the steel industry. Reluctant about the strike from the beginning, he introduced another motion that went back to the Secretary of Labor's opening proposal to extend the wartime compromise. Acceptance of employee representation and freedom for unions to recruit members independently during wartime had brought large membership gains, stimulated the AFL to push for full union recognition in 1919, and could eventually lead to union domination of plant grievance systems. Gompers therefore had his reasons, but coming when it did, his reversal amounted to tacit surrender on the central issue of union recognition months before the steel strikers were finally defeated on the field. While Gary might have accepted this solution before the strike, with victory in sight he and a majority of the employers' group now spurned it.[28]

Rockefeller did not. Having failed to persuade Gary to accept his plan before the strike, he had taken his key advisers along to the conference with the serious intention of setting industrial relations in the entire country on a sound permanent basis. When Gompers reversed himself after the conference's deadlock, in Gary's absence from the public group Rockefeller won its support for the AFL President's new resolution. The group also approved of Secretary Wilson's plan for a national system of industrial conflict adjustment similar to the system King had crafted for Canada and Colorado featuring regional hearing panels and adding a tripartite national board under an impartial umpire. NWLB officials had urged such a system since the spring. With these proposals on the table, Rockefeller obtained a majority vote of the public group for a resolution calling for Chairman Bernard Baruch to request that President Wilson reconstitute the conference. This was the turning point for which he had been waiting.[29]

Rockefeller's motion called for the dismissal of the employer and employee groups, which were leaving anyhow, and the invitation of fifteen or twenty of the "biggest names in the country" to join those of the public group who wished to continue deliberations. According to Baruch's letter to the President, the renewed conference would revert to the original purpose of considering various methods of employee representation along with the plan for conflict resolution. This new conference's report could then become the basis for another tripartite gathering that could recommend legislation to Congress.[30]

President Wilson, or whoever acted on his behalf, complied with Baruch's request and set the date of the new conference for 1 December. Secretary Wilson was designated chairman, but his duties mediating the steel and coal strikes meant that real responsibility fell to the vice chairman, Herbert Hoover. With an eye to the Republican nomination for President in 1920, Hoover added this task to his ongoing work as director of the American Relief Association and his new presidency of the mining engineers' national organization. The fact that he had converted his relief program from federal to private auspices the previous summer would certainly have ingratiated him with Rockefeller Foundation officials who thought private philanthropy and credit could best solve Europe's problems. That change also provided a model for Hoover's subsequent shift of the industrial relations problem from the public to the private sphere through his leadership of the new industrial conference. Both actions coincided with Rockefeller's social religion: brotherly love, not legal coercion, must be the answer.[31]

Rockefeller's pivotal role in renewing the industrial conference did not imply that he controlled everything from Gompers' abandonment of labor's demand for union recognition through Baruch's letter to the President and Secretary Wilson's passing chairmanship of the new conference on to Hoover. Yet Rockefeller's leadership in the development of industrial relations after the 1913–1914 Colorado strike and his extensive behind-the-scenes activity during the October industrial conference—along with Gompers' cooperative policy with big business and Hoover's advocacy of humanized scientific management—suggested a significant influence of Rockefeller and his advisers upon the second industrial conference.

All these men shared a global view of modern economic life with Raymond Fosdick, who apparently became Rockefeller's top adviser while in Washington during the first conference in October. He attended the initial sessions of the International Labor Organization (ILO) there as a League of Nations official. The month before, he had written Rockefeller from London urging his support for the League as a buttress to world economic and social stability. The ILO linked Rockefeller's industrial relations policy with that cause. Undoubtedly, Fosdick participated in the conference strategy sessions of the Rockefeller circle and a group of executives from major corporations that had adopted the employee representation plan.[32]

This "Special Conference Committee" sought to advance the Rockefeller approach of winning workers' consent to managerial authority rather than aggravating their hostility. Its aim was to soften Gary's overtly antiunion open shop stance, believing that could not block the rising power of organized labor. The Committee continued to meet secretly until the late 1930s when Senator Robert M. LaFollette, Jr.'s civil rights committee exposed it as a violation of the Wagner Act's protection of labor's right to organize. From early 1920 on it was aided by a team of labor experts in the law office Fosdick opened to serve Rockefeller. After a few years that team took the name Industrial Relations Counselors, Inc. to carry on King's work of setting up employee representation systems in large corporations. Fosdick's office also became the center of Beardsley Ruml's effort to develop a social science that could inform labor management and guide the whole of Rockefeller's financial and philanthropic "stewardship." A notable example of this undertaking was the research of Elton Mayo at Harvard in industrial psychology. The core concern throughout was the avoidance of class conflict as epitomized by the Bolshevik revolution.[33]

Before his auspicious return to Washington in October 1919, Fosdick had assessed international labor from his League office in London. To his brother he wrote that

> labor should organize. I am coming more and more to believe that the open shop is fundamentally a wrong principle and while it may have fitted things as they existed five years ago, it cannot possibly suit the temper of this age. But the better labor is organized and the greater the degree of solidarity between labor unions, the greater is the menace of a labor dictatorship by the minority, just as it is in Russia today. The obvious answer and the answer which I know will occur to your mind, is education—the mellowing influence of the school and the church. If we had a century or two to work this thing out in, I think that the answer would be the right one; but we haven't a century or two. This matter is going to come to a crisis in the next decade; and it is going to come, I fear, in passion and hatred in the same temper in which this railroad strike is developing now in England.[34]

Fosdick bore this underlying vision through the 1920s when he reorganized the uniquely influential international Rockefeller philanthropic complex.

Hoover expressed an almost paranoid version of this view. To him, Bolshevism was but the extreme end of worker resistance to managerial discipline. Coming home the same month as Fosdick, after coordinating much of Europe's economy for nine months, he reported,

> Two convictions are dominant in my mind. The first comes from contact with stupendous social ferment and revolution in which Europe is attempting to find solution for all its social ills by practical experiments in Socialism. My conviction is that this whole philosophy is bankrupting itself from a startling quarter in the extraordinary lowering of productivity of industrial commodities to a point that, until the recent realization of this bankruptcy, was below the necessity for continued existence of their millions of people.
>
> My second conviction is older but has been greatly hardened, and that is that a greater appreciation of the enormous distance that we of America have grown away from Europe in the century and a half of our national existence, in our outlook on life, our relations toward our neighbors and our social life and political ideals. The supreme importance of this Americanism neither permits us to allow the use of this community for experiment in social diseases, nor does it permit us to abandon the moral leadership we have undertaken of restoring order in the world.

Hoover neatly associated Fosdick's highly successful, Rockefeller-backed campaign against prostitution and sexual infection among servicemen with his own struggle against Marxism. America must not, he stated, "experiment in foreign social diseases." Europe's "groping for the method of nearer equality of opportunity and better distribution of the results of industrial production . . . [was] dominated by Marxian socialism." Only a difference of intensity, Hoover thought, marked "the Bolshevik form, through which there has been over-night Communization of all property, and . . . the milder form of legislative nationalization of industry."[35]

To Hoover, the obvious antidote to sexual and ideological infection was the work ethic. While he saw the need for "the better division of the products of industry," his whole emphasis was upon "the steady development of higher productivity." The world's economic system "must be founded upon the maximum exertion of every individual within his physical ability and upon the reduction of waste both nationally and individually." Not surprisingly, he concluded that "this bankruptcy of the Socialist idea should, if reaction is to be prevented, return the guardianship of this problem from the radical world to the liberal world of moderate men, working upon the safe foundation of experience."[36]

Such a man was John D. Rockefeller, Jr. As soon as he had seen Hoover take control of the renewed industrial conference, Rockefeller "threw himself" into the Interchurch World Movement. Led by John R. Mott, like so many of the modernizing missionary endeavors Rockefeller had long underwritten, its investigation of the steel strike would lead to a suggested "conference" relationship in industry not unlike his own plan. In the spring of 1920 while preparing a promotional article for the Interchurch, Rockefeller envisioned the church stimulating in peacetime the "spirit of sacrifice, of high resolve, of response to the call of duty . . . which led the nations onto the mountain top and gave new hope for the future of the world" during the war. The church alone, he thought, could halt "the reaction which has since followed [bringing] to the surface with equal prominence the lower traits of selfishness, extravagance, indolence and lawlessness, which reveal human nature at its worst." People realize, he held, "that law and order are based upon the principles of righteousness, justice and fair dealing which the church more than any other institution stands for and maintains in the community. They know that financial credit and the stability of trade and commerce rest upon the integrity of a promise, far more than upon a contract, however securely drawn, or a bond, however coercive it may be. . . . The great credit system, which alone makes possible the vast business of this country is based upon integrity." Coming to the gist of his argument, he observed that "in no field of human relationships is the spirit of brotherhood on which the church was founded more profoundly needed than in industrial relations. . . . The men in the Colorado coal fields who some years ago had been on strike for many months and in whose minds the most intense bitterness had grown up, responded to the genuine spirit of brotherhood when it was made manifest among them, while personal contact and the rubbing of elbows soon dispelled hatred and bitterness and established mutual confidence and good will." Overlooking labor's signal defeat in the 1919 steel strike, Rockefeller took a rosy view of his solution to the problem of industrial relations. He believed that it would help "in laying the foundation for a better understanding and friendlier relations in industry. . . . For true it is that the greatest thing in the world is love."[37]

To one of his wealthy friends from whom he had solicited a contribution, he affirmed that the Interchurch would help "to stabilize the business interests of the city and free them from the almost chronic disturbance and loss which needless industrial disputes of the day are subjecting them to."[38] And at the peak of his enthusiasm during the fund drive in April 1920, he sought a $50 million to $100 million permanent endowment for the Interchurch from his father. "I do not think we can overestimate the importance of this Movement," he wired. "As I see it, it is capable of having a much more far-reaching influence than the League of Nations in bringing about peace, contentment, goodwill and prosperity among the peoples of the earth."[39]

Yet despite Rockefeller's earnest effort and several million dollars from his own family, he could not prevent the failure of the Interchurch financial appeal as separate from the successful denominational drives it coordinated. Afterward, he had to be rescued from his embarrassingly deep legal involvement in the Movement's debts by Raymond Fosdick. Final Senate rejection of President Wilson's treaty in March 1920 had made Fosdick's position untenable as the leading American official in the League of Nations. Fosdick turned full-time to Rockefeller's service, virtually as chancellor.[40]

Meanwhile, Hoover had carried out his leadership of the second industrial conference between December 1919 and March 1920. Hoover's letter of appointment from President Wilson's office had expressed the hope "that the working man will feel himself induced to put forth his best effort, that the employer will have an encouraging profit, and that the public will not suffer at the hands of either class." A similar letter to Secretary of Labor Wilson added the wish "that this conference may lay the foundation for the development of standards and machinery within our industries by which these results may be obtained." Hoover himself wrote a fellow engineer that he expected "the industrial conference now sitting under my immediate chairmanship" to evolve "a definite plan for handling these matters" of labor management and profit sharing. But Hoover's plans turned out to be somewhat different from those of the administration.[41]

Hoover took "a very positive stand on the general theory of the Conference that we were dealing with unrest and appeal to public opinion, and for that reason it was desirable that the country should know that we had at least given some thought to the questions underlying social unrest," one participant later commented. The way in which Hoover actually shifted the problem of industrial relations from the public to the private sphere is indicated by a legal brief in his papers from early in the proceedings. Citing the Supreme Court's ruling on the Adamson eight-hour day law for interstate railroads, the brief held that Secretary Wilson's proposed bill for adjusting railroad labor disputes was unconstitutional because the Court had distinguished between legislation on hours from that on wages: "The Court reiterated that it was the right of the parties to agree to a standard of wages free from legislative interference.... This decision, therefore, would seem only to sustain the power of Congress to act when the parties have not voluntarily done so."[42] This theory provided constitutional legitimacy for the Rockefeller plan, maintaining the separation between voluntary contract and governmental coercion, society and state, private and public. On uncertain terrain, it turned the tide of battle away from increasing legal protection of labor's rights.

While Hoover's conference was meeting, a management journal edited by a friend of his ran a symposium on industrial relations. A statement by Charles Evans Hughes, 1916 Republican presidential candidate long associated with the Rockefellers, also argued against labor legislation, although as Chief Justice in 1937 he would lead the Supreme Court's acceptance of the landmark Wagner Act. Now, however, his statement, like Hoover's, asserted managerial control of production, urged labor diligence, and recommended company shop councils. Neither agreed with former President Taft, cochairman of the War Labor Board, who recommended continuation of the wartime experiment in government supervision of employee representation and freedom for union recruitment.[43]

The conference's transfer of industrial relations from public regulation to private volition emerged implicitly in a preliminary report of December 1919: "The right relationship between employer and employee in large industries can be promoted only by the deliberate organization of that relationship."[44] The point became explicit by the end of the conference in March 1920, as indicated in a memorandum in Hoover's files: "It is the belief of the conference that bargains as to standards are not of such a nature as to lend themselves to enforcement and must rest at present at least upon good faith on both sides. It is obvious that if collective bargaining is to have any development in the country, the fidelity of employees and employers to such agreement are the prerequisites for its extension."[45] Rockefeller's religion had gained ascendency over President Wilson's politics, private power over public policy.

In the final report, corporate managerialism completely replaced industrial democracy:

> The guiding thought of the Conference has been that the right relationship between the employer and employee can best be promoted by the deliberate organization of that relationship. That organization should begin within the plant itself. Its object should be to organize unity of interest and thus to diminish the area of conflict, and supply by organized cooperation between employers and employees the advantages of that human relationship that existed between them when industries were smaller. Such organization should provide for the joint action of managers and employees in dealing with their common interests. It should emphasize the responsibility of managers to know men at least as intimately as they know materials, and the right and duty of employees to have a knowledge of the industry, its processes and policies. Employees need to understand their relation to the joint endeavor so that they may once more have a creative interest in their work.[46]

The report in these words simply translated the King-Rockefeller plan into the idiom of scientific management.

Emphasizing the essential issue, the report insisted that the relationship of capital and labor "is not a field for legislation, because the form which employee representation should take may vary in every plant. . . . [T]he Conference proposes a system of settlement close at hand under governmental encouragement, and a minimum of regulation. The entrance of the Government into these problems should be to stimulate further cooperation."[47] Under Hoover's guidance the second industrial conference interpreted out of existence Secretary Wilson's proposed legislation which had been the premise of its calling. The only role left to government in the final report was to promote private solutions to industrial disputes on management's terms: "Its basic idea is stimulation to settlement of differences by the parties in conflict, and the enlistment of public opinion toward enforcing that method of settlement."[48] Nor can this outcome be isolated from the collapse of the steel strike and the defeat of labor's greatest drive to that time to secure the principle of union recognition in collective bargaining. As with the prewar Colorado strike, victory over labor in the field of industrial battle was required to establish the managerial scheme of employee representation that retarded worker control and facilitated corporate discipline.

Hoover and Rockefeller had dined together in January 1920, to discuss "questions involved in the industrial conference." Yet when Rockefeller's endorsement of the final report was requested, he feigned ignorance of the subject of industrial relations on which he had been posing as an expert for some years. He deferred to Mackenzie King, who had just painfully finished his own formal study for the Rockefeller Foundation, *Industry and Humanity*. King, in his typically orotund style, lauded the "consummate skill" with which the report "seeks to preserve the widest measure of individual freedom in industry generally . . . paralleled as it is by a presentation which makes apparent the greater security which comes to the individual through the essentially collective relationship arising out of the quasi-monopolistic nature of these particular classes of employment [where public rights are seriously affected]."[49]

With endorsements of this sort, Hoover's group submitted the report to the President. Yet the conference members did not ask the administration to seek legislation, nor did they make such a request itself. Instead of being sent to Congress, the report was forwarded to businessmen and academics. The largest number of copies was sent to Clarence Hicks, the personnel manager at Jersey Standard and the leader of the Special Conference Committee. Thus did Rockefeller receive back the ball he seems to have passed to Hoover the previous fall. And, as then, he enjoyed the full cooperation of labor's top spokesman. While Hoover's conference members paid for printing and his relief office in New York provided mailing lists, the report was distributed, at government expense, by the Chief Clerk of the Labor Department—Samuel Gompers![50]

The issue of labor legislation could not be entirely stilled by these maneuvers though. It was raised later in the spring of 1920 by the Senate Committee on Education and Labor. At these hearings W. Jett Lauck, staff director for both the prewar U.S. Industrial Commission and the wartime Labor Board, argued for the setting of specific principles in labor adjudication. Lauck held that this had been the reason for extending the industrial conference and that the result of Hoover's evasion of this aim had been "to make agreement more difficult than before and to create a spirit of conflict rather than of cooperation." The report, he said, had nullified its entire usefulness by preventing the application of any principles to industrial disputes."[51]

When Senator Kenyon challenged Hoover about his aversion to going "too far in the elaboration of principles," Hoover referred to the same theory of gradual progress that King had avowed in his letters to Rockefeller several years before:

> As to the question of a code, the opinion of the conference was that if we start to establish a code we will enter an area of unending contention and conflict, and that many of those things are highly undetermined, and some kind of structure could be set up, such as is proposed in this report, and that the structure at first would develop out of precedent and out of experience and probably be the foundation of an industrial code. In other words, that this development must take place, as the law has developed, out of experience rather than out of legislation.

Hoover held the line against any legal guarantees for labor for the foreseeable future. Instead, he stressed labor's need to work harder: "above all things to try to restimulate the creative instinct in labor." Drawing the crucial line of defense for Rockefeller's scheme, he added, "I will say about this report that the portion which has received criticism from organized labor is the portion that has set out the organization of shop councils, all of which is purely voluntary organization and has no relationship to legislation."[52] It would take the Wagner Act of 1935 to move beyond that line.

Hoover bearded the labor lion in its own den later in 1920. Having failed to persuade a gathering of executives using the shop council plan, possibly the Special Conference Committee, to meet with the AFL Executive Council, he did so on his own. He urged the labor leaders to accept the employee representation scheme. The engineering profession, he told them, had moved in recent years from the view

> that industry was a matter of processes and machines to the idea that industry is a human problem [and that] the problem of labor is one that should be solved from the standpoint of the human rights of each individual.... [P]erhaps cooperation

> comes as near as anything else [to the right approach. Yet] one of the criticisms of organized labor is that it tends to curtail production.... Organized labor could not do more to raise itself in the esteem of the American people than to give its co-operation to solve that particular question. [F]or if every atom of production was realized, it would eliminate a large measure of unemployment. [Therefore], I suggest that the American Federation of Labor embrace the idea of the shop council ... [as] the way of settling the entire problem.... The engineers will do nothing except agree—and it is worth your while to do this; there will be the interested third parties.[53]

If Gompers had expected much reciprocal "cooperation" from Hoover at this low point in the history of the union movement in America, these remarks made clear Hoover's deeply rooted ideological bias against organized labor.

By the time of Hoover's encounter with the AFL leaders, Fosdick had met with Rockefeller and King at "The Eyrie," the heir's summer residence on the Maine coast. King had returned to Canadian politics and soon became the perennial prime minister, while Fosdick added King's duties to his own. As part of his reorientation of Rockefeller philanthropy through the development of a new, integrated social science, he shifted the remnant of the Interchurch under Rockefeller's control toward community studies. Contrary to his intention, the major project of this Institute of Social and Religious Research emphasized class differences and slipped into print in 1929 as Robert and Helen Lynd's celebrated *Middletown*. On a vastly larger scale Fosdick employed Beardsley Ruml to redirect the Laura Spelman Rockefeller Memorial, recently dedicated to Rockefeller's late mother by his father, from charities for women and children to deeper theoretical problems. The Memorial profoundly influenced social research through its grants to university work like Elton Mayo's and to coordinating bodies like the Personnel Research Foundation, the Social Science Research Council, the National Bureau of Economic Research, and the Council on Foreign Relations, to name but a few of the most important. Both as Secretary of Commerce and as President, Hoover drew heavily on Rockefeller-financed experts as well as on direct grants for his own projects.[54]

This collaboration is well illustrated with reference to the coal industry, a major subject of Hoover's Waste in Industry studies in 1921 and a prime example of Rockefeller's industrial relations program. Early in 1920 Hoover stated that "no adequate solution can be found except through organized cooperation of the operators, labor, railroads and large consumers. Under existing laws as to combinations, such cooperation cannot be carried on. Therefore, we believe that some federal legislation is necessary permitting such cooperation under competent government authority."[55] His study of the coal industry, however, found no place for a representative of labor. On the other hand, Hoover later wrote Fosdick about a threatened strike: "During the past six weeks, we have been unceasing in our efforts to bring about exactly the steps you have suggested and I am in hopes we will see success before the week is out."[56] Hoover's aide, Edward Eyre Hunt, worked closely with Rockefeller people regarding unemployment in the industry over the years, promoting increased productivity and further cartelization on the apparent assumption that profits would be invested elsewhere to employ displaced workers. As Ellis Hawley notes, while Hoover's "faith in the ability of enlightened businessmen to create an economic utopia remained unshaken," the failure of Rockefeller's labor policy in the coal industry was fully documented in 1934 by Mary Van Kleeck and Ben Selekman of the Russell Sage Foundation. One result of that failure was the near collapse of the United Mine Workers union and the lapse of Hoover's friendship with its leader, John L. Lewis.[57]

In its larger historical context, the relationship between John D. Rockefeller, Jr., and Herbert Hoover in connection with President Wilson's industrial conferences in 1919–1920 illumines many dimensions of the transition from the Progressive Era to the New Era. Especially noteworthy was Hoover's subtle transfer of effective action in the field of industrial relations from the public political sphere to the private economic realm. The American Federation of Labor's aversion to governmental intervention in industrial relations coincided enough with that of Hoover and Rockefeller to facilitate that shift. Ironically, this helped to undermine labor's effort to organize independently. The privatization of industrial relations reversed the policy of the Wilson administration before and during the war which had encouraged both Rockefeller-style shop councils and union growth. With the new balance of power between capital and labor after the defeat of the steel strike of 1919, labor's loss of government support proved disastrous. The widespread belief that modern society was moving toward worker control within industrial democracy was soon dispelled. Late in 1920 Hoover well stated the view of the state's role in industrial relations which allowed capital to prevail. In a letter to the editor of *Industrial Management*, Hoover wrote: "While I am no believer in extending the bureaucratic functions of Government, I am a strong believer in Government intervening to induce active cooperation in the community itself."[58] That was precisely Rockefeller's attitude.

NOTES

1. David M. Kennedy, *Over Here* (New York: Oxford University Press, 1980); Robert K. Murray, *Red Scare* (New York: McGraw-Hill, 1955); David Brody, *Labor in Crisis* (New York, J. B. Lippincott, 1965); and Burl Noggle, *Into the Twenties* (Urbana: University of Illinois Press, 1974); Haggai Hurvitz, "Ideology and Industrial Conflict: President Wilson's First Industrial Conference of October, 1919," *Labor History* 18 (1977): 509–24; Gary Dean Best, "President Wilson's Second Industrial Conference, 1919–1920," *Labor History* 16, (1975): 505–20; Lawrence

E. Gelfand, ed., *Herbert Hoover: The Great War and Its Aftermath, 1914–23* (Iowa City: University of Iowa Press, 1979); Ellis W. Hawley, ed., *Herbert Hoover as Secretary of Commerce, 1921–1928: Studies in New Era Thought and Practice* (Iowa City: University of Iowa Press, 1981); Gary Dean Best, *The Politics of American Individualism* (Westport, Conn.: Greenwood Press, 1975); Robert H. Zieger, *Republicans and Labor, 1919–1929* (Lexington: University of Kentucky Press, 1969); Raymond B. Fosdick, *John D. Rockefeller, Jr.* (New York: Harpers, 1956). Samples of Rockefeller's articles and speeches on the subject are collected in his book, *The Personal Relation in Industry* (New York: privately printed, ca. 1922).

2. This thesis is based on Charles E. Harvey, "John D. Rockefeller, Jr., and the Interchurch World Movement," *Church History* 51 (June 1982): 189–209; and "John D. Rockefeller, Jr., and the Social Sciences," *Journal of the History of Sociology* 2 (Fall 1982): 1–31.

3. The "organizational synthesis" is most closely associated with *Business History Review* and the works of Alfred D. Chandler, Jr. and Louis Galambos. The major statement is Chandler's *The Visible Hand* (Cambridge: Harvard University Press, 1977). David F. Noble, *America by Design* (New York: Oxford University Press, 1977) deals with engineers and the role of government in the corporate system. G. William Domhoff continues the emphasis on wealthy families, recently in *Who Rules America Now?* (Englewood Cliffs, N.J.: Prentice-Hall, 1983). Robert Arnove, ed., *Philanthropy and Cultural Imperialism* (Boston: G. K. Hall, 1980) carries on the debate about influences on social thought. Guy Alchon, *The Invisible Hand of Planning: Capitalism, Social Science, and the State in the 1920s* (Princeton: Princeton University Press, 1985) and Robert M. Collins, *The Business Response to Keynes, 1929–1964* (New York: Columbia University Press, 1981) emphasize the role of Beardsley Ruml, director of the Laura Spelman Rockefeller Memorial, more than Rockefeller's role.

4. Virtually unique in emphasizing Rockefeller's role is Irving Bernstein's classic, *The Lean Years: A History of the American Worker, 1920–1933* (Boston: Houghton-Mifflin, 1960). See also Stephen Scheinberg, "The Development of Corporate Labor Policy, 1880–1940" (Ph.D. diss., University of Wisconsin, 1966); Kim McQuaid, "A Response to Industrialism: Liberal Businessmen and the Evolving Spectrum of Capitalist Reform, 1886–1960" (Ph.D. diss., Northwestern University, 1975); Stuart Brandes, *American Welfare Capitalism, 1880–1940* (Chicago: University of Chicago Press, 1976); Samuel Haber, *Efficiency and Uplift* (Chicago: University of Chicago Press, 1964); Robert Ozanne, *A Century of Labor-Management Relations at McCormick and International Harvester* (Madison: University of Wisconsin Press, 1967). On the international picture see Arno J. Mayer, *Politics and Diplomacy of Peacemaking* (New York: Alfred A. Knopf, 1967); Charles S. Maier, *Recasting Bourgeois Europe* (Princeton: Princeton University Press, 1975); John M. Thompson, *Russia, Bolshevism and the Versailles Peace* (Princeton: Princeton University Press, 1966).

5. Louis Hartz, *The Liberal Tradition in America* (New York: Harcourt-Brace, 1955); and James Weinstein, *The Corporate Ideal in the Liberal State, 1900–1918* (Boston: Beacon Press, 1968).

6. James R. Green, *The World of the Worker* (New York: Hill and Wang, 1980), esp. 67–99; David Montgomery, *Workers' Control in America* (New York: Cambridge University Press, 1979); Daniel T. Rodgers, *The Work Ethic in Industrial*

America (Chicago: University of Chicago Press, 1978), esp. 57–64; Melvin L. Urofsky, *Big Steel and the Wilson Administration* (Columbus: Ohio State University Press, 1969); Valerie Jean Conner, *The National War Labor Board* (Chapel Hill: University of North Carolina Press, 1983); Robert D. Cuff, "The Politics of Labor Administration during World War I," *Labor History* 21 (1980): 546–69; Haggai Hurvitz, "The Meaning of Industrial Conflict in Some Ideologies of the Early 1920's" (Ph.D. diss., Columbia University, 1971); Robert H. Zieger's perceptive "Herbert Hoover, the Wage-Earner, and the 'New Economic System,' 1919–1929," in *Herbert Hoover as Secretary of Commerce*, 82–112.

7. Bernstein, *Lean Years*, 144–89.

8. George S. McGovern and Leonard F. Guttridge, *The Great Coalfield War* (Boston: Houghton Mifflin, 1972); Graham Adams, Jr., *Age of Industrial Violence* (New York: Columbia University Press, 1966); Stephen J. Scheinberg, "Rockefeller and King: The Capitalist and the Reformer," in *Mackenzie King*, ed. John English and J. O. Stubbs (Toronto: Macmillan, 1978), 89–104.

9. McGovern and Guttridge, *Great Coalfield War*, 250–68. For a period piece on the Secretary of Labor by his wartime publicity man, later a noted business statistician, see Roger W. Babson, *W. B. Wilson and the Department of Labor* (New York: Brentano's, 1919).

10. Bernstein, *Lean Years*, 159–62; and Fosdick, *Rockefeller*, 143–66.

11. Hurvitz, "Meaning of Industrial Conflict"; Cuff, "Politics of Labor Administration"; and McGovern and Guttridge, *Coalfield War*.

12. Fosdick, *Rockefeller*, passim; C. Howard Hopkins, *John R. Mott* (Grand Rapids, Mich.: Eerdmans, 1980); Charles E. Harvey, "Religion and Industrial Relations," *Research in Political Economy* 4 (1981): 199–227; and Harvey, "Speer Versus Rockefeller and Mott," *Journal of Presbyterian History* 60 (Winter 1982): 283–300.

13. David Burner, *Herbert Hoover* (New York: Alfred A. Knopf, 1978); and Emily Rosenberg, *Spreading the American Dream* (New York: Hill and Wang, 1982).

14. Ellis W. Hawley, "The Great War and Organizational Innovation: The American Case," unpublished paper 1984; Robert D. Cuff, "Herbert Hoover, the Ideology of Voluntarism, and War Organization During the Great War," in *Herbert Hoover: The Great War*, 23–39; Craig Lloyd, *Aggressive Introvert* (Columbus: Ohio State University Press, 1972).

15. Conner, *War Labor Board*, passim; Urofsky, *Big Steel*, 248–333; Brandes, *Welfare Capitalism*, 119–34; Cuff, "Politics of Labor Administration"; David Brody, *Steelworkers in America* (Cambridge: Harvard University Press, 1960), 199–262.

16. Harvey, "Speer Versus Rockefeller and Mott," 286–88; and the anonymous *War Work of John D. Rockefeller, Jr.*, commissioned and published by his wife in the early 1920s. The *New York Times* gave the drive extensive coverage and featured numerous advertisements for it.

17. Raymond B. Fosdick, *Chronicle of a Generation* (New York: Harper, 1958); and Darryl L. Revoldt, "Raymond B. Fosdick" (Ph.D. diss., University of Akron, 1982).

18. Herbert Hoover, *American Epic* (Chicago: Regnery, 1961), 2:236; Raymond B. Fosdick, *Letters on the League of Nations* (Princeton: Princeton University Press, 1966); essays by Eugene P. Trani, Robert H. Van Meter, Murray Rothbard, and Carl Parrini in *Herbert Hoover: The Great War*; Michael J. Hogan, "Revival and

Reform: America's 20th Century Search for a New Economic Order Abroad," *Diplomatic History* 8 (1984): 287–310.

19. William Preston, Jr., *Aliens and Dissenters: Federal Suppression of Radicals, 1903–1933* (Cambridge: Harvard University Press, 1963).

20. Murray, *Red Scare*, 110–19; Federal Council of Churches, *Report of Special Meeting* (New York: FCC, 1919), 43–47; Rodgers, *Work Ethic*, 57–64.

21. Arthur S. Link, *Woodrow Wilson: Revolution, War and Peace* (Arlington Heights, Ill.: AHM Publishing, 1979), 104–28; Kennedy, *Over Here*, 231–96; Urofsky, *Big Steel*, 284–88; Brody, *Labor in Crisis*, 100–102.

22. Hurvitz, "Wilson's First Industrial Conference," 513; Noggle, *Into the Twenties*, 31–65; Robert Himmelberg, "Business, Antitrust Policy, and the Industrial Board of the Department of Commerce, 1919," *Business History Review* 42 (1968): 1–23; Murray Rothbard, "Herbert Hoover and the Myth of Laissez-Faire," in *A New History of Leviathan*, ed. Ronald Radosh and Murray Rothbard (New York: E. P. Dutton, 1972), 111–45.

23. Best, *Politics of American Individualism*, 38–69; and programs and lists are among photocopy material from W. B. Wilson's papers in the National Archives available in Box 50, Pre-Commerce Papers, Herbert Hoover Papers, Herbert Hoover Library, West Branch, Iowa, hereafter cited as PC-HHP.

24. W. B. Wilson to W. Wilson, 30 August 1919; W. Wilson to My dear Sir, 3 September 1919, ibid.

25. "Address Delivered by Hon. W. B. Wilson . . . 6 October 1919," ibid.

26. Brody, *Labor in Crisis*, 112–46, 171–78; Eldon G. Ernst, "The Interchurch World Movement and the Great Steel Strike of 1919–1920," *Church History* 34 (June 1970): 212–23; Eldon G. Ernst, *Moment of Truth for American Protestantism* (Missoula, Mont.: Scholars' Press, 1972).

27. Brody, *Labor in Crisis*, 176–77; Bernstein, *Lean Years*, 170–89.

28. "Minutes of Meetings of the Group Representing the Public, National Industrial Conference," and (Secretary of Interior) Franklin K. Lane to W. B. Wilson, 24 October 1919, Box 50, PC-HHP.

29. Brody, *Labor in Crisis*, 147; Bernstein, *Lean Years*, 146–47; Public Group Minutes; [W. B. Wilson], "Outline of Plan for Adjustment of Labor Disputes," Box 50, PC-HHP; Conner, *National War Labor Board*, 174–76.

30. Lane to W. B. Wilson, 24 October 1919 attributed the "biggest names" idea to Rockefeller, adding "I understand this is quite agreeable to your view"; and Bernard M. Baruch to The President of the United States, 24 October 1919, Box 50, PC-HHP.

31. Woodrow Wilson to the Ladies and Gentlemen of the Industrial Conference, undated, ibid.

32. Secretary of Interior Lane presided over the first conference in October, while Secretary of Labor Wilson officiated at the simultaneous meetings of the International Labor Organization also in the nation's capital. My interpretation is based on material in Rockefeller's and Fosdick's papers cited in Harvey, "John D. Rockefeller, Jr. and the Social Sciences."

33. Bernstein, *Lean Years*, 167–69; Ozanne, *A Century of Labor-Management Relations*, 156–61; Clarence J. Hicks, *My Life in Industrial Relations* (New York: Harpers, 1941), 135–39. Hicks had moved from International Harvester to Colorado Fuel and Iron to Jersey Standard and led the Committee.

34. Raymond B. Fosdick to Harry Emerson Fosdick, 9 September 1919, Box 5, Raymond Fosdick Papers, Seeley Mudd Library, Princeton, New Jersey, and Fosdick, *The Old Savage and the New Civilization* (Garden City, N.Y.: Doubleday, 1929).

35. Hoover typescript for talk to the mining engineers, 16 September 1919, Box 26, PC-HHP. Zieger, "New Economic System," 102, notes that "[Hoover] was thoroughly familiar with the employers in the Special Conference Committee."

36. Hoover transcript for talk, 16 September 1919.

37. John D. Rockefeller, Jr., "Why I Am a Church Member," unpublished manuscript, 1920, Box 40, the Papers of John D. Rockefeller, Jr., Record Group 2, Rockefeller Archive Center, Pocantico Hills, New York.

38. Rockefeller to William Fellowes Morgan, 7 May 1920, ibid.

39. Rockefeller to John D. Rockefeller, 21 April 1920, ibid.

40. Harvey, "Religion and Industrial Relations," 209–24.

41. Woodrow Wilson to Herbert Hoover, 19 November 1919, Box 51; Woodrow Wilson to W. B. Wilson 19 November 1919, Box 51; Hoover to Thomas T. Read, 16 December 1919, Box 26, all in PC-HHP.

42. W. O. Thompson to H. J. Waters, 6 March 1920, Box 52 and memorandum attached to a letter from Hoover's secretary, Ed. D. Kneass, to Secretary of the Industrial Conference, 11 December 1919, ibid.

43. Reprints of statements by Hughes, Hoover, and Taft printed in response to Franklin K. Lane, "Lasting Lessons of the Labor Crisis," *Industrial Management* 59 (February 1920): 94–98, Box 53, PC-HHP.

44. *Preliminary Statement of Industrial Conference* (Washington, D.C.: Government Printing Office, 1919), 3.

45. Memorandum in Hoover's files dated 3 March 1920, Box 52, PC-HHP. There was no formal report of the first conference, but the National Industrial Conference Board which led the employer group published the pamphlet, *The Vital Issues of the Industrial Conference* (Boston: NICB, 1919).

46. *Report of Industrial Conference Called by the President, March 6, 1920*, 6–8.

47. Ibid., 29–30.

48. Ibid., 32.

49. Rockefeller to Hoover, 5 January 1920; Hoover to Rockefeller, 10 January 1920; Rockefeller to Hoover, 16 January 1920; Rockefeller to Hoover, date obscure; all in Box 16, PC-HHP. Rockefeller forwarded King's comments to several conference members with his own deferential remarks in Rockefeller to Julius Rosenwald, 26 February 1920. Stanley King wrote Ed. Kneass, 10 March 1920: "Mr. Hoover asked me yesterday for another copy of W. L. Mackenzie King's letter to John D. Rockefeller, Jr., regarding our proposals and I take pleasure in handing it to you. Mr. Hoover wants this to use in connection with his talk with the special correspondents." All in Box 52, PC-HHP. Hoover elaborated his own views in *American Individualism* (Garden City, N.Y.: Doubleday, 1923); Rockefeller's book on industrial relations was published the same year.

50. Gompers' correspondence, Box 51, PC-HHP.

51. U.S. Congress, Senate, Committee on Education and Labor, *Industrial Conference Hearing... on Report of Industrial Conference*, 66th Cong., 2nd sess., 1920, 1–24, esp. 16–17, 21; and W. Jett Lauck and Claude S. Watts, *The Industrial Code* (New York: Funk and Wagnalls, 1922).

52. Ibid., 25–42, esp. 26–32, 42. Hoover praised King's Canadian system and opposed a recent Kansas law that provided for state settlements. William Appleman Williams, *Some Presidents* (New York: Random House, 1972), 42, lauds Hoover as a "leader of the public in coming together in cooperative action"; but Joan Hoff Wilson, *Herbert Hoover: Forgotten Progressive* (Boston: Little, Brown, 1975), 90–100, argues that Hoover stressed shop councils while only giving lip service to real collective bargaining.

53. Extracts from "Minutes of the Executive Council of the AFL" along with "Hoover Confers with AFL Executive Council on Economic and Industrial Conditions," *New York Times* article of 12 November 1920, Box 26, PC-HHP. The debate continued when Gompers printed his own comment and Hoover's "A Plea for Cooperation" in the *American Federationist* 28 (January 1921): 33–35, 39–40. Cf. Brody, *Labor in Crisis*, 147.

54. See Harvey, "Robert S. Lynd, John D. Rockefeller, Jr. and *Middletown*," *Indiana Magazine of History* 79 (December 1983): 330–54; and Harvey, "John D. Rockefeller, Jr., and the Social Sciences."

55. *Annual Banquet of American Institute of Mining and Metallurgical Engineers, Wednesday, February 16th, 1920, Waldorf-Astoria*, a brochure with program notes on Hoover address at the "Open Forum on the State of the Bituminous Coal Industry," and correspondence between Hoover as AIMME president and his vice president on the study of the coal industry, both in Box 25, PC-HHP.

56. Hoover to Fosdick, 28 June 1922, with other letters later in 1922 about matters raised by George J. Anderson of the group in Fosdick's office that became Industrial Relations Counselors, Inc. in 1924 and about a meeting with Hoover attended by Fosdick and Rockefeller Foundation president George Vincent late in 1922, all in Box 228, PC-HHP.

57. Hunt organized Hoover's "Waste in Industry" studies, which Hoover carried over from the AIMME in 1920 to the Federation of American Engineering Societies in 1921 and the Department of Commerce thereafter, and the two collaborated with Rockefeller associates like Arthur Wood, Bryce Stewart, and Joseph H. Willits in promoting similar policies; Edward Erye Hunt, F. G. Tryon, and Joseph H. Willits, *What the Coal Commission Found* (Baltimore: Williams and Wilkins, 1925), 242, 244, 331; Ellis W. Hawley, "Secretary Hoover and the Bituminous Coal Problem, 1921–1928," *Business History Review* 42 (1968): 247–70; Mary Van Kleeck and Ben Selekman, *Miners and Management* (New York: Russell Sage Foundation, 1934); Melvin Dubofsky and Warren Van Tine, *John L. Lewis* (New York: Quadrangle/New York Times, 1977).

58. Hoover to John R. Dunlap, 19 November 1920, Box 53, PC-HHP.

3

Interwar Air Defense Planning: The Role of the President's Aircraft Board

Stephen D. Bodayla

Of the many weapons employed for the first time in World War I, the airplane had the greatest national defense implications. European strategists immediately recognized the potential of the airplane and began to plan for its integration into their defenses. It was not until 1925, however, that the first realistic and comprehensive American air defense plan, contained in the report of the President's Aircraft Board, was completed.

The American delay was the result of unwillingness of the military establishment to accept the airplane as the weapon of the next war. The reasons for this are myriad and include: skepticism about the usefulness of airplanes in view of their range limitations; the belief that America was secure within its oceanic womb; the unwillingness of the Navy to accept the secondary role the development of an air force would eventually bring it; reluctance to make the financial commitment necessary to develop an effective air force; and a determination never again to involve the United States in the kind of large-scale warfare which would require the use of airplanes. Many military planners firmly believed that Japan would be America's next enemy. It would constitute no threat to North America and could be defeated with traditional naval warfare. Resistance to the development of an air force therefore was considerable.[1]

The champion of air power during and after World War I was the charismatic, brilliant, but impulsive General William Mitchell. Most histories of air development call him the catalyst to a growing national recognition of the need to develop America's air defense capabilities. Many are critical of his methods, however.[2]

Mitchell, the son of a United States senator, entered the Army during the Spanish-American War as a private but was quickly commissioned a lieutenant. He served in Cuba during the conflict and in the Philippines immediately afterwards. He remained in the Signal Corps and rose rapidly in rank becoming a captain at age twenty-four and the youngest man ever assigned to the Army General Staff at age thirty-three. He was an impressive and dynamic young officer.[3]

Army aviation was housed in the Signal Corps and hence the genesis of Mitchell's interest in airplanes. In 1911, Congress made its first-ever appropriation for aviation—$125 thousand for the Signal Corps' aviation section which was commanded for a time by Mitchell. He did not fly a plane until he was thirty-seven but quickly became a passionate proponent of the new weapon.

Upon American entrance into World War I, Mitchell (who was already in Europe as an aeronautical observer) joined the Allied forces in France. There "with great energy but little authority" he began planning for an American expeditionary air force.[4] He served on the staff of General John J. Pershing and developed the American Expeditionary Force's Aviation Program in the summer of 1917. Mitchell demonstrated courage and intelligence in leading the air force and advanced from major to the temporary rank of brigadier general while taking increasingly important commands. During this time he was greatly influenced by the advanced views of independent use of airplanes of British and French officers.

After the war Mitchell, as Assistant Chief of the Air Service, continued his advocacy of the airplane calling for the modernization and enlargement of the nation's tiny air force. He favored an air force independent of the Army and Navy or, alternatively, a single Department of Defense which would coordinate sea, air, and ground forces. Most Navy leaders, supported by Pershing, denied that the airplane would revolutionize future warfare and the War Department continued to plan with the battleship as the key strategic weapon. Frustrated by their intransigence, Mitchell arranged for a series of sensational demonstrations of the airplane's capabilities. In succession he staged an across-the-nation air race and a series of demonstrations of the ability of airplanes to sink an invading naval force. In 1921 and 1923 he accomplished the latter through the aerial bombing of captured German ships and of obsolete American naval vessels. The Navy rationalized his successes and resistance to the airplane remained high.[5]

Ironically, the same wartime lessons that had provided inspiration for Mitchell's unabashed airplane advocacy taught other military leaders differently. The war offered no proof, they argued, that the airplane had a capability for decisive action in war. Thus independence for aviation could not be justified, although it was valued as a servant of the Army and Navy in reconnaissance and ground support duties. In 1919, the Dickman Board, set up to study the lessons to be learned by the Army from World War I, originated this argument and it became the basis of opposition to a separate air force for much of the following decade. The Navy seconded the Dickman argument with Assistant Secretary of the Navy Franklin D. Roosevelt voicing its opposition.[6]

Despite attempts to squash Mitchell's proposals, his headline-grabbing activities and his steady flow of articles, interviews, and speeches aroused sufficient public and congressional interest as to prompt several official attempts at examining the questions he was raising.

In 1923 the Lassiter Board, composed of several General Staff officers and chaired by Major William Lassiter, was created to study Major General Mason M. Patrick's call for a new aviation policy. It concluded that "unless steps are taken to improve conditions in the Air Service it will in effect be practically demobilized at an early date." The Board recommended higher peacetime levels and suggested goals for expansion of the Air Service in time of war. It held that although certain units of the Air Service should be assigned to direct support of the Army, the remainder should be formed into a reserve under the General Headquarters where it could be used for ground support or in independent operations. These changes would be brought about by a proposed ten-year development program which would bring the peacetime level of the air force to 4,000 officers, 25,000 enlisted men, 2,500 aviation cadets, 2,534 airplanes, 20 airships, and 38 balloons with the capacity to expand in war to 22,628 officers, 172,994 enlisted men, 8,756 airplanes, 31 airships, and 134 balloons.

The Lassiter Board further recommended that the Army and Navy work out their aviation requirements together.[7] Secretary of War John W. Weeks concurred with the Lassiter report and sent it to the Joint Board with the blockbuster recommendation that Congress should consider all future appropriations for Army and Navy aviation jointly. The Army and Navy strongly opposed the suggestion, but the question suddenly became academic with the death of Warren Harding (who was somewhat open to well-argued military expenditure proposals and intrigued by the possibilities of the airplane) and the ascension to the presidency of Calvin Coolidge. Coolidge's commitment to fiscal austerity was incompatible with the heavy spending which the implementation of the Lassiter recommendations would entail. The report was placed on a back burner.

In the spring of 1924 a special committee of the House of Representatives was appointed to study alleged monopolistic practices of the aviation industry. Under Chairman Florian Lampert, the inquiry expanded into a lengthy study of aviation in general. The committee would not file a report until 14 December 1925.[8] Mitchell appeared before the panel and made numerous allegations regarding the state of preparedness of the nation's air defense, the indifference of his superiors to the pitiful condition of the air force, the deliberate manipulation of information to cover up the lack of air defense planning, and other related charges. There is no denying the truth of some of Mitchell's contentions, but his hyperbolic presentation damaged his credibility, antagonized his superiors, and generally is believed to have done his cause harm. Other events of 1925, however, would overshadow the ongoing Lampert investigation.[9]

Throughout 1924 and into 1925 Mitchell escalated his attacks on the

War Department and Congress for what he saw as their shortsightedness. Aircraft appropriations continued to fall short of the levels he considered minimal. His sensational public statements and publications increasingly alienated him from the military establishment. When his term as Assistant Chief of the Air Service expired in April 1925, he was not reappointed to the post. His temporary rank of brigadier general reverted to the permanent rank of colonel and he was reassigned as Air Officer, Eighth Corps, at Fort Sam Houston, Texas. Clearly, the intention was to silence the nation's most prominent aerial kvetch.[10]

Then, in one week in September 1925, a naval seaplane was lost on a nonstop flight from San Francisco to Hawaii and the U.S. Navy dirigible *Shenandoah* was destroyed on a goodwill flight. From exile in Texas, Mitchell used these tragedies as vehicles for the denunciation of the Navy and War Departments charging them with "incompetency, criminal negligence and almost treasonable administration of the national defense." His attacks were so bold and sensational that no one doubted that a court-martial would result.[11]

President Coolidge, undoubtedly moved to action by the controversy, appointed a President's Aircraft Board to study "the best means of developing and applying aircraft to the national defense."[12] The public learned of the creation of the Board on 13 September 1925, when newspaper stories reported the appointment of nine prominent Americans to conduct the study. Actually, Coolidge had decided to form such a panel long before the *Shenandoah* tragedy and the subsequent Mitchell charges.

On 11 March 1925, Coolidge wrote to Dwight Whitney Morrow that "I may like to have you look into the subject of airplanes for me."[13] Morrow had been Coolidge's classmate at Amherst College and was for more than a decade a senior partner with J. P. Morgan & Co. While he had been an adviser to the Allied Maritime Transportation Council during World War I, he had never flown in an airplane and was unfamiliar with the military use of planes.

When Coolidge announced the Board's formation in September 1925, Mitchell expressed delight at its appointment. The Aircraft Board was clearly selected to avoid charges of bias. Its members were prominent and respected men of unquestioned integrity. Morrow was selected unanimously to chair the Board. Other members included Judge Arthur C. Denison of the Sixth Circuit Court of Appeals; Senator Hiram Bingham of the Military Affairs Committee; Representative James S. Parker of the House Interstate and Foreign Commerce Committee; retired General James G. Harbord who had been Pershing's Chief of Staff during the war and was now president of Radio Corporation of America; retired Admiral Frank F. Fletcher (an early supporter of aviation); William F. Durand of Stanford University, President of the American Society of Mechanical Engineers and a member of the National Advisory Committee for Aeronautics; Howard E. Coffin, consulting engineer and aeronautics expert; and Representative Carl Vinson of the House Naval Affairs Committee. Coolidge ordered the Board to present its findings by the end of November. This short deadline has been widely but erroneously interpreted as an attempt by Coolidge to divert public attention from the Mitchell court-martial scheduled to begin in late October and expected to last many weeks. Coolidge was hoping, it is argued, to obviate public reaction to the punishment Mitchell would certainly receive for his brashness from the court-martial panel by providing an anti-Mitchell perspective in the form of a prestigious Aircraft Board report.[14]

While this is a theory commonly expressed by both those friendly to Mitchell and his critics, it reflects a misperception of the relationship between Coolidge and Morrow. The two men had remained friendly toward one another since college. Morrow held Coolidge in high esteem and Coolidge undoubtedly returned that regard, but they certainly were not cronies. Coolidge had no friends in the traditional sense. He had known Morrow for more than three decades and thus knew well Morrow's independent approach to issues. The President could not have known what Morrow's views would be. Coolidge had little patience for drawn-out proceedings and long reports. He undoubtedly wanted this airplane controversy settled once and for all. The manner of his appointment of the Board and the early deadline given it were not unique to this situation but rather were typical of his administrative style.[15]

The Aircraft Board opened its hearings on 21 September 1925 and met daily until 16 October. In those weeks it heard testimony from a wide range of experts with many varying interests and perspectives. Among them were Acting Secretary of War Dwight F. Davis, Secretary of Commerce Herbert Hoover, Secretary of Navy Curtis D. Wilbur, Army Chief of Staff Major General John J. Hines, the Postmaster General, and numerous Army and Navy men, both aviators and not. The star attraction among the ninety-nine witnesses, of course, was Colonel Billy Mitchell.

Even Mitchell apologists bemoan his testimony. Rarely in his long public life did Mitchell give a bad performance. However, before the Board he was at his very worst. He arrived to loud applause and considerable media interest on 29 September. He proceeded to read to the Board from his recently published *Winged Defense*. His statement droned on and even friendly observers described it as monotonous and very dull. After several hours Mitchell stopped to inquire if the Board had heard enough but was encouraged by Chairman Morrow to continue his statement until he was finished. The effect was deadly. Parrying questions was Mitchell's forte, yet little opportunity arose for such give-and-take and thus neither Mitchell's charm nor wit were showcased. After a day and a half his testimony ended, and most observers agreed that he had offered little that was new.

Basically, Mitchell's testimony merely reiterated charges he had made many times before. He called for a separate air force. He described the current condition of the Air Service as utterly inadequate to be useful in time of war. He predicted that the next war would begin with an air attack. When pressed as to where such an attack might originate, he argued that England, in alliance with other powers, might mount the offensive against the United States—presumably from Canada. However, he was forced to admit that this was improbable.[16]

Approximately half of the witnesses before the Board were air officers. Most shared Mitchell's gloomy evaluation as to the poor state of preparedness of the nation's air force and agreed that it should be separated from the Army and Navy. Mitchell's strongest support probably came from Chief of the Air Service, Major General Mason M. Patrick, who testified that he recommended "that the Air Service be given semiautonomous status, that it be formed into an air corps, and that the chief of that corps report to the Secretary of War."[17]

Faced with a late November deadline, the Aircraft Board labored long hours to conclude its work. The testimony itself consisted of many hundreds of pages when transcribed and was bound in four volumes. The report, though much briefer, was extremely difficult to write since Chairman Morrow insisted that it be unanimously approved. It appears that Morrow felt that a unanimous report would settle for the foreseeable future the raging controversy and would place the nation in the best possible air defense position. After reading the four volumes of testimony, Morrow hammered out a report that was acceptable to the other members of the Board with barely enough time to have it printed and to the President on 30 November 1925.[18]

Although the President's Aircraft Board report constituted the first realistic and comprehensive air defense planning of the interwar period, some argue that there was little new among the Board's recommendations. More accurately, the Board built upon a foundation of suggestions and recommendations made over several years by leading aviation experts and groups and presented those ideas in a single, palatable package reinforced by the prestige and political clout of the nine prominent and well-connected Americans who made up the Board. Thus for the first time, ideas that had long been bandied about received serious attention. The report could not compete for headlines with the sensational Mitchell stories, but it was far more effective in bringing about change than Mitchell had been in his years of controversy.

In its findings the Board responded to some of the more controversial issues. It argued that there was no danger of an aerial attack in the foreseeable future: "No airplane capable of making a transoceanic flight to our country with a useful military load and of returning to safety is now in existence." The effective radius of flight for bombing operations, the report stated, was between two hundred and three hundred miles. An attack upon the continental United States was considered to be so improbable that the report called fear of such an attack to be "without reason."[19]

The report acknowledged the possibility that the next war might begin in the air, although not over the United States, but maintained that "in all probability it will wind up as the last war did, in the mud."[20] As to Mitchell's implication that we might be attacked by air from Canada, the Board declared that it would be "wholly unreasonable" to create a defense system predicated on an attack from Canada or Mexico.

The Aircraft Board took a firm stance in opposition to the creation of a separate department for the air force. Much to the delight of the Army and Navy, the report stated that "we do not consider that air power, as an arm of the national defense, has yet demonstrated its value—certainly not in a country situated as ours—for independent operations of such a character as to justify the organization of a separate department. We believe that such independent missions as it is capable of can be better carried out under the high command of the Army or Navy, as the case may be."[21] On the other hand, the report called for the creation of new Assistant Secretaries of War, Navy, and Commerce with the exclusive responsibilities of coordinating the activities of their departments with respect to aviation.[22]

The report paid proportionately more attention to the problems of the Army Air Service than any other subject. After indicating the great difficulty the Board had in resolving conflicting information regarding the size of the air force, the quality of the aircraft available, the actual personnel trained to fly, and other such routine matters, the report made numerous important recommendations. The name Air Service should be changed to Air Corps to more accurately reflect its role as "an air force acting alone on a separate mission" rather than exclusively in the traditional auxiliary or service role. The new Assistant Secretary of War would provide "sympathetic supervision and counsel" and would promote "close cooperation between aviation and the other parts of the Army." He would be "especially useful" in matters of procurement: if expenditures were under the scrutiny of a civilian head "much of the feeling on the part of Congress that there was extravagance, and on the part of the Air Service that there was parsimony might be avoided."[23]

The report suggested that aviation be given special representation on the Army General Staff even though it might necessitate waiving some of the qualifications for membership and would contradict one of the fundamental principles of the General Staff that no member represent any particular service. The good to be gained, the report argued, justified such a departure from the general rule.

Since there was a shortage of Air Service field officers, the Board recommended that the Secretary of War be allowed to assign air officers to flying commands with appropriate temporary rank. In recognition of the hazardous nature of flying, the report called for extra pay for flyers in peace as well as war. As additional reward, it was recommended that a special aviation medal and ribbon be granted for extraordinary heroism in peace or war.[24]

Many of the Board's recommendations were clearly reflections of its realization that morale within the Air Service was extremely low. While the Board did not agree with many of the sweeping changes called for by Mitchell and his supporters, it did demonstrate sensitivity to the difficult conditions under which these officers labored and sought to respond to their grievances and reward their efforts.

Finding a "serious shortage" of flying cadets and Air Service reserve officers, the Board called for suitable appropriations for needed training planes and subsidiary flying fields for use by the reserve. There should be a "very considerable increase" in the number of institutions providing ground instruction in the fundamentals of military aviation. Annual summer training in flying should be given to members of the Air Corps Reserve Officers' Training Corps, so that they could qualify as military aviators. A careful study of the desirability of increasing the use of enlisted men as military pilots was also recommended.[25]

The report gauged the current strength of the Air Service at 912 officers and 8,722 enlisted men with 396 planes available for use in the case of war. While sidestepping the controversy Mitchell inspired as to whether the planes were obsolete and dangerous, the Board called this a "transition period" with new and approved types of planes ready for production in quantity to take the place of older models. Therefore, it recommended that for five years Congress provide special appropriations for the purchase of new planes. In this the Board took issue with the Lassiter Board's ten-year air expansion program saying it did not consider it wise to make definite plans for such an extended period. It is probable that the Board opted for a five-year plan because Morrow knew that Coolidge would be unwilling to commit his successor to the ten-year plan.[26]

In most instances the Board's report made recommendations for naval aviation that paralleled those made for the Army Air Service. It was suggested that naval aviators be granted representation in both the Office of the Chief of Naval Operations and the Bureau of Navigation. Surely to the chagrin of the Navy brass, the report suggested that "within a proper spirit of cooperation... the naval high command will find real opportunity to utilize the special knowledge and counsel of the naval aviator." The Board also called for improved training for air personnel, the possible use of enlisted men as pilots, the granting of temporary rank to naval air officers when appropriate, and other recommendations similar to earlier suggestions for the Army.[27]

The Aircraft Board devoted more attention to civilian air service and the aircraft industry than might be expected in a study of air defense. The Board felt the subjects could not be separated. It recommended that the military and civilian services remain distinctly separate. Its operating principle was that "peace-time activities of the United States have never been governed by military considerations." Drawing upon nineteenth-century Prussia as its example, the Board argued that "the union of civil and military activities would breed distrust in every region to which our commercial aviation sought extension." While this position might be interpreted as an antimilitarist stance, it more likely was an indication of a concern by board members about the free enterprise system being compromised by government involvement in the private sector.

The Board was particularly concerned about the relationship of the aircraft industry to the national defense. It judged its importance to be vital and estimated that the aircraft industry could contribute approximately fifteen thousand airplanes to the nation's air force in the first year of a major emergency and still more in the second and subsequent years. Yet, the report held, the current methods of irregular government ordering of airplanes was detrimental to a healthy aircraft industry. Board recommendations aimed at creating a sound industry, so that it might be of maximum benefit to the nation in case of war. There should be a greater continuity of orders for military aircraft and adoption of a standard rate of replacement. Production orders should be given only to companies which maintained design staffs of reasonable size and kept them active. Government competition with civil industry should be halted. Provision should be made for small orders for experimental aircraft designs. Finally, government aviation research should be expanded.[28]

The tone of the Aircraft Board report was conciliatory. It acknowledged throughout the honest differences of opinion of those who gave testimony. It pointed out how difficult it was to know which perspective offered was the best for the nation's air defense. The report admitted that the Board had difficulty agreeing on a unanimous report which was achieved only through "mutual accommodation and understanding." It suggested that the contesting parties work out their problems in a similar manner.

The Aircraft Board conducted hearings through 16 October 1925. Less than two weeks later, on 28 October, the Mitchell court-martial hearings began. On 30 November the Aircraft Board's report was made public and on 17 December Mitchell was found guilty of conduct prejudicial to good order and military discipline. Suspended from rank, command, and duty for five years, Mitchell resigned on 1 February 1926. In some ways the Aircraft Board report vindicated Mitchell in that implicitly its recommendations admitted the poor state of air defense preparedness.

Coincidentally, three days before the announcement of the guilty verdict in Mitchell's court-martial, the Lampert Committee presented its long-awaited report. In essence, it agreed with Mitchell when it found that an independent air force should be established to serve as a coordinate armed force in a single national defense department. It also agreed with Mitchell and the Lassiter Board on such issues as aircraft procurement and the general condition of the aircraft industry. Like the Lassiter report, the Lampert Committee's findings lacked the prestige of the Aircraft Board's conclusions.[29]

From the White House on down, the Aircraft Board's work was hailed for its objectivity and thoroughness. Morrow was widely praised for his leadership of the panel. Only hard-core Mitchell supporters found occasion to criticize aspects of the Board's conclusions. The success of the Aircraft Board can most effectively be measured in terms of congressional implementation of its recommendations. By this gauge it was remarkably successful. A flurry of legislation followed the digestion of the report.

Probably the most important piece of legislation to be spawned by the Aircraft Board report was the Air Corps Act of 2 July 1926. This act changed the name of the Army's air arm from Air Service to Air Corps. It created the office of Assistant Secretary of War to help foster military aviation. An air section was established in each General Staff division. Most importantly, the Secretary of War was authorized to increase the level of available planes to 1,800 (an increase of 36 percent over current levels) and to purchase up to 400 replacements annually to maintain that number. Since only 605 planes had been constructed since World War I, the effective authorized increase was nearly 200 percent. The bill also authorized the expansion of manpower by a 32 percent increase in the allotment of Regular Army commissioned personnel designated to the Air Corps which would raise the level to 1,650. Enlisted personnel could be increased to 71 percent to 15,000.[30]

In 1926 Congress also enacted the Air Commerce Act. This bill placed control of civil aviation within the Commerce Department. The government assumed responsibility for building and maintaining airways. All aircraft must be registered and minimum standards of aircraft safety were established. As was foreseen by the Aircraft Board, improvements in civil aviation would have immeasurable benefits for the nation's air force in time of war. President Coolidge displayed more interest in and enthusiasm for civil aviation than for military aviation expansion. This has been variously attributed to his instinctive frugality, a larger concern for the nation's budget, or an inherent pacifism which caused reluctance to allocate additional funds for military purposes. The best explanation is probably a blend of the three.

The President's Aircraft Board successfully served several functions. It gave full and fair hearing to the many varying opinions regarding the current state and future significance of the airplane to the nation's defense. Unlike preparers of previous studies, the Board had no ax to grind and hence the President, Congress, and the American public readily accepted its recommendations. From the perspective of Mitchell and his staunchest supporters, the Board did not go far enough in its recommendations. Yet given the inclinations of the President, the budget-minded Congress, and isolationist public opinion, the Board's moderate and reasonable proposals went a long way towards strengthening America's air defense. It is improbable that more could have been achieved in the prevailing political environment. The Aircraft Board was the primary and most successful attempt at air defense planning in the interwar period.

Presidential commissions have become frequent phenomena in twentieth-century America. Often their primary purpose appears to be to reduce the immediate pressure on the President and limit the political damage which would result from lengthy media focus on some acute problem. Rarely do the recommendations of these commissions become part of the long-term planning process. The President's Aircraft Board is typical of other twentieth-century commissions in that it was set up hurriedly in response to a crisis with possible political implications and was given a short deadline by which to present its report. It is atypical in that it seems to have exceeded its charge by providing more extensive recommendations than requested and thereby inspiring a program for long-range air defense. The President's Aircraft Board served Coolidge well, since to a large degree, it dissipated the Mitchell controversy while facilitating long-range air defense planning. The Warren, Kerner, and Tower commissions served their presidents far less well.

NOTES

1. For the Navy's perspective, see William R. Braisted, *The United States Navy in the Pacific, 1909–1922* (Austin: University of Texas Press, 1971); and Harold and Margaret Sprout, *Towards a New Order of Sea Power: American Naval Policy and the World Scene* (Princeton: Princeton University Press, 1943).

2. See for example, Carroll V. Glines, Jr., *The Compact History of the United States Air Force*, new and rev. ed. (New York: Hawthorne Books Inc., 1980); and Herbert M. Mason, Jr., *The United States Air Force: A Turbulent History* (New York: Charter Press, 1976).

3. Over the decades Mitchell has been a popular subject for biographers. The most objective accounts are Alfred F. Hurley, *Billy Mitchell: Crusader for Air Power*, new ed. (Bloomington: Indiana University Press, 1975); and Burke Davis, *The Billy Mitchell Affair* (New York: Random House, Inc., 1967). Mitchell's papers are in the Library of Congress.

4. James Lea Cate, "William Mitchell," *Dictionary of American Biography*, Supplement II (New York: Charles Scribners Sons, 1958), 460.

5. Hurley, *Billy Mitchell*, 64–71. A recent look at one of Mitchell's extravaganzas is William M. Leary, "Billy Mitchell and the Great Transcontinental Air Race of 1919," *Air University Review* 35 (May–June 1984): 64–76.

6. R. Earl McClendon, *The Question of Autonomy for the United States Air Arm* (Montgomery, Ala.: Air University Library, 1950), 43–44.

7. *Report of a Committee of Officers....* (Lassiter Board Report), 27 March 1923 (Washington, D.C.: Government Printing Office, 1923).

8. U.S. Congress, House, *Inquiry into Operations of the United States Air Ser-*

vices, Hearings before the Select Committee of Inquiry into Operations of the United States Air Service, 68th Cong., 1st sess., 1925.

9. Hurley, *Billy Mitchell*, 95–98.

10. Ibid.

11. *New York Times*, 6 and 7 September 1925.

12. Calvin Coolidge to Curtis D. Wilbur and Dwight F. Davis, 12 September 1925, Calvin Coolidge Papers, Library of Congress, reproduced in *Report of President's Aircraft Board* (Washington, D.C.: Government Printing Office, 1925), 1.

13. Coolidge to Dwight W. Morrow, 11 March 1925, Morrow Papers, Amherst College, Amherst, Mass.

14. See for example Harold Nicolson, *Dwight Morrow* (New York: Harcourt, Brace & Co., 1935), 281–86; Hurley, *Billy Mitchell*, 101–2; and Davis, *Billy Mitchell Affair*, 225–32.

15. The longstanding Coolidge-Morrow relationship is difficult to understand. On the surface at least, no two men could be more dissimilar. Morrow was gregarious, affable, and progressive. Coolidge, of course, was otherwise. Anne Morrow Lindbergh does not view Coolidge as being among her father's close friends. She sees them bound together only by their shared Amherst College experience. Interview with Anne Morrow Lindbergh, 17 June 1980, Darien, Conn.

16. *Hearings Before the President's Aircraft Board* (Washington, D.C.: Government Printing Office, 1925), 499–502, 553–59.

17. Ibid., 72–74.

18. Hiram Bingham to Edward Lowry, 28 February 1934 and William F. Durand to Lowry, 6 July 1934, Morrow Papers.

19. *Report*, 10–12.

20. Ibid., 7.

21. Ibid., 14.

22. Morrow was clearly aware of the problems a continued divided military aviation might cause in future wars but was confident they could "work it out." Morrow to Major General H. E. Ely, 22 December 1925, Morrow Papers.

23. *Report*, 19.

24. Ibid., 20–21.

25. Ibid., 21.

26. The number of planes available for use in war was one of the most difficult statistics for the Board to obtain. The Army tended to count anything with wings. Mitchell discounted all but the most modern aircraft. The Board adopted General Patrick's definition of "standard plane" and number.

27. *Report*, 24–25.

28. Ibid., 28–29.

29. Edwin H. Rutkowski, *The Politics of Military Aviation Procurement, 1926–1934* (Columbus: Ohio State University Press, 1966), 189–90.

30. Ibid., 21–22. It should be pointed out that full implementation of the act did not occur. Coolidge delayed the onset of some of its provisions as he was allowed under the bill. Congress and the Bureau of the Budget felt there was no need to increase immediately air personnel since the procurement of aircraft was so slow. None of this reduced the quality of the plan however.

4

The Air Corps Five-Year Program: A Study in Planning

Jerold E. Brown

Passage of the Air Corps Act,[1] signed into law by President Calvin Coolidge on 2 July 1926, marked a major turning point in the history of military aviation in the United States. From the end of the First World War to the mid–1920s, the United States Air Service had languished. For all practical purposes it hardly existed as a viable fighting force. Ninety-five percent of its experienced officers and skilled enlisted technicians had been discharged or left the service for better pay and opportunities in the postwar civilian economy. Those who remained faced an uncertain future, poor pay, inferior equipment, and dilapidated housing. During the postwar decade living conditions at Air Service stations and flying fields increasingly worsened since little money was available to maintain the temporary wartime buildings, further compelling men to seek opportunity in the civilian sector. The Air Service lived off of its wartime surplus equipment and aircraft; research and development were minimal.

A return to traditional isolationism, fiscal conservatism, and the general antimilitary bias of Americans, coupled with a reaction against the peace settlement in Europe and a feeling that the United States should never again become involved in a war in Europe, militated against more adequate provision for military needs in general and the fledgling Air Service in particular. In large part, the plight of the postwar Army was generally unseen and unknown. What the public did see, and what continued to vex the higher echelons of the Army and War Department, was the increasing dissent and criticism of Brigadier General William Mitchell who refused to be ignored. Mitchell had mastered the use of contemporary media to keep the aviation issue alive before Congress and the public. Although Congress periodically dealt with the state of the nation's defenses in the years following the First World War, it declined to act decisively on the issues Mitchell raised or to rescue the Air Service from the dismal state into which it had fallen. Frustrated and outraged, Mitchell finally went too far. His unsupportable (some might argue they were calculated) charges against the Army, War Department, and Navy Department leadership led to his court-martial and eventual resignation from the service. His highly publicized court-martial, however, spurred the President and Congress to action. The result was the Air Corps Act of 1926.

Based on recommendations by the President's Aircraft Board (the Morrow Board) and a growing body of information and ideas gathered through congressional hearings and investigations over more than half a decade,[2] the Air Corps Act signified a long-sought recognition from Congress and the President that the air arm had indeed been woefully neglected since the end of the World War. The act reorganized and raised the status of the air arm from that of a "service" to a coequal branch with other combat arms such as infantry, cavalry, field artillery, and coast artillery. It further provided for a new assistant secretary of war to represent aviation interests in the War Department and to act as spokesman before Congress and two new assistant chiefs of the Air Corps to share administrative responsibilities. Most importantly, the Air Corps Act provided for a major program to rebuild and revitalize the flagging air arm—a five-year program to increase "the efficiency of the Air Corps of the Army and for its further development."[3]

The Five-Year Program represented an unprecedented attempt at long-range planning in the United States. Implementation of the program would cross the boundaries of presidential administrations, successive congresses, and chiefs of staff; other men than those initiating the program would be responsible for its successful conclusion. Success would depend on foresight, a clear understanding of goals, timely availability and synchronization of resources, and a close cooperative effort by the President, Congress, the War Department, the Chief of Staff, and the leadership of the newly created Air Corps. Although the program ultimately failed to achieve its goals and fulfill the aspirations of its congressional proponents and aviation leaders, it was a significant experiment in planning at the national level before such planning became generally accepted in the United States.

When the Five-Year Program expired in 1932 far short of its original goals, War Department and Air Corps leaders sought to establish responsibility for the failure. They blamed the program's failure on budgetary restrictions, especially cuts made by the Bureau of the Budget throughout the program, and the deepening depression that precipitated cancellations of the program's final increment.[4] Undoubtedly these factors played a significant role in the course of the program, but they do not entirely account for either the failure or the accomplishments of the program.[5] To grasp fully the causes of the Five-Year Program's failure, one must look at the Air Corps Act, the plan itself, the agents responsible for implementing it, and how they interacted.

A major problem with the Five-Year Program was the nature of the Air Corps Act. While Section 8 of the act provided for the Five-Year Program, general goals of the program appeared throughout the act. The act established broad policy, but provided no means to carry out that policy. Nor did Congress consider the act to be an authorization for appropriations. The act was more like an authorization to seek authorization. The act did not compel the President to act, it merely authorized him to act: "The President is hereby authorized . . . "[6] While the act was very specific in some respects, it was open to broad interpretations in others. It was at once too flexible, yet it lacked flexibility. Some obstacles inherent in the act were easily overcome; others were not. The program was seriously flawed from the outset, therefore, because the enabling legislation failed to provide an appropriate framework for planning.

For instance, the act stipulated that the Five-Year Program commence with fiscal year 1927. But the bill did not become law until after the start of the fiscal year. This left the Plans Division of the Air Staff, the agency responsible for detailed planning, no time to study, review, and propose appropriate supporting legislation. While some discussion preceded passage of the act, planners could not finalize detailed plans until they knew the law's definitive form. They could only know this for certain when President Coolidge signed the bill into law. Thus Congress was asking the Chief of the Air Corps to deliver a plan before it had clearly defined the parameters. The result of this timing was to delay, by mutual agreement, the first increment of the program until fiscal year 1928.[7] Although future dislocations within the program were not tied to the delay in launching the first increment, this delay was indicative of the inherent problems in the legislation.

Even with the additional year the delay gave the Plans Division to produce a workable plan, it did not complete a final version of the plan until 1 July 1927, the day the program officially commenced. The War Department approved the plan two weeks later.[8] As is often the case, however, projecting figures on paper is a relatively easy task compared to implementation.

The Air Corps Act determined the program's overall limits. But those limits were neither attainable, given the unwillingness of Congress to expand the Army as a whole, nor realistic in terms of Air Corps needs. Section 2, for example, established the basic strength of the Air Corps at 1,514 company and field grade officers, plus 4 general officers, and 16,000 enlisted men. This was 64 percent and 83 percent above the respective strengths as of 30 June 1927. Spreading the required increase over five increments (and planning for 15,000 rather than 16,000 enlisted men), the plan called for annual additions of 9 percent to 11 percent (see table 1). As table 2 shows, while the Air Corps did not attain the mandated strength, both officer and enlisted strength did increase considerably from 1927 to 1932. But mere statistics do not tell the full story. Congress did not provide for a general increase in overall Army strength to allow for the Air Corps buildup. This meant that other branches would lose strength, not just relatively but absolutely, to the Air Corps. In later increments of the program when shortages

Table 1
Summary of Requirements for Five-Year Program by Annual Increment

	Available 1927		F.Y. 1928		F.Y. 1929		F.Y. 1930		F.Y. 1931		F.Y. 1932	
	Off	EM	Off	EM	Off	EM	Off	EM	Off	EM	Off	EM
Personnel Required	919	8,697	1,100	9,590	1,237	10,838	1,374	12,086	1,512	13,334	1,650*	15,000
Increase			181	893	137	1,248	137	1,248	138	1,248	138	1,666
Serviceable Aircraft			1,186		1,345		1,520		1,659		1,800	
Increase					159		175		139		141	
New Housing Units Required												
Officer	249		82		192		732		423		348	
NCO	167				60		1,152		456		487	
EM	2,223		1,560		2,182		2,654		2,277		2,177	

*Includes 150 officer students.

Technical Construction Required		
Hangars	125	$5,200,000
Field Shops	20	1,684,800
Depot Shops	8	1,280,000
Field Warehouses	24	1,123,200
Depot Warehouses	6	3,000,000
Hq & Ops Bldgs	68	1,360,000
Photo Bldgs	16	576,000
Arms & Parachute Bldgs	25	375,000
Radio Bldgs	27	270,000
School Bldgs	7	280,000
Gas & Oil Storage		412,000
Paint, Oil & Dope Houses	23	115,000
Improve Landing Fields		2,058,000
Night Flying Equipment		340,000
		$18,074,500
F.Y. 1928		523,240
F.Y. 1929		2,153,760
F.Y. 1930		5,364,940
F.Y. 1931-1932		10,032,560
		$18,074,500

Source: 145.91–346, Albert F. Simpson Historical Research Center, Maxwell AFB.

Table 2
Personnel Growth under Five-Year Program

	Available 1927		1928		1929		1930		1931		1932	
	Off	EM	Off	EM	Off	EM	Off	EM	Off	EM	Off	EM
Required	919	8,697	1,100	9,590	1,237	10,838	1,374	12,086	1,512	13,334	1,650	15,000
Increase			181	893	137	1,248	137	1,248	138	1,248	138	1,666
Actual Strength	902	9,077	1,025	9,493	1,143	10,890	1,271	12,032	1,291	13,194	1,281	13,369
Increase			123	416	118	1,397	128	1,142	20	1,162	-10	175
Shortage			75	97	94	+52	103	54	221	140	369	1,631

Source: *Reports of the Secretary of War to the President, 1927–1932.*

Table 3
Cadets Undergoing Flying Training, End of Fiscal Year—30 June

1926	142
1927	125
1928	280
1929	403
1930	378
1931	421
1932	325
1933	238
1934	310

Source: *Reports of the Secretary of War to the President, 1926–1934.*

developed in other arms, the Chief of Staff and the Secretary of War raised this issue before Congress and warned of its ultimate consequences.[9] This issue might have been resolved while Congress was considering the legislation, but War Department spokesmen did not pursue the question during the hearings lest Congress delay further.

Another example of the program's impracticality was the provision for 2,500 flying cadets. Even if 2,500 qualified candidates could have been accommodated at existing or projected training facilities, the Air Corps could have offered commissions to no more than 10 percent of each class. In fact, from 1926 to 1933 the Air Corps did not train a total of 2,500 flying cadets. The average was 289 per year (see table 3). Only about 250 of those who survived the rigorous training and qualified were offered commissions, many of those in reserve status.[10] Training men who could not be effectively utilized was a waste of valuable resources and an indication of a poorly conceived and coordinated plan.

Aircraft procurement was another area where specificity, on the one hand, and unclear language, on the other, led to uncertainty, confusion, and serious consequences for the program. Section 8 of the Air Corps Act read:

> The Secretary of War is hereby authorized to equip and maintain the Air Corps with not to exceed one thousand eight hundred serviceable airplanes, . . . together with spare parts, equipment, supplies, hangars, and installations necessary for the operation and maintenance thereof. In order to maintain the number specified above, the Secretary of War is hereby authorized to replace obsolete or unserviceable aircraft from time to time: *Provided,* That the necessary replacement of aircraft shall not

exceed approximately four hundred annually: ... *And Provided Further,* That the total number of planes authorized in this section shall include the number necessary for the training and equipment of the National Guard and the training of the Organized Reserves as may be determined by the Secretary of War.

Inasmuch as the latter provision would significantly reduce the number of aircraft available for training and operation of the Air Corps, one might assume that it would have been a major point of contention. Surprisingly, it was not. The sticky point in Section 8 was the term "serviceable." Did "serviceable" include obsolescent but airworthy aircraft? Did it include machines undergoing periodic maintenance and overhaul? How many aircraft must one carry in inventory to have a given number "serviceable"? One estimate was that 2,058 aircraft on hand would provide 1,800 "serviceable" planes. The issue was debated and argued within the War Department and before Congress throughout the duration of the Five-Year Program and beyond. The Chief of the Air Corps and the Secretary of War differed in their interpretations of the term. In an attempt to settle the dispute, the Judge Advocate General issued a legal opinion. He sided with the Secretary of War.[11] Even that opinion did not resolve the issue. "Serviceable" was one of those terms that could never be defined to the satisfaction of all concerned parties. Although aware of the controversy, Congress chose not to clarify the term in any subsequent legislation. The basic problem persisted of planning around such a vague and nebulous term.

As significant as the serviceability issue seemed at the time, it was only important if the mandated limit of aircraft could have been attained. According to the final revision of the Five-Year Program, aircraft were to increase between 8 percent and 13 percent annually (see table 1). In addition to adding new units each year, the Air Corps also had to replace a percentage of existing aircraft that would wear out, be destroyed in accidents, or become obsolete. The Air Corps estimated the normal replacement rate at about 12.5 percent. In fact, the rate was much higher. The simple arithmetic progression of increase tended to become a geometric progression for acquisition purposes. Over the period of the Five-Year Program the Air Corps actually acquired, through purchase and contract, 2,368 aircraft—well above the annual limit of 400 originally imposed by Congress.[12] As table 4 shows, even this seemingly large number of acquisitions could not bring the number of serviceable aircraft to 1,800, however they were defined. Five years after the program commenced the Air Corps had succeeded in reducing its initial shortage by a little more than half, leaving a shortage of 129 aircraft. Therefore, the debate over serviceability was moot.

Administration penny-pinching and congressional reluctance to go beyond the limits set by the Bureau of the Budget did not alone account for this failure. Congress, in fact, substantially increased appropriations for

Table 4
Aircraft under Five-Year Program

	1928	1929	1930	1931	1932
Aircraft Required	1,186	1,345	1,520	1,659	1,800
Increase		159	175	139	141
On Hand	939	1,273	1,319	1,476	1,671
Actual Increase		334	46	157	195
Shortage	247	72	201	183	129

Source: *Reports of the Secretary of War to the President, 1928–1932.*

aircraft procurement between 1927 and 1932 (see table 5). Net dollars for aircraft purchases nearly doubled for the first increment and reached 230 percent of the pre-program appropriation by the fourth increment. Even this increase in funds was insufficient to provide for ongoing replacements and a net increase in aircraft to achieve the program's goal.

To some extent, the aircraft shortfall was due to the rapidly advancing aeronautical technology of the period which directly affected the cost of new machines. By 1931 the Air Corps was purchasing a whole range of technical devices not in service in 1927 including such items as the Vandykes turbo supercharger and Sperry artificial horizons and directional gyros. Unit cost rose as this new technology came on line. In 1927, for example, the Air Corps paid $7,750 for a Consolidated Aircraft PT1 trainer. It paid Douglas Aircraft $9,320 for a BT–2B trainer in 1931, an increase of 20 percent over the earlier model. The price of spares rose commensurately. A Wright JB5 engine cost $4,448 in 1927; the newer Wright R–1820-E cost $5,719 in 1931, an increase of 28.5 percent.[13] Not only did advancing technology push up costs, it also caused an increase in the rate of obsolescence of existing machines, further accelerating the necessary rate of replacement. Air staff planners who failed to understand and forecast the impact of rapidly evolving technology shared responsibility with the administration and Congress for the limited success in this phase of the Five-Year Program.

Although the shortfall of aircraft posed a problem for the program, even more serious was the problem of acquiring the proper types of aircraft. At the outset of the program, the Secretary of War and the Chief of the Air

Table 5
Procurement Appropriations for Aircraft under Five-Year Program

Date Passed	F.Y.	Authority	Cash	Plus Contract Authorization	Less Award to Pay Contracts	Net Available
15 Apr 1926	1927	44 *Stat.* 269	$6,754,000	$3,000,000	$2,150,000	$7,604,000
23 Feb 1927	1928	44 *Stat.* 1120	9,492,500	4,495,000	3,000,000	13,987,500
23 Mar 1928	1929	45 *Stat.* 338-339	11,257,445	5,000,000	3,995,000	16,257,445
28 Feb 1929	1930	45 *Stat.* 1361-1362	18,439,280		2,250,000	16,189,280
4 Mar 1929	1929	45 *Stat.* 1665	3,250,000		3,250,000	0
28 May 1930	1931	46 *Stat.* 445	17,573,723			17,573,723
23 Feb 1931	1932	46 *Stat.* 1290	15,296,231			15,296,231
14 Jul 1932	1933	47 *Stat.* 677	11,525,728			11,525,728

Corps had complete discretion regarding what types of aircraft to purchase. From the middle of the second increment onward, however, some officers and Assistant Secretary of War (Air) F. Trubee Davison repeatedly warned that the program was "out of balance."[14] One of the keys to this "balance" was the types of aircraft being acquired, i.e., training, bombardment, pursuit, transport, and so forth. Some officers thought that combat types were being acquired while sacrificing the latest training and transport types. Others felt that not enough emphasis was placed on combat types. This was essentially a doctrinal dispute based on the wider debate taking place in the Air Corps and Army. Although Congress was aware of the developing crisis for several years, it chose not to act. Only after the program's final increment was cancelled did Congress step in to mandate procurement of specific types of aircraft.[15] Too late to affect the program in any case, this type of congressional interference was neither desirable nor necessary. It was, moreover, indicative of faulty planning in the Plans Division, poor judgment and an inability by the Chief of the Air Corps and the Secretary of War to resolve the doctrinal question, and Congress' failure to establish and maintain systematic oversight of the program.

The problem of maintaining a balance in the Five-Year Program went beyond the types of aircraft being purchased. The program encompassed four seemingly disparate areas: personnel, aircraft, housing, and technical construction. Yet these four areas were closely related. Alterations, delays, or changes in one area would inevitably affect or distort other areas. Nevertheless, Congress and the War Department chose to deal with each area more or less as a distinct entity. The way they chose to deal with each area significantly influenced the program's overall development.

Aircraft procurement, for example, was handled one way. Congress established very specific rules for procurement of aircraft. Section 10 of the Air Corps Act required public advertising of all specifications, an established bidding procedure, and open awarding of contracts. Congress appropriated funds for procurement through War Department annual appropriation bills. The appropriations committees of Congress—not the military affairs committees—reviewed contracts, held hearings, and interviewed staff officers supporting requirements and estimates. Congress mandated appropriations for aircraft procurement not as maximum but as minimum expenditures.[16] This latter provision compelled the Air Corps to let contracts whether or not those contracts represented the best deal the Air Corps could negotiate at the moment.

Housing and technical construction were handled yet another way. Inadequate housing was not limited to Air Corps stations; it was endemic throughout the Army. The housing situation was a legacy of the First World War. Between April 1917 and November 1918, the War Department had accumulated thousands of acres of land and constructed tens of thousands of temporary housing units. Often built with green lumber, these structures had an expected life span of five years. Nevertheless, a decade later a large percentage of active duty personnel were still living in this wartime housing. Due to the nature of its construction and the lack of adequate maintenance funds, housing was in disrepair, dilapidated, and decaying. Such poor living conditions affected both morale and reenlistment rates. Because the Air Corps had no permanent housing prior to the war, it suffered to a greater degree than the rest of the Army from these conditions.[17]

Throughout the first half of the 1920s, Congress wrestled with the problems of surplus real estate and deteriorating housing. Anxious to reduce the budget, but increasingly sensitive to the rising chorus of criticism about Army housing conditions, Congress sought a satisfactory but cheap solution to its dilemma. Successive congresses investigated, held hearings, and considered numerous proposals and bills.[18] Finally in March 1926, Congress passed S. 1129 which created the Military Posts Construction Fund (MPCF). Proceeds from the sale or disposal for all War Department real estate since November 1918 were to be paid into the MPCF which would then be used to finance new housing.[19] Thus Congress solved a vexing problem without direct cost to the public treasury and backed neatly into providing new Army housing without raising serious objections in a period of fiscal conservatism.

Unfortunately, the task of rebuilding Army housing was far greater than originally anticipated. Congress initially authorized and appropriated funds for new housing based on money available in the MPCF in its first year of existence (see table 6). Thereafter, the fund failed to grow as quickly as demand for construction. When it became apparent that the sale of surplus real estate would not generate sufficient money, Congress resorted to supplementing the MPCF with general treasury funds. The treasury share of Army housing appropriations rose from 40 percent in 1927 to 93 percent in 1932, or more than 80 percent of the $74 million invested in housing through the MPCF. Yet in spite of these considerable resources, conditions remained substandard at many military posts. As Chief of Staff General Douglas MacArthur noted in his annual report for 1933:

> Many officers and men are living under deplorable and, in some cases, even unsanitary conditions. Large numbers of enlisted men are housed in dilapidated buildings erected during the war as temporary shelters. At one post numbers of junior officers occupy quarters in which bathrooms serve also as kitchens. At others officers and enlisted men and their families are living in old shacks that offer little in the way of modern conveniences and which, moreover, are exceedingly expensive to maintain.[20]

The War Department estimated the cost of completing all Army housing construction at $135 million—nearly double the amount already expended on the program.[21]

Inasmuch as housing requirements for the Five-Year Program (see table

Table 6
Housing and Technical Construction Legislation under Five-Year Program

Date	Authorization Act	Housing AC	AC%	Technical AC	AC%	Appropriation Act	Cash Other	Note
4 May 1926	Pub. 177 69-I 44 Stat. 395-6	5,770,000 1,376,000	24%					Military Posts Construction Fund
3 Jul 1926						2nd Deficiency Act 1926 44 Stat. 877-8	2,250,000 3,520,000	Cash Contract auth. 44 Stat. 395-6
23 Feb 1927						WD Annual App. Act 1928 44 Stat. 1115	(3,520,000)	To pay contracts 44 Stat. 878
25 Feb 1927	Pub. 641 69-II 44 Stat. 1235-6	5,080,000 2,383,000	46%					3,680,000 MPCF 1,400,000 Treas.
3 Mar 1927	Pub. 764 69-II 44 Stat. 1390-91	7,115,000 2,814,000	40%					
22 Dec 1927						1st Deficiency Act 1927 45 Stat. 35-36	6,162,000 126,000	44 Stat. 1235-36 44 Stat. 1390 3,680,000 MPCF 2,482,000 Treas.
18 Feb 1928	Pub. 61 70-I 45 Stat. 129-30			6,695,691 5,662,691	84%			
23 Mar 1928						WD Annual App. Act 1929 45 Stat. 334-5	5,084,000 2,115,000	44 Stat. 1390-91 45 Stat. 129-30 Contact auth.
26 May 1928	Pub. 518 70-I 45 Stat. 748-50	13,268,284 5,851,950	42%	6,499,500 6,499,500	100%			
29 May 1928						2nd Deficiency Act 1928 45 Stat. 926-7	1,107,975 2,685,000	45 Stat. 129-130 Contract auth.

25 Feb 1929	Pub. 806 70-II 45 Stat. 1301-5	17,185,610 7,278,560	 42%	5,552,842			
28 Feb 1929					WD Annual App. Act 1930 45 Stat. 1358	14,441,950 (4,800,000) 3,000,000	45 Stat. 748 To pay contracts 45 Stat. 335, 926 Contract auth. 4,800,000 MPCF
4 Mar 1929					2nd Deficiency Act 1929 45 Stat. 1664-65	1,103,000	45 Stat. 1301-05
28 May 1930					WD Annual App. Act 1931 46 Stat. 440-1	16,062,860 (3,000,000) 2,773,000	45 Stat. 129, 300 1258, 1301, 1425 To pay contracts 45 Stat. 1358 Contract auth. 2,589,000 MPCF 13,473,860 Treas.
3 Jul 1930	Pub. 535 71-I 46 Stat. 1014-15	14,930,880 7,632,120	 51%				
6 Feb 1931					1st Deficiency Act 1931 46 Stat. 1074-75	730,030 504,800	Housing Technical
23 Feb 1931					WD Annual App. Act 1932 46 Stat. 1285-86	20,695,990 (2,773,000) 3,000,000	45 Stat. 129, 748, 1301, 46 Stat. 781, 1014 To pay contracts 46 Stat. 441 Contract auth. 1,500,000 MPCF
14 Jul 1932					WD Annual App. Act 1933 47 Stat. 673	(2,250,000)	To pay contracts 46 Stat. 1286

6) dovetailed conveniently with the Army housing program, Congress chose to handle Air Corps requirements through the MPCF. Under the initial authorization and appropriation bills for the MPCF, Air Corps stations had received about 24 percent of construction dollars. When Congress took up two authorization bills at the beginning of 1927, just prior to the commencement of the first increment of the Five-Year Program, Congress increased the Air Corps' share to 42 percent. Of $74 million appropriated for Army housing from 1926 to 1933, Congress designated 43 percent for Air Corps projects, an extraordinarily high percentage considering that the Air Corps comprised less than 15 percent of total Army strength during the period. The housing situation improved markedly at all but a few Air Corps posts.

Nevertheless, the result of having Air Corps housing and technical construction—handled in the same manner as housing and later combined with housing bills—fall under a parallel program was to somewhat disassociate those aspects of the Five-Year Program from personnel and aircraft. The two-step procedure Congress had evolved to do business influenced the program's development as much as the unwillingness of Congress to appropriate funds. The first step was to pass an authorization bill based on proposals submitted by the War Department. The House Committee on Military Affairs received the proposed authorization bill, held hearings, and sent its recommendation to the full House. As a rule, the House Committee on Military Affairs approved and the House passed nearly everything requested by the War Department. In most cases, the Senate concurred with minor amendments usually restoring projects deleted in the House.[22] But an authorization bill once passed by Congress merely permitted the War Department to return to Congress with a request for appropriations. Moreover, authorization carried no assurance that an appropriation was forthcoming or that individual projects would not be subsequently eliminated or pared down. Authorization also carried no assurance that the first projects authorized would be the first funded. The appropriation committees dealt with appropriation bills; a different panel of legislators reviewed and passed them on to the full Congress for consideration. The time interval between passage of an authorization bill and passage of supporting appropriations varied considerably. Funds might be available as soon as one month or as long as three years after authorization (see table 6). Some authorized projects were never funded. While this procedure assured thorough scrutiny of all War Department requests by Congress, it was not conducive to efficient and timely fulfillment of those requests. Moreover, since Air Corps requirements were included in a larger package, coordination with other aspects of the Five-Year Program was sacrificed. Once again, the system did not provide oversight procedure for either all or part of the program.

In no other area of the Five-Year Program were the limitations of congressional control and the inherent weaknesses of the original plan more ap-

Table 7
Annual Appropriation for Air Corps, Army: "improvement of stations"

Date	Fiscal Year	Authority	Appropriation
15 Apr 1926	1927	44 *Stat.* 269	300,000
23 Feb 1927	1928	44 *Stat.* 1120	1,062,930
23 Mar 1928	1929	45 *Stat.* 338	1,736,619
28 Feb 1929	1930	45 Stat. 1361	3,598,376
28 May 1930	1931	46 *Stat.* 445	2,724,073
23 Feb 1931	1932	*	

* Item removed from Air Corps, Army, and placed under Quartermaster.

parent than in the development of technical facilities. The plan of 1927 called for the modernization and development of thirty-one existing or temporarily closed stations plus the construction of two new fields. Improvements included new buildings to replace obsolete or deteriorated structures, new lighting equipment for expanded night flying, and more hard-surfaced, all-weather runways, taxiways, and aprons. The estimate to accomplish this was a modest sum, $18,074,500 (see table 1), over five years. As the Five-Year Program unfolded, however, development of technical facilities increasingly strayed from the intent of the original planners. So different was the actual course of development that it hardly resembled the plan of 1927.

As in the case of Army housing, administration fiscal restraint could not alone be held responsible for the failure to develop technical facilities as planned. In three bills passed from February 1928 to February 1929, Congress authorized $17,715,033, or 98 percent of the original estimate for technical construction (see table 1). Congress subsequently funded nearly all of these authorized projects. In addition to appropriations for designated projects, Congress substantially increased discretionary money the Air Corps could use to upgrade and maintain existing facilities. The annual War Department appropriation act included an item for "improvement of stations" under the heading "Air Corps, Army." Prior to the initiation of the Five-Year Program, Congress had allowed $300 thousand annually for this purpose. During the four years of the Five-Year Program, however, Congress appropriated over $9 million under this heading (see table 7), seven times the annual pre-program level. This item alone added 50 percent to available Air Corps resources for improving its technical facilities.

One other source of funds for developing Air Corps facilities was available to the Air Corps, the pork barrel. Individual congressmen and delegations introduced or supported a host of bills and amendments for projects in their respective districts over and above administration budget restrictions. Most of these special interest bills concerned the purchase of small tracts of land adjacent to existing Air Corps property or limited construction projects. Both authorization and appropriation bills emerged from this process. Scott Field at Belleville, Illinois; Bolling Field in the District of Columbia; Maxwell Field, Montgomery, Alabama; Selfridge Field, Mount Clemens, Michigan; Hensley Field, Grand Prairie, Texas; Governors Island, New York City; and Tucson Field, Tucson, Arizona each received money through special interest bills and amendments.[23] No evidence indicates that Congress diverted or withheld money from projects slated for development under the Five-Year Program in favor of pork barrel projects.[24] Neither the War Department nor the Air Corps objected to any special interest legislation. On the contrary, they welcomed this valuable source of dollars for desirable but otherwise unscheduled projects.

Like Army housing, Air Corps technical facilities generally improved from 1927 to 1932. New hangars and other technical buildings as well as improvements to runways and landing fields appeared at most Air Corps stations. Nevertheless, after spending more than originally estimated, the Chief of the Air Corps called for an additional $15,941,489 in May 1933 to complete the program begun in 1927.[25] This latter sum did not include projects underway but not yet complete or a number of projects previously funded but postponed with the cancellation of the Five-Year Program. A handful of stations slated for improvement in 1927 had not yet received any new construction when the program expired. Facilities at these stations had deteriorated to an even worse state than at the outset of the program.[26] The program appeared to have fallen far short of its goal.[27]

However, the problem was not so much the lack of progress as the appearance of the lack of progress. The fault lay with a poorly conceived plan that could not be implemented as conceived. The planners had hoped to rectify years of neglect with a single sweep of the broom. They planned construction projects at every operating station, scheduled the reopening of March Field, inactive since 1922, and projected construction of two new fields. Yet when it came time to implement the plan, they readily abandoned it and resorted to more pragmatic methods of doing business that the Army always had employed in peacetime. The result was to rely on ad hoc compromises that favored certain projects at the expense of others. This significantly increased the cost of the entire program while creating a physical plant very different from that envisioned in the 1927 plan. Examples abound of both unanticipated and calculated changes that influenced the development of technical facilities under the Five-Year Program. For instance, the original estimate of $18 million, even pre-Depression dollars, seems excessively low for a plan as ambitious as that submitted by the Plans Division in 1927. One can only speculate whether the estimate was deliberately low to assure War Department and congressional approval or simply miscalculated, based on a failure to appreciate the scope of the task at hand. In any case, the ultimate cost to resurrect and rebuild Air Corps ground facilities was several times the 1927 estimate.

The excessively low estimate to carry out the 1927 plan was further emphasized when, like Topsy, the plan just grew. Instead of two new fields, the Air Corps actually established five new fields, initiated preparations at a sixth site, and purchased land that doubled the size of another field.[28] Randolph Field, the vaunted "West Point of the Air," was one of the two new fields in the original plan. Built on land donated by a group of San Antonio, Texas businessmen and dedicated in 1930, Randolph Field ultimately cost more than $15 million, ten times the original estimate.[29] Barksdale Field, located in Bossier Parish, Louisiana, was not included in the original plan. It became necessary when Fort Crockett, Texas, the site designated to host the Third Attack Group, was found to have inadequate space for expansion. Constructed on twenty-three thousand acres donated by local government and civic groups, Barksdale Field cost more than $7 million to develop.[30] Faulty engineering surveys at two sites, Albrook Field in Panama and Benton Field at Alameda, California at first delayed construction, then necessitated considerable additional resources to develop adequately the two sites.[31] Not only was the original cost of the program clearly underestimated, but the Plans Division had allowed no funds for contingent expenses or unanticipated expansion once the program was underway.

No other case better exemplifies the departure from the original plan during implementation of the Five-Year Program than Rockwell Field. One of the earliest fields acquired by the Army for aviation purposes, Rockwell Field was located on North Island in San Diego Bay. It was one of only two Air Service fields that had any permanent construction when the First World War ended. Slated for further development in the 1927 plan, Congress appropriated $518 thousand for construction at Rockwell in the program's first increment. But a long, bitter dispute with the U.S. Navy with whom the Army shared North Island deterred the War Department from investing in additional permanent construction lest it lose that investment to the Navy. Instead, the Air Corps solicited and received offers of free land from Marin County and the city of Alameda, California on which to relocate Rockwell's major activities. At the War Department's request, Congress then withdrew and reappropriated the Rockwell funds for construction at the two new sites. Later, however, when engineering problems appeared at the Alameda site and both the Chief of the Air Corps and the Chief of Staff were replaced, the Air Corps reversed its decision to leave North Island and decided to remain there. Returning to Congress, the War Department requested money to construct the facilities proposed in the original plan. After lengthy debate, Congress appropriated funds for Air Corps development on North Island. Nevertheless, the Army eventually lost North Island to the Navy.[32]

Not only did Air Corps indecisiveness jeopardize the future of Rockwell Field—and contribute to its eventual loss—but also the entire affair showed an incredible lack of foresight regarding long-term Air Corps needs. All of the circumstances involved in the controversy over North Island as well as the limitations of Fort Crockett, the search for a home for the Air Corps Tactical School, and other problem areas existed prior to the Air Corps Act of 1926. Experienced planners would have considered these issues and provided for appropriate contingencies. Instead, planners in the Office of the Chief of the Air Corps produced a plan based on statistical goals but without clearly articulated overall objectives. They reacted as events unfolded as often as they determined those events. The plan's flexibility was one of weakness rather than strength. Yet paradoxically, the weakness of the original plan allowed the Air Corps to establish a number of previously unplanned but excellent and enduring facilities.

The planners' lack of foresight was surpassed only by the absence of agreement among Air Corps, War Department, and congressional leaders on priorities, the status of development from increment to increment, and adjustments once the program had gone awry. Nothing better illustrates this absence of agreement than the divergence between the annual assessments of the program by the Secretary of War and his subordinates. At the end of the first increment, for instance, Secretary of War Dwight Davis reported that progress during the year had been "most gratifying."[33] On the other hand, Assistant Secretary of War (Air) Davison pointed out in the same volume of reports that aircraft had fallen short of the required number and housing was behind schedule. Only one-fifteenth of the enlisted housing and one-hundredth of the non-commissioned officer housing was completed during the year.[34] Such contrary assessments of the year's progress perhaps could be explained by the difference in perspectives of the two parties and the early state of the program's development. That argument might be confirmed if the differing views were later reconciled. They were not.

In his annual report for 1930, the new Secretary of War, Patrick J. Hurley, claimed that aircraft deliveries were abreast of schedule, the full complement of enlisted personnel for the third increment was on hand, and the program was budgeted to completion and should be completed on time.[35] Major General James E. Fechet, Chief of the Air Corps, was not so sanguine. He maintained that "the full objectives of the Third Increment have not been met due to lack of sufficient facilities, shortage of senior officer personnel, and lack of equipment."[36] The next year, 1931, Hurley continued to present a rosy picture of progress. "The Air Corps 5-year program," he reported, "proceeds satisfactorily."[37] In contrast to Hurley's optimism, Davison flatly stated that the program was meeting its goals only in enlisted strength; it was behind in every other respect.[38] This disagreement continued in 1932. Although the program was moribund, Hurley wrote that "progress on the 5-year program has been, considering the economic condition of the country, very satisfactory."[39] Davison, on the other hand, came right to the point: "It has not been completed."[40] Hurley's caveat notwithstanding, one wonders if he and Davison were addressing the same program.

A number of factors perhaps could account for the wide discrepancy between the views of the secretaries and their subordinates. Sheer unbridled optimism, restraint imposed by the chief executives, or inexcusable ignorance of the true state of development may have led to the secretaries' uncritical assessments. A natural tendency to minimize what could be accomplished with the funds Congress provided and a growing feeling of frustration at not being able to achieve all they desired may explain the pessimistic pronouncements of Davison, Fechet, and other serving officers. Whatever the source of the controversy, Congress had every opportunity to learn the actual status of the program and effect certain adjustments. It chose not to do so.

Beginning in November 1928, only five months into the program's second increment, Davison appeared before a subcommittee of the House Committee on Appropriations, then considering the War Department appropriation bill for fiscal year 1930. Davison advised the members of the subcommittee that housing and technical construction were way behind schedule. Furthermore, Davison testified, posts brought into existence as part of the Five-Year Program were major problem areas.[41] The committee listened but made no significant changes in the bill it was considering.

Davison continued this line of testimony when he appeared before a subcommittee of the House Committee on Military Affairs seven weeks later. By this time, Davison's warnings had begun to sound like the monotonous refrain from a too-often heard tune. At the same time Davison was appearing before the House committee, Major General Charles P. Summerall, then Chief of Staff, was repeating much the same litany before a subcommittee of the Senate Committee on Appropriations. Numerous shortages in the Air Corps program, especially in technical construction, persisted, Summerall advised the Senators, due to budget restrictions set by the President and the Bureau of the Budget. The Senate did restore a few items cut earlier by the House, but then compromised most of the gains away in conference.[42] This was to be the pattern during the remainder of the program.

Late in November 1929, Summerall and Fechet returned to the House Committee on Appropriations. Over the next several weeks, they discussed at length the program's status as it neared the halfway point. They advised the committee that the program was unbalanced, housing was still critically short, equipment was not keeping pace with increasing personnel, and some aircraft were sitting in the open because hangars were being used to store hay which was more perishable than aircraft. Especially onerous to the Air Corps was Congress' practice of including contract authorization provisions in construction appropriations. The contract authorization provision allowed the Air Corps to let contracts in a fiscal year for equipment or services that would not be completed or delivered until the next or subsequent fiscal year. The contractor would be paid in the year the contract was concluded. Thus the Air Corps could expedite deliveries and construction by contracting in advance, and Congress could postpone appropriating money for an additional year. But the Air Corps objected. The system required part of the next appropriation to pay the contract obligation limiting future purchasing power. In its report on the bill under consideration, the Appropriations Committee acknowledged that there were some problems with the Five-Year Program, especially in housing, aircraft, and personnel. The committee sent the amended bill to the full House, eliminating the contract authorization provision—not because the Air Corps so strenuously objected but for economy—and cut more than $2 million from the housing program. The committee then claimed that it was not responsible for this cut: "Whether or not permanent housing to the extent indicated is necessary or will need to be provided is not for this committee to determine."[43] Who was responsible, then? The committee did not say. Nor did the committee show any interest in why the Five-Year Program was failing or what should be done about it.

Davison and Fechet were both in a combative mood when the Senate Committee on Appropriations took up the House-approved bill in mid–April. Davison vehemently attacked the cuts made by the House, charging that changes in the housing program were a serious embarrassment to the War Department. Fechet seconded Davison and pleaded as well for more funds for technical construction. The Senate restored some of the cuts made by the House, but it also restored the unwanted contract authorization provision.[44] Like the House committee, the Senate committee called for neither a thorough reassessment nor an investigation for the Five-Year Program.

The year 1930 was a replay of 1929. In June, Summerall, Fechet, and Major Frank Kennedy, Chief of the Air Corps Buildings and Grounds Division, appeared before the House Committee on Military Affairs reciting what they had said a dozen times. Then the committee tinkered with the details of the bill under consideration but made no substantive changes. In November, the House Committee on Appropriations took up the annual War Department appropriation bill which was to include the final increment of the Five-Year Program. Fechet made one last attempt to impress on the committee the dire state of the program. He told the members of the subcommittee that the fourth increment would not be completed at the end of the fiscal year, and that something had to be done if the program was to be salvaged. In spite of Fechet's warning, the committee's report presented an optimistic outlook for the Five-Year Program, the Army housing program, and technical construction. The committee proceeded to recommend an overall cut in the Bureau of the Budget estimate for the War Department in keeping with the general policy of reducing expenditures to conform to reduced revenues.[45] For all practical purposes, this move spelled the end of the Five-Year Program.

Fechet's successor inherited the duty of officially declaring the Five-Year Program a failure. On 5 January 1932, Major General Benjamin Foulois, Chief of the Air Corps for only two weeks, appeared before the subcommittee of the House Committee on Appropriations for the last time on behalf of the program. The final increment, scheduled for fiscal year 1932, had at first been delayed, then cancelled. The program would not be completed, Foulois told the panel, "and even if it were complete at that time, in accordance with the interpretations of the law under which we have been operating and submitting estimates from 1928 to 1932, inclusive, the United States Army would not have a well-balanced and properly equipped force."[46] Once again, the committee listened, but it was too late to act. In any case, most of the members had already written off the program. Perhaps they had heard all of this too many times. After a long delay, the committee's report acknowledged that the program had indeed failed to attain its objectives, but it hardly delved into the causes. "We have not been keeping pace with attrition."[47] That was as profound as the report would get. Neither House nor Senate committee attempted to resurrect the program or call for a general investigation to determine why the program fell short of its goals. There would be no postmortem.

If a postmortem had been conducted, it would have found that the Air Corps benefited significantly from the Five-Year Program. An increased strength level; more newer and better aircraft in its inventory; new housing and technical buildings at most of its stations; and a number of new stations in operation or nearing completion combined to enhance the Air Corps. Nevertheless, the goals established by the Air Corps Act of 1926 and the expectations of aviation leaders had not been fully met. A multitude of causes were responsible for that failure. Historians have previously identified a number of those causes, including the onset of the Depression that triggered general budget cuts, the lack of support by both chief executives in office during the period, and the failure of Congress to override the restrictions placed on appropriations by the Bureau of the Budget.

A number of other equally significant factors clearly contributed to the failure to achieve the Five-Year Program's goals. Among these factors was the faulty enabling legislation that set numerical goals but represented neither a clear consensus as to what the new air force should look like nor how to create it. Congress compounded the inherent faults in the original legislation by failing to delegate or establish oversight responsibility to a standing, special, joint, or ad hoc committee. The congressional committees that dealt with aspects of the program concentrated on the program's details, not its overall direction or progress.

The planners in the Office of the Chief of the Air Corps must also shoulder a share of the responsibility for the program's shortcomings. They seriously underestimated the resources necessary to achieve even the limited goals set by the Air Corps Act. Subsequent changes in the original plan significantly increased the program's actual cost, but the rigid and inflexible budget system was unresponsive to the changing circumstances and requirements. Thus, the program was denied the commensurate increase in appropriations necessary to implement it fully.

Another factor that influenced the progress of the Five-Year Program was the shortage of trained and experienced planners in the Air Corps. There was no formal training for air staff planners in the 1920s. Most of the staff officers who worked in the Office of the Chief of the Air Corps learned their craft on the job. The majority of Air Corps officers were aviators who had come to the Air Corps to fly, not to work on the staff.[48] They tended to be younger and less experienced in staff work than their counterparts in other branches of the Army. While the experience gained during the period from 1926 through 1932 would pay ample dividends a decade later, its absence was evident in the course of the Five-Year Program.

Finally, one of the foremost causes for the program's shortfall was the lack of coordination both within and between the planning circles of the Air Corps, the War Department, the administration, and the committees of Congress concerned with various aspects of the program. This lack of coordination was indicative of a failure to understand that planning is a comprehensive and ongoing process in which the constituent parts must be dealt with in detail while preserving the integrity of the plan as a whole. The fate of the Five-Year Program, therefore, demonstrated the institutional limits of planning in the United States before the coming of the New Deal.

NOTES

1. 44 Stat. 780–90 (1926).

2. U.S. Congress, House, *United Air Service, Hearings before the Committee on Military Affairs*, 66th Cong., 2nd sess., 1919–1920; House, *Investigation of the Air Service, Hearings before the Committee on Rules*, 68th Cong., 1st sess., 1924; House, *Inquiry Into Operations of the United States Air Service, Hearings before the Select Committee on Inquiry Into Operations of the United States Air Service*, 68th Cong., 1st sess., 1924; House, *Air Service Unification, Hearings before the Committee on Military Affairs*, 68th Cong., 2nd sess., 1925; House, *Department of Defense and Unification of Air Service, Hearings before the Committee on Military Affairs*, 69th Cong., 1st sess., 1926.

3. 44 Stat. 783 (1926).

4. F. Trubee Davison, "Annual Report of the Assistant Secretary of War,"

Report of the Secretary of War to the President, 1932, 39; statement of MG B. D. Foulois in U.S. Congress, House, *War Department Appropriation Bill for 1933 Military Activities, Hearings before the Committee on Appropriations*, 72nd Cong., 2nd sess., 5 January 1932, 992–1002, 1037–43; statement of MG J. E. Fechet, House, *War Department Appropriation Bill for 1931 Military Activities, Hearings before the Committee on Appropriations*, 71st Cong., 2nd sess., 7 December 1929, 634–35; statement of MG C. P. Summerall, Senate, *War Department Appropriation Bill, 1930, Hearings before the Committee on Appropriations*, 70th Cong., 2nd sess., January 1929, 60.

5. Alfred Goldberg, ed., *A History of the United States Air Force, 1907–1957*, (Princeton: D. Van Nostrand Company, 1957), 37; Carroll V. Glines, Jr., *The Compact History of the United States Air Force* (New York: Hawthorn Books, Inc., 1963), 122; Herbert Molloy Mason, Jr., *The United States Air Force: A Turbulent History* (New York: Mason/Charter, 1976), 105–7; Irving Brinton Holley, Jr., *Buying Aircraft: Materiel Procurement for the Army Air Forces* (Washington, D.C.: Office of the Chief of Military History, 1964), 48–52, 63–65; Edwin H. Rutkowski, *The Politics of Military Aviation Procurement, 1926–1934: A Study in the Political Assertion of Consensual Values* (Columbus: Ohio State University Press, 1966), 6, 215–17.

6. 44 Stat. 783 (1926).

7. *History of United States Air Force*, 36, claimed that lack of funds was responsible for the delay.

8. Albert F. Simpson Historical Research Center, Maxwell AFB, 145.91–346, hereafter USAFHC.

9. *Report of the Secretary of War to the President, 1930*, 3 and *Report of the Secretary of War to the President, 1933*, 33.

10. See for example, Assistant Secretary of War Davison, "Annual Report of the Assistant Secretary of War," ibid., 1932, 40–41; U.S. Congress, House, *H. Rept. 97*, 71st Cong., 2nd sess., 1930, 4.

11. Ibid., 1931, 31.

12. U.S. Congress, House, *H. Rept. 1215*, 72nd Cong., 1st sess., 1932, 15.

13. Ibid., 1931, 254–59.

14. "Report of the Assistant Secretary of War," ibid., 1929, 90; statement of MG J. E. Fechet, U.S. Congress, House, *War Department Appropriation Bill for 1931 Military Activities, Hearings before the Committee on Appropriations*, 71st Cong., 2nd sess., December 1929, 633–44; statement of F. Trubee Davison, Senate, *War Department Appropriation Bill for 1931, Hearings before the Committee on Appropriations*, 71st Cong., 2nd sess., April 1930, 1–4; Chief of the Air Corps, *Annual Report, 1930*, 83; "Naval Aviators and the Air Corps 'tell all': Examination and Cross-Examination," *Aviation* 31 (June 1932): 261–63.

15. 47 Stat. 676–77 (1932).

16. See for example, 44 Stat. 269 (1926), 1120 (1927); and 45 Stat. 338 (1928), 1361–62 (1929).

17. U.S. Congress, House and Senate, *Sale of Surplus Real Estate by the War Department, Joint Hearings before the Committees on Military Affairs*, 68th Cong., 2nd sess., 1924–1925, 6, 18, 40; Senate, *S. Rept. 13*, 69th Cong., 1st sess., 1925, 20–21, 32; *Report of the Secretary of War to the President, 1926*, 35; Chief of the

Air Corps, *Annual Report, 1926*, 34–35; "Report of the Assistant Secretary of War," *Report of the Secretary of War to the President, 1927*, 44.

18. U.S. Congress, House, *War Expenditures, Hearings before the Select Committee on Expenditures in the War Department*, 66th Cong., 1st sess., 1921; House, *H. Rept. 1406*, 66th Cong., 3rd sess., 1921; House, *Real Estate: Survey of Real Estate Owned and Controlled by War Department, Hearings before the Committee on Military Affairs*, 66th and 67th Cong., 1921, 1922, pts. 1 and 2; House and Senate, *Sale of Surplus Real Estate by the War Department, Joint Hearings before the Committees on Military Affairs*, 68th Cong., 2nd sess., 1924, 1925; 43 Stat. 487 (1924).

19. 44 Stat. 204–6 (1926).

20. "Report of the Chief of Staff," *Report of the Secretary of War to the President, 1933*, 42.

21. Ibid.

22. See for examples, U.S. Congress, Senate, *S. Rept. 918*, 70th Cong., 1st sess., 1928; *S. Rept. 1593*, 70th Cong., 2nd sess., 1929; *H. (Conf.) Rept. 850*, 70th Cong., 1st sess., 1928, 6.

23. See for examples, U.S. Congress, *House, H. Rept. 452*, 70th Cong., 1st sess., 1928; *H. Rept. 576*, 70th Cong., 1st sess., 1928; *H. Rept. 383*, 71st Cong., 2nd sess., 1930; *H. Rept. 384*, 71st Cong., 2nd sess., 1930; *H. Rept. 1589*, 71st Cong., 2nd sess., 1930; *H. Rept. 2424*, 71st Cong., 3rd sess., 1931; *H. Rept. 2588*, 71st Cong., 3rd sess., 1931; *H. Rept. 2589*, 71st Cong., 3rd sess., 1931; *H. Rept. 2898*, 71st Cong., 3rd sess., 1931.

24. When Congressman Edward M. Irwin of Illinois attempted to divert funds already authorized for Selfridge Field to Scott Field, Illinois, the chairman of the subcommittee responsible for such bills, W. Frank James, soundly chastised Irwin for stepping out of bounds. U.S. Congress, House, *Various Bills for Construction and Acquisition of Land, Hearings before the Committee on Military Affairs*, 71st Cong., 2nd sess., 1931, 60–62.

25. B. D. Foulois to John J. McSwain, Chairman, House Committee on Military Affairs, 1 May 1933, USAFHC, 145.91–50.

26. U.S. Congress, House, *H. Rept. 1511*, 72nd Cong., 1st sess., 1932, 2–26, gives a complete summary of all construction projects authorized since 1927 and details of those projects undertaken.

27. "A.C. Building Program—Status as of July 1, 1932," chart appended to Chief of the Air Corps, *Annual Report, 1932*, showed that only a small percentage of construction had been completed. However, the chart is seriously misleading since it was based on $120 million in total projects under eight headings. At no time did the Air Corps propose that much construction.

28. The fields established between 1927 and 1932 included Randolph Field, San Antonio, Texas; Albrook Field in Panama; Barksdale Field, Bossier Parish, Louisiana; Hamilton Field, Marin County, California; and Benton Field, Alameda, California. The Air Corps acquired land adjacent to Bolling Field on Anacostia Flats, District of Columbia, to build what became known as New Bolling Field and land to develop Hickham Field in Hawaii.

29. *Randolph Field Dedication, June 20–21, 1930*, dedication program, USAFHC, K287.86; and "Some Facts on the Air Corps Training Center," *Air Corps News Letter*, 1 March 1938, 14–16.

30. "World's Largest Airport Reservation," *Manufacturers Record* 103 (June 1934): 25.

31. U.S. Congress, House, *Construction at Army Air Corps Posts, Hearings before the Committee on Military Affairs*, 70th Cong., 2nd sess., 1929, 4; and Chief of the Air Corps, *Annual Report, 1932*, 2–3.

32. Jerold E. Brown, "Army-Navy 'Cooperation' in the Interwar Years: The Case of North Island," *Periodical*, forthcoming.

33. *Report of the Secretary of War to the President, 1928*, 2.

34. "Report of the Assistant Secretary of War," ibid., 68.

35. Ibid., 1930, 2–3.

36. Chief of the Air Corps, *Annual Report, 1930*, 83.

37. *Report of the Secretary of War to the President 1931*, 3.

38. "Report of the Assistant Secretary of War," ibid., 30.

39. Ibid., 1932, 5.

40. "Report of the Assistant Secretary of War," ibid., 40.

41. U.S. Congress, House, *War Department Appropriation Bill for 1930, Hearings before the Committee on Appropriations*, 70th Cong., 2nd sess., 1928, 421–22.

42. U.S. Congress, House, *Construction at Army Air Corps Posts, Hearings before the Committee on Military Affairs*, 70th Cong., 2nd sess., 1929, 2–4; Senate *War Department Appropriation Bill for 1930, Hearings before the Committee on Appropriations*, 70th Cong., 2nd sess, 1929, 60; *S. Rept. 1565*, 70th Cong., 2nd sess., 1929; *H. (Conf.) Rept. 2619*, 70th Cong., 2nd sess., 1929, passim.

43. U.S. Congress, House, *H. Rept. 97*, 71st Cong., 2nd sess., 1930, 10 and see 2–13; House, *War Department Appropriation Bill for 1931 Military Activities, Hearings before the Committee on Appropriations*, 71st Cong., 2nd sess., 1929, 30–35, 633–44.

44. U.S. Congress, Senate, *War Department Appropriation Bill for 1931, Hearings before the Committee on Appropriations*, 71st Cong., 2nd sess., 1930, 1–3, 93–94; and House, *H. (Conf.) Rept. 1598*, 71st Cong., 2nd sess., 1930.

45. U.S. Congress, House, *1932 Increment Army Housing Program and Technical Air Corps Construction, Hearings before the Committee on Military Affairs*, 71st Cong., 2nd sess., 1930, 2, 29–34; *H. Rept. 1852*, 71st Cong., 2nd sess., 1930; *H. Rept. 1870*, 71st Cong., 2nd sess., 1930; House, *War Department Appropriation Bill for 1932 Military Activities, Hearings before the Committee on Appropriations*, 71st Cong., 3rd sess., 1930, 681, 691, 721–30, 750–51; *H. Rept. 2179*, 71 Cong., 3rd sess., 1931, 2–5, 9–13.

46. U.S. Congress, House, *War Department Appropriation Bill for 1933 Military Activities, Hearings before the Committee on Appropriations*, 72nd Cong., 2nd sess., 1932, 1042–43, also see 992–94, 999–1000, 1002.

47. U.S. Congress, House, *H. Rept. 1215*, 72nd Cong., 1st sess., 1932, 15.

48. The National Defense Act of 1920 required 90 percent of Air Service officers to be qualified pilots, 41 Stat. 768–69 (1920).

5

Creating the Organizational Nexus for New Deal National Planning

Patrick D. Reagan

Not surprisingly, scholars have tended to associate national planning with New Deal reform. With the Great Depression acting as catalyst, modern American national planning came to public attention in the 1930s. Traditional studies of New Deal planning implicitly began with an a priori definition of national planning as an attempt by the federal government to impose its coercive power from above on the voluntary institutions of the private sector in ways that challenged the tenets of the American faith in individualism.[1] Clearly then our usual perception of national planning in the United States focuses on the 1930s with an intellectual emphasis on a definition of planning that has not been examined in light of historical evidence. Recent work by historians studying the pre–New Deal period leads to questioning of the presuppositions behind this traditional view of the origins of New Deal planning. Did national planning in the United States only begin as part of the New Deal's response to the crisis of the Depression? Does the traditional definition of national planning hinder our understanding of how planning evolved within the context of the American concern for preserving nineteenth-century voluntarism in the wake of the vast changes wrought by the organizational revolution of the late nineteenth and early twentieth centuries? Did Progressive reform set precedents for planning that laid the groundwork for later efforts? Did mobilization for World War I pave the way for the associational experiments of the Hooverian twenties? Did Hooverian planning networks created in the high tide of New Era capitalism engender ad hoc institutional paths followed by the planners who ended up on Roosevelt's New Deal planning board in the thirties? If the New Deal relied so thoroughly on the federal government for its planning work, why did strictly state-oriented planning wither in the wake of demobilization after World War II? Were the voluntary efforts of the twenties as important in the long sweep as the statist experiments of the New Deal and mobilization for World War II? When examined closely, the history of five New Deal planners before 1933 gives tentative answers to these questions.[2]

From July 1933 to August 1943, planners appointed by President Franklin D. Roosevelt to the National Resources Planning Board (NRPB) directed New Deal efforts at state-sponsored national planning. In response to the Great Depression, New Deal planners established a permanent shelf of public works projects that could be drawn on as a countercyclical tool to respond to downturns in the business cycle, created regional planning boards in New England and the Pacific Northwest, founded state planning boards in a majority of the states, developed the policy of compensatory spending usually credited to Keynesian economists, and led the fight for executive branch reorganization to bring order to the welter of New Deal alphabet soup agencies. During World War II, Roosevelt's planners conducted industrial war production site location studies, created the Roster of Specialized and Scientific Personnel to ensure appropriate use of human resources, and engaged in postwar planning that led to passage and implementation of the G.I. Bill of Rights. Yet before these people could employ the state as the agent of national planning, they garnered ideas and institutional experience in the private sector or in organizations that blurred the lines between private sector and public sector. Roosevelt's planners came from upper-class backgrounds and worked in mainstream American institutional settings—business corporations, professional associations, social science research organizations, and organized philanthropies. By 1933 that institutional experience helped to generate shared ideas about bringing together various organized groups into harmonious cooperation with one another. The planners' experience from 1900 to 1933 led them to reject nineteenth-century liberal distinctions between separate private and public sectors. They believed in modern twentieth-century managerial and technical expertise as a way of promoting economic stabilization through fostering cooperation among organized groups be they private, public, or private/public. Their advocacy of intertwining public and private organizations under the leadership of technical elites implied that democracy and national planning were antithetical. Nevertheless, the planners sought to build what they sincerely believed was a kind of democratic national planning operating through a political system that included access to leaders, representative interest groups, and by inference, the citizenry as a whole. The history of modern American national planning mirrored the growth of the organizational society that dominated the life of modern America which had become an urban-industrial nation.[3]

In attempting to promote social and economic balance between organizational groups, American national planning—unlike its European counterparts—drew on the voluntarist tradition to conserve elements of the past while looking forward to the future. Over time, planning eventually took on a conservative tone. Yet the conservative implications of national planning as a policy process seeking institutional balance and socioeconomic stabilization stemmed from the work of the first generation of planners. The planners' ideas took time, effort, and institutional support to develop. Through historical study of the people, ideas, and institutions which evolved into the planning nexus, the scholar can trace the emerging path to planning which remained obscured by seemingly divergent interests. When looked at as part of an emerging set of institutional connections that led to the New Deal planning board, the planners' careers take on more significant meaning. Their achievements as advisory national planners to President Franklin D. Roosevelt and New Deal reform indicated their importance to the national planning process in the American context. These planners came to New Deal planning through analogous stages of intellectual development, establishment of reputations, and forming of institutional networks. Early life and education of the planners gave an elite coloration to their views enhanced by respectable professional credentials. Between 1900 and 1917, the planners laid the foundation for their own specialized work and made contact with a number of important people and institutions. Participation in industrial life through business corporations, city planning, professional work in political science, economics, and psychology during the Progressive Era led into diverse mobilization work during World War I. The experience of mobilizing voluntary associations under the auspices of the federal government in 1917–1918 led naturally into efforts to create what Ellis Hawley has called the "associative state" during the 1920s under the leadership of Secretary of Commerce Herbert Hoover. Hooverian planning during the New Era created widening networks that led some of the participants to Roosevelt's planning agency in the early months of the New Deal.[4]

The planners were not without names and faces. They came from such representative institutional backgrounds as business corporations, city and regional planning, academic social science disciplines, and organized philanthropy. In July 1933 President Roosevelt appointed three men to serve on the National Planning Board under the Public Works Administration as authorized by Title II of the National Industrial Recovery Act. At the Board's head sat Roosevelt's uncle, Frederic A. Delano, a respected Chicago businessman and city planner. University of Chicago political scientist Charles E. Merriam became the philosophical guiding light of the agency. Columbia University institutional economist Wesley Clair Mitchell served as the third member until his resignation in late 1935. In 1936 a new two-member Advisory Committee intended to represent the business community replaced Mitchell's position. On the recommendation of Delano, Merriam, and Public Works Administrator Harold L. Ickes, President Roosevelt appointed Boston manufacturer Henry S. Dennison and Macy's Department Store treasurer Beardsley Ruml to replace Mitchell. Together Delano, Merriam, and Mitchell directed the nation's first experiment in governmental planning from 1933 through 1935 as members of the National Planning Board. From

1935 through 1943, Dennison and Ruml took Mitchell's place and joined Delano and Merriam on the National Resources Committee and the National Resources Planning Board.[5]

Beginning life with the advantages of entry into upper-class and middle-class families with access to specialized education in the nation's newly reorganized universities, Delano, Merriam, Mitchell, Dennison, and Ruml took various routes to national planning. Each planner gradually established professional expertise and a national reputation in a certain institutional arena. Involvement in Progressive reform and mobilization for the Great War led to a widening of intellectual horizons and institutional networks. Eventually each played some role in the emerging associational state apparatus created by Secretary of Commerce Herbert Hoover during the New Era of the 1920s. But what differentiated these men from thousands of other actors in the organizational society of the early twentieth century was their direct link from Hooverian efforts to the New Deal. Through the wrenching prism of the Great Depression, these people became Roosevelt's New Deal planners. Not surprisingly, their paths to national planning were convoluted, hardly inevitable, and clearly not in any straight-line progression that a later scholarly analysis might imply. Yet their search for ways to integrate the best of voluntarist precedents from the nineteenth century with new organizational activities of the twentieth century in order to create planning mechanisms—private, public, and mixes of the two—came from their experience in attempting to serve their class, professions, organizations, and country.

All five of the planners came from well-to-do families of the late nineteenth-century and received superb educational credentials. Born in 1863, Frederic A. Delano was the son of a Hudson River valley aristocrat who had made his fortune in the China trade and industrial investments in coal, copper, and dock properties. Delano attended Harvard University to study topography, geology, and engineering before his 1885 graduation with a degree in natural history. Born in 1874, Charles E. Merriam studied at Lenox College in Hopkinton, Iowa where his father worked as a grocer, the postmaster, and Lenox trustee. In 1896 Merriam moved on to Columbia University to study political science at the leading school in the country. By 1900 Merriam had earned his doctorate and landed a position as the first political scientist at the new University of Chicago. Born in 1874 to a Rushville, Illinois doctor, Wesley Clair Mitchell entered the University of Chicago in 1892 with the first class. Mitchell soon turned to the study of economics under classical economist J. Laurence Laughlin and gadfly institutional economist Thorstein Veblen. Born in 1877 to a successful Boston manufacturer of jewelry boxes and paper products, Henry S. Dennison attended Harvard University where he studied chemistry until his graduation in 1899. Born in 1894 to a Cedar Rapids, Iowa brain surgeon, Beardsley Ruml studied psychology at Dartmouth College, then went on for a doctorate in the new field of mental testing at the University of Chicago. Each of the planners started with the advantages of an elite education which made possible both entry into mainstream institutional life and rapid career advances.[6]

Though their career paths diverged, the planners represented what might be thought of as wings of a nascent national planning movement. Delano represented the corporate liberal linking of business management and city planning. Merriam moved from what his biographer Barry Karl terms "the academic entrepreneur" to become a social science research manager uniting academic social scientists in a new national umbrella organization, the Social Science Research Council. Mitchell represented the economic research wing of planning from his position as research director of the National Bureau of Economic Research. Dennison proved an astute corporate liberal businessman interested in using the Dennison Manufacturing Company as a social laboratory to experiment with welfare capitalist reforms, social research, and scientific management. Beardsley Ruml, an intensely enigmatic man, moved from academic to applied psychology to his leadership as a philanthropic manager of the Laura Spelman Rockefeller Memorial. The planners' different routes to planning eventually brought them together in various organized activities during the Progressive Era, mobilization for the Great War, and the New Era of managerial capitalism in the 1920s.

After graduating from Harvard in 1885, Delano took advantage of family contacts to enter the Aurora, Illinois shops of the Chicago, Burlington, and Quincy Railroad. Between 1885 and 1905, he moved up the corporate managerial ladder through strikebreaking service, engineering skill, marriage to the daughter of the railroad's first vice president, and promotion. By 1901 Delano served as the corporation's general manager at Chicago. Shortly after election to the prestigious Chicago Merchants' Club in 1902, Delano began talks with insurance executive Charles D. Norton that led to city planning. Delano incorporated his plans for consolidation of the city's railroad terminals into the 1908 Chicago City Plan. Architect Daniel Burnham employed a corps of experts in usual Progressive style to draft the Chicago Plan later implemented with support from the Chicago business community.[7]

Between 1905 and 1914 Delano finished his career in railroad management serving in high positions for railroads facing economic difficulties—the Wheeling and Lake Erie, the Pittsburgh-Wabash, and the Chicago, Indianapolis and Louisville railroads. In 1908 he received election as president of the American Railway Association and overseer of Harvard University. At the same time he served on boards of various Chicago businesses, social clubs, and voluntary associations. In 1913 Delano briefly served as railroad representative on President Wilson's Commission on Industrial Relations until his resignation in August 1914 to become a vice-governor of the newly established Federal Reserve Board. In World War I, he resigned from the

Board to take an officer's commission in Paris as Director of Transportation for the American Expeditionary Force under General Atterbury, ex–vice president of the Pennsylvania Railroad.[8]

During the 1920s Delano engaged in voluntary associational work promoting city and regional planning. As a trustee of the Russell Sage Foundation, he helped Charles D. Norton obtain financial support for the Regional Plan of New York and Its Environs (RPNY). With Norton's death in 1923, Delano became head of the RPNY which conducted extensive surveys of the New York area published in multivolume works modeled after earlier Progressive Era socioeconomic investigations. As head of the Washington, D.C. Committee of One Hundred of the American Civic Association, Delano pushed for creation of the National Capital Park and Planning Commission in 1924. President Coolidge appointed Delano to the Commission in 1926. As head of the Commission from 1929 to 1943, Delano directed planning for the expansion of the capital city's roads, parks, and buildings. Delano, then, represented the managerial–city planning wing of an emerging organizational nexus of planning.[9]

Merriam's path to planning took a considerably different course. Between 1900 and 1911, Merriam moved up the academic ladder to a full professorship in the Department of Political Science at the University of Chicago. In several books on American political theory written in this period, Merriam developed his idea of "social lag." The emergence of organized interest groups, Merriam argued, called for a modernization of the political party system, so that parties could act as mediators between groups. From 1904 to 1919, Merriam branched out into municipal reform politics as an independent Republican from the University-area Seventh Ward (Hyde Park). As alderman to the Chicago City Council from 1909 to 1911 and 1913 to 1917, Merriam became involved in city planning efforts focused on the areas of revenues, personnel, and public administration. He argued that municipal government should operate like a business–efficiently. Using techniques developed by academic social scientists, reformers could promote administrative reorganization of Chicago's government.[10]

During World War I, Merriam was High Commissioner of the Rome, Italy branch of the Committee on Public Information gaining experience in creating links between voluntarist activities and the state. Throughout the 1920s, Merriam encouraged social science research at the University of Chicago using the wider community as a social laboratory, consolidated contacts with philanthropists at the national level, and advocated formation of a Social Research Council modeled after the war-engendered National Research Council. In 1923 with the help of his brother John, a prominent paleontologist and president of the Carnegie Institute of Washington, D.C., Merriam cooperated with Director Beardsley Ruml of the Laura Spelman Rockefeller Memorial (LSRM) to found the Social Science Research Council (SSRC). Merriam advocated interdisciplinary research projects in the social sciences as seen in his essays in *New Aspects of Politics* (1925) and his presidential leadership of the American Political Science Association. Merriam invested time, energy, and philanthropic monies in building up the SSRC to bring about cooperation between professional associations of political scientists, sociologists, economists, statisticians, psychologists, historians, and anthropologists. Financed primarily through grants from the LSRM, the SSRC cooperated with such research organizations as the National Research Council, the National Bureau of Economic Research, and the Brookings Institution on work for subcommittees of the Unemployment Conference of 1921 sponsored by Secretary of Commerce Herbert Hoover.[11]

In the late 1920s, Merriam declined a proffered position with the newly reorganized Rockefeller Foundation but did take a position with the new Spelman Fund of New York, successor philanthropy to the LSRM in sponsoring public administration research. The Spelman Fund would help finance the creation of state planning boards in the 1930s. Merriam's associational work of the 1920s culminated with his participation on President Hoover's Research Committee on Social Trends (PRCST) from 1929 to 1933. PRCST historian Barry Karl has noted that the Committee included many of the leading social scientists of the day and its work led into the more politicized social research of the 1930s. Merriam represented the social science research wing of the emerging planning movement.[12]

Serving with Merriam on the PRCST was institutional economist Wesley Clair Mitchell of Columbia University. Mitchell had taught economics at the University of Chicago, the University of California at Berkeley, and Columbia University while working on his seminal studies of fluctuations in the economic cycle. After publication of *Business Cycles* (1913), Mitchell's reputation grew leading to widening contact with other social scientists. During World War I, Mitchell worked with Edwin F. Gay, former dean of the Harvard Graduate School of Business Administration, and Henry S. Dennison on mobilization work for the government. Mitchell moved on to head the Price Section of the War Industries Board. Wartime experience led Mitchell to conclude that statist research and planning efforts were much too limited and incomplete.[13]

In 1920 Mitchell and Edwin F. Gay founded the National Bureau of Economic Research (NBER) for the scientific study of national income distribution. During the 1920s the NBER conducted several studies on the business cycle and unemployment and seasonal operation of the construction industry for subcommittees of the Unemployment Conference of 1921. In 1927 Mitchell succeeded Merriam as chairman of the SSRC. In 1929 the NBER completed the first national survey of economic conditions published in two volumes as *Recent Economic Changes*. Mitchell acted as research director for the study which included the key chapter on corporate management by Henry S. Dennison. That same year, Mitchell became research director and Merriam vice-chairman for the President's Research Committee on Social Trends. The Laura Spelman Rockefeller Memorial helped finance both of these social research projects which resulted in the landmark summary volumes, *Recent Economic Changes* and *Recent Social Trends*. American social science had arrived as a potential component in the national planning process. As head of both the National Bureau of Economic Research and the Social Science Research Council, Mitchell represented the economic research branch of the social science research wing of the organizational nexus of planning.[14]

Henry S. Dennison came to planning through reorganization of the family corporation, broadened contacts in Boston, war mobilization work in 1917–1918, and associational efforts throughout the 1920s. After his Uncle Charles gained control of the Dennison Manufacturing Company in Framingham, Massachusetts in 1906, he and Henry embarked on an ambitious reorganization of the firm. From 1911 through 1920, Dennison placed control of the company into the managers' hands through a 1911 stock ownership plan, integrated production and sales, and implemented welfare capitalist reforms to create employee loyalty. Dennison consciously planned and created an Employment Department (1914), an Unemployment Insurance Reserve Fund (1916), and a company union, the Works Committee (1919).[15]

At the same time, Dennison moved into broader Boston circles made possible by his leadership of the local Chamber of Commerce. He met liberal businessmen such as Edward A. and Lincoln Filene while also engaging in reform work sponsored by the American Association for Labor Legislation such as advocacy of old age pensions and private unemployment insurance plans. His most useful contact proved to be Dean Edwin F. Gay of the Harvard Graduate School of Business Administration. During mobilization for World War I, Dennison acted as Gay's assistant at the Division of Planning and Statistics for both the Shipping Board and the War Industries Board. At the suggestion of Bernard Baruch, head of the War Industries Board, Gay and Dennison formed the Central Bureau of Planning and Statistics. In October 1919, Dennison served as a business representative on President Wilson's First Industrial Conference which unsuccessfully tried to resolve the issues in the steel strike of 1919. Voluntarist and statist experience served businessman Dennison well on his way to becoming a national planner.[16]

During the 1920s Dennison came into his own with associational work in socioeconomic research, management education, and scientific management. In 1919 he and Edward A. Filene established the Twentieth Century Fund to conduct research regarding industrial democracy which later expanded into broader social and economic research. In 1922 Dennison helped found a Boston-area trade association, the Manufacturers' Research Association. The year before he had served as president of the Taylor Society. Throughout the decade, Dennison promoted education, organization, and professionalization of management as seen in his formation of the National Personnel Association in 1922. That group was later renamed the American Management Association with a European branch, the International Management Institute, headquartered in Geneva, Switzerland.[17]

By the late 1920s Dennison had become a representative corporate liberal businessman. While a member of the planning staff which organized the agenda for the Unemployment Conference of 1921, Dennison became interested in business cycle theory. He discussed possible ways of dealing with the ups and downs of the cycle with people such as his friend Edwin F. Gay, first dean of the Harvard Graduate School of Business Administration; Wallace B. Donham, Gay's successor at the Business School; and institutional economist and recognized business cycle authority, Wesley Clair Mitchell. In 1929 Dennison joined one of the Hooverian subcommittees stemming from the 1921 conference which researched and drafted the landmark, two-volume study, *Recent Economic Changes*. In his "Management" chapter for that work, Dennison reviewed the changes in business corporations since the late nineteenth century by drawing from ideas and experience within his own firm since 1900. Managerial leadership reinforced Dennison's faith in voluntarist corporate planning.[18]

In 1929 Dennison tried to found the Business Research Council to bring together prominent corporate liberal businessmen in an umbrella national organization modeled after the Merriam-Ruml inspired Social Science Research Council. With the onset of the Depression, both the Council and many of the Dennison Manufacturing Company's welfare programs failed. In discussions with participants in a Harvard study group directed by Edwin Gay, members of the U.S. Chamber of Commerce's Committee on the Continuity of Business and Employment, and representatives on the Department of Commerce's Business Advisory and Planning Council, Dennison consciously moved toward the idea of government-sponsored—but voluntarist, corporate-oriented—national planning. Service on the Industrial Advisory Board of the National Recovery Administration during the early New Deal led Dennison to hope for cooperation between business, government, labor, and research experts. By the time of his appointment to the New Deal planning board in early 1936, Dennison represented the corporate liberal business wing of the organizational nexus of national planning.[19]

Beardsley Ruml proved the most elusive of the planners. After graduate work in psychology at the University of Chicago, Ruml followed his undergraduate mentor in psychology, Walter Van Dyke Bingham, to the Carnegie Institute of Technology as a faculty member in the first department of applied psychology in the nation. After American entry into the Great War, Ruml joined Bingham, Walter Dill Scott, and his graduate mentor, James R. Angell, on the Committee for Classification of Personnel in the Army (CCP) in the Adjutant General's Office of the War Department. Ruml developed reliability tests for occupational placement of draftees by the Test

Trades Division of the CCP. After the wartime mobilization experience, several of the CCP alumni formed two short-lived industrial psychology consulting firms, the Scott Co. of Philadelphia and the Personnel Research Federation.[20]

Ruml followed his old mentor James R. Angell to the Carnegie Corporation as assistant to the president in 1921. When Angell moved on to the presidency of Yale University, he recommended Ruml to Rockefeller adviser Raymond B. Fosdick for temporary philanthropic survey work. Fosdick recommended that Ruml be appointed head of the smallest of the Rockefeller philanthropies, the Laura Spelman Rockefeller Memorial (LSRM). In 1921 the Memorial held a $74 million principal with an annual working capital of $4 million. Ruml proposed a plan to reorient the LSRM with concentration on building a national social science research network drawing on private research institutes, major universities, and cooperative public sector federal research bureaus. As director of the LSRM in the 1920s, Ruml implemented his plan granting almost one-fourth of the total monies appropriated to the University of Chicago and Merriam's new Social Science Research Council.[21]

The Memorial also funded projects for subcommittees of the Unemployment Conference of 1921 conducted by the National Bureau of Economic Research, the National Research Council, and the Social Science Research Council. The LSRM provided money for two major Hooverian planning efforts of the New Era which resulted in publication of *Recent Economic Changes* (1929) and *Recent Social Trends* (1933). Ruml, Merriam, and Mitchell helped establish SSRC fellowships which sponsored such scholars as Gunnar Myrdal who would later direct the classic study, *An American Dilemma* (1944). From 1925 the LSRM cooperated with the SSRC in holding annual social science research planning conferences on the campus of Ruml's undergraduate alma mater, Dartmouth College, in Hanover, New Hampshire. These conventions both brought together the nation's leading social scientists and allowed for the planning of future projects by the policy making body of the SSRC, the Problems and Policy Committee. Social science researchers directed by philanthropic managers such as Ruml became voluntarist agents in the nexus of planning.[22]

In 1929 Ruml helped in the reorganization of the Rockefeller philanthropies along corporate divisional lines with a new Social Science Division of the Rockefeller Foundation and the Spelman Fund of New York replacing the LSRM. Originally headed by Ruml and later by Merriam, the Spelman Fund financed projects in public administration in the 1930s and the 1940s. In 1931 Ruml served as dean of the new Social Science Division of the University of Chicago helping President Robert Hutchins reorganize the school into divisional units with emphasis on the research-oriented graduate programs. In 1934 Ruml took up the position of treasurer of the R. H. Macy Department Store in New York City. Throughout the 1930s, Ruml continued to act as an informal policy adviser to New Deal administrators though incomplete records and Ruml's concern for staying out of the public eye leave the particulars hidden. Ruml represented the managerial-philanthropic wing of the organizational network that culminated with membership on the New Deal planning agency in early 1936 alongside his fellow business representative, Henry S. Dennison.[23]

New Deal planning grew out of the organizational nexus that emerged from the personalities, ideas, experiences, and institutional networks of the men who became the nation's planners. From 1900 to 1933 these five men took diverse paths to planning that brought them together in the associational activities of private, private-public, and public sector projects and organizations based on modifications of the corporate model first developed by America's business managers in the late nineteenth and early twentieth centuries. Overemphasizing differences between the Hooverian associationalism of the New Era and the Rooseveltian planning of the New Deal overlooks the continuity of people, ideas, and institutional networks. Actually, the move from Hooverian voluntarism to the Rooseveltian positive state took a direct and documented route through the President's Research Committee on Social Trends (1929–1933). In the Merriam-inspired and Mitchell-written "Review of Findings" at the front of the two-volume summary report, *Recent Social Trends*, published in the spring of 1933, the Committee recommended creation of an advisory national planning agency. Not surprisingly, both Charles E. Merriam and Wesley Clair Mitchell joined Frederic A. Delano on the National Planning Board appointed several months later. When Mitchell resigned in late 1935, both Delano and Merriam recommended the appointment of Henry S. Dennison and Beardsley Ruml to serve as the new Advisory Committee.[24]

The planners' experience before 1933 laid the groundwork for New Deal planning efforts which occurred between July 1933 and August 1943 when the board was abolished by a Congress ignorant of its work. Each of the planners had come to a definition of national planning as an ongoing process which would involve the use of social science research experts advising the policy-making political leaders in the executive and legislative branches of the federal government. As part of this advisory planning process, the planners sought to promote education and cooperation among major organized groups such as the liberal element of the corporate sector of the business community, organized labor, and all levels of government—corporatist members of the organizational society. In taking national planning beyond Hooverian voluntarism in the midst of the enormous wreckage of the Great Depression, the New Deal planners logically and naturally extended their ideas, organizational networks, and experience from the pre–1933 period. What they failed to recognize was the elite hue they gave to the planning process. Unorganized people had no place in the planners' organizational nexus. Nevertheless, each of the planners continued to insist that advisory national planning by a technical elite working with the federal government and organized interest groups would bring about "democratic national planning." They did offer both a new description of the American socioeconomic structure and a new prescription for the future. Having seen interaction between voluntary associational groups across private/public sector lines, the planners argued that the atomistic individuals of Adam Smith's self-regulating economy had been transformed into corporate-sized molecules operating in what they hoped would create a harmonious society of co-operating groups of citizens, their representative organizations, and rationally-informed political leaders in both the White House and the Congress.

Using voluntarist precedents of the pre–1933 period, the planners sought to promote intergroup cooperation in place of the ever-feared competition or conflict observed by various Depression-era commentators. The New Deal planning agency's job then became one of encouraging voluntary co-operation through an intangible mix of private and public sector work in order to avoid the imposition of compulsory state power. In this sense, their ideal of national planning under the New Deal sought to achieve a highly conservative aim of promoting and maintaining social and economic stability through the use of technical expertise and intergroup cooperation. In the long view, they hoped to bring this about by extending a modified version of corporate practice into the public realm of American life so as to unite—rather than divide—private and public sectors. As we know, the idea never quite worked out that way.[25]

Between 1933 and 1943, the New Deal planners sought to build their planning ideal through promotion of business-government cooperation, advocacy of public works planning as a countercyclical fiscal tool, creation of regional and state planning boards, executive branch reorganization, and gradual movement toward the idea of compensatory spending policy as a way to use public sector fiscal policy to complement downturns in private sector economic activity. Yet the closer the planners got to actual political influence, the more controversial many of their ideas became. By the spring of 1943, the planners became embroiled in a bitter debate in Congress over postwar planning that led to abolition of the planning board. Cries of "creeping socialism" and unfavorable comparisons of American national planning with Fascist, Nazi, and Soviet planning made a mockery of a decade of a distinctly American version of planning.[26]

Yet after the predominantly statist-oriented experiments of the New Deal and World War II mobilization planning, the planners' ideas took on new life in the older form of voluntarist, private sector-oriented organizational forms represented in such postwar planning organizations as the National Planning Association and the Committee for Economic Development. Yet remnants of the New Deal's emphasis on the role of the positive state remained in the guise of the Council of Economic Advisers created by the Employment Act of 1946.[27] Historical understanding of the creation of the organizational nexus that led to New Deal national planning should remind us that our sometimes provincial concern for neatly-packaged ages can leave important developments out of the larger history of the emergence of modern America. Neither the voluntarist-inspired committee system of the Hooverian, Republican-dominated New Era of the 1920s nor the statist-oriented experimentation of the Rooseveltian, Democratic-dominated New Deal of the 1930s can fully lay claim to a monopoly on the historical evolution of American national planning.

In light of the history of these New Deal planners, we can reach some tentative answers to those questions raised by recent scholars of American planning. American national planning emerged long before the crisis of the Great Depression. Our traditional European-oriented definition of national planning as constituting the use of coercive state power to control—to command—the private sector misses the historical context of *American* planning efforts. Planners in the United States built the organizational networks for national planning in response to the concerns and needs of Progressive reformers, wartime mobilizers of 1917–1918, and the associationalists of the New Era centered especially around Secretary of Commerce Herbert Hoover. New Deal planners took part in this evolving planning nexus and proved to be the latest wave on the incoming tide of national planning. Never fully rejecting the nineteenth-century tradition of voluntary action, American planners also never fully accepted the dictates of the twentieth-century positive state as painted by academic theorists. Rather, American national planners, including those New Deal planners discussed here, sought to define a middle way between an outmoded voluntarism and a new dawn perceived as a bureaucratic nightmare operated by the state. Knowing this, we hardly should show surprise in discovering that when New Deal and World War II statist-oriented planning withered, the mixed forms remained. We only now are beginning to understand the importance of these peculiarly American planning institutions in the postwar period.[28]

During the 1930s and since, opponents of national planning on the right feared the use of overweening state power, while seeking to bring about a return to the golden age of private sector voluntarism which never existed in pure form. Advocates of planning on the left hoped for the use of state power as a way to control the overbearing power of corporate America, all the while declaiming that a return to the past could only sacrifice the future. Perhaps the final irony is that neither the hopes nor the fears of either group came to pass. New Deal national planning involved an attempt to bring together technical experts as advisers to political leaders and representatives of organized groups in both the private and the public sector in order to promote economic stabilization and social cooperation. The postwar years saw the emergence of a modernized liberalism willing at times to draw on either the tradition of voluntarism or the positive state while experimenting with a newer tradition that combined elements of both. The final legacy of the New Deal planners remains shrouded in these ambiguous planning efforts—voluntarist, statist, and combinations of the two—a conclusion that we may find disconcerting. But human agency often plays out on the ironic stage of history. Our role remains that of attempting to understand that stage, rather than trying to redirect it to fit our own contemporary fears or hopes.

NOTES

1. Arthur M. Schlesinger, Jr., *The Age of Roosevelt, Vol. II: The Coming of the New Deal* (Boston: Houghton Mifflin, 1958), 282–84; Paul K. Conkin, *The New Deal* (1967; Arlington Heights, Ill.: AHM Publishing, 1975), 2nd ed. 46; R. Alan Lawson, *The Failure of Independent Liberalism: 1930–1941* (New York: Capricorn Books, 1971), 61–84; Richard H. Pells, *Radical Visions and American Dreams: Culture and Social Thought in the Depression Years* (New York: Harper and Row, 1973), 43–95; Otis L. Graham, Jr., *Toward a Planned Society: From Roosevelt to Nixon* (New York: Oxford University Press, 1976).

2. Robert Wiebe, *The Search for Order: 1877–1920* (New York: Hill and Wang, 1967); Alfred D. Chandler, Jr., *The Visible Hand* (Cambridge: Harvard University Press, 1977); Stephen Skowronek, *Building a New American State* (Cambridge and New York: Cambridge University Press, 1982); Paul A. C. Koistinen, "The 'Industrial-Military Complex' in Historical Perspective: World War I," *Business History Review* 41 (1967): 367–403; Murray H. Rothbard, "War Collectivism in World War I," in *A New History of Leviathan*, ed. Murray N. Rothbard and Ronald Radosh (New York: E. P. Dutton, 1972), 66–110; Robert D. Cuff, *The War Industries Board* (Baltimore: Johns Hopkins University Press, 1973); Cuff, "We Band of Brothers—Woodrow Wilson's War Managers," *Canadian Review of American Studies* 5 (Fall 1974): 135–148; Cuff, "Herbert Hoover, the Ideology of Voluntarism and War Organization During the Great War," *Journal of American History* 64 (September 1977): 358–72; Ellis W. Hawley, "Techno-Corporatist Formulas in the Liberal State, 1920–1960: A Neglected Aspect of America's Search for a New Order," unpublished 1974 paper; Hawley, *The Great War and the Search for a Modern Order* (New York: St. Martin's Press, 1979); Hawley, "The Great War and Organizational Innovation: The American Case," unpublished 1984 paper; Hawley, "Herbert Hoover, the Commerce Secretariat, and the Vision of an 'Associative State," 1921–1928," *Journal of American History* 61 (June 1974): 116–40; David M. Kennedy, *Over Here: The First World War and American Society* (New York: Oxford University Press, 1980); special issue on "Corporate Liberalism," *Business History Review* 52 (Autumn 1978); Guy Alchon, *The Invisible Hand of Planning: Capitalism, Social Science, and the State in the 1920s* (Princeton: Princeton University Press, 1985); Ellis W. Hawley, " 'Industrial Policy' in the 1920s and 1930s," in *The Politics of Industrial Policy*, ed. Claude E. Barfield and William A. Schambra, (Washington, D.C.: American Enterprise Institute for Public Policy Research, 1986), 63–86; Richard S. Kirkendall, *Social Scientists and Farm Politics in the Age of Roosevelt* (Columbia: University of Missouri Press, 1966); Theda Skocpol and Kenneth Finegold, "State Capacity and Economic Intervention in the Early New Deal,"

Political Science Quarterly 97 (1982): 255–78; Ellis W. Hawley, *The New Deal and the Problem of Monopoly* (Princeton: Princeton University Press, 1966); Ellis W. Hawley, "A Partnership Formed, Dissolved, and In Renegotiation: Business and Government in the Franklin D. Roosevelt Era," in *Business and Government: Essays in 20th-Century Cooperation and Confrontation*, ed. Joseph R. Frese and Jacob Judd (Tarrytown, N.Y.: Sleepy Hollow Press, 1985); Albert U. Romasco, *The Politics of Recovery: Roosevelt's New Deal* (New York: Oxford University Press, 1983); Theda Skocpol, "Legacies of New Deal Liberalism," *Dissent* 30 (Winter 1983): 33–44; Theodore Lowi, *The End of Liberalism* (New York: W. W. Norton, 1969, 1979); Otis L. Graham, Jr., "The Planning Idea From Roosevelt to Post-Reagan," in *The New Deal Viewed From Fifty Years*, ed. Lawrence E. Gelfand and Robert J. Neymeyer (Iowa City: Center for the Study of the Recent History of the United States, 1983), 1–19; Barry D. Karl, *The Uneasy State* (Chicago: University of Chicago Press, 1983).

3. Patrick D. Reagan, "The Architects of Modern American National Planning" (Ph.D. diss., Ohio State University, 1982). The analysis in this essay stems from the insights of the organizational school of modern American history summarized in key articles including Alfred D. Chandler, Jr. and Louis Galambos, "The Development of Large-Scale Economic Organizations in Modern America," *Journal of Economic History* 30 (1970): 201–17; Louis Galambos, "The Emerging Organizational Synthesis of Modern American History," *Business History Review* 44 (1970): 279–90, and "Technology, Political Economy, and Professionalization: Central Themes of the Organizational Synthesis," ibid. 57 (Winter 1983): 471–93; Robert D. Cuff, "American Historians and the 'Organizational Factor'," *Canadian Review of American Studies* 4 (Spring 1973): 19–31; and Ellis W. Hawley, "The Discovery and Study of a 'Corporate Liberalism'," *Business History Review* 52 (1978): 309–20; Thomas J. McCormick, "Drift or Mastery? A Corporatist Synthesis for American Diplomatic History," *Reviews in American History* 10 (1982): 318–30; John Lewis Gaddis, "The Corporatist Synthesis: A Skeptical View," and Michael J. Hogan, "Corporatism: A Positive Appraisal," *Diplomatic History* 10 (1986): respectively, 357–62, 363–72.

4. Clifford J. Hynning, "Administrative Evolution of National Planning in the Pre–New Deal Era," *Plan Age* 5 (June 1939): 157–89; Hawley, "Herbert Hoover, the Commerce Secretariat, and the Vision of an 'Associative State' "; Patrick D. Reagan, "From Depression to Depression: Hooverian National Planning, 1921–1933," *Mid-America* 70 (1988); Barry D. Karl, "Presidential Planning and Social Science Research: Mr. Hoover's Experts," *Perspectives in American History* 3 (1969): 347–409.

5. Technically the planning board had several names: the National Planning Board (1933–1934), the National Resources Board (1934–1935), the National Resources Committee (1935–1939), and the National Resources Planning Board (1939–1943). Only Charles E. Merriam of the NRPB published his view of the agency's history, in two short articles, "Planning Agencies in America," *American Political Science Review* 29 (1935): 197–211, and the "The National Resources Planning Board: A Chapter in American Planning Experience," ibid. 38 (1944): 1075–88. Wesley Clair Mitchell gathered his essays on planning in *The Backward Art of Spending Money and Other Essays* (New York: McGraw-Hill, 1937) though he did not comment on the planning board in particular. The best published works

on New Deal planning include Otis L. Graham, Jr., "The Planning Ideal and American Reality: The 1930s," in *The Hofstadter Aegis*, ed. Stanley Elkins and Eric McKitrick (New York: Alfred A. Knopf, 1974), 257–99; and Graham, *Toward A Planned Society*; Philip W. Warken, *A History of the National Resources Planning Board, 1933–1943* (New York: Garland, 1979) and Marion Clawson, *New Deal Planning: The National Resources Planning Board* (Baltimore: Johns Hopkins University Press, 1981).

6. Biographical information on the individual planners is in the Frederic A. Delano Papers, Franklin D. Roosevelt Library, Hyde Park, New York; David Cushman Coyle, "Frederic A. Delano: Catalyst," *Survey Graphic* 35 (July 1946): 252–54; Barry D. Karl, *Charles E. Merriam and the Study of Politics* (Chicago: University of Chicago Press, 1974); Joseph Dorfman, "Wesley C. Mitchell (1874–1948)," *Economic Journal* 59 (September 1949): 448–58; Lucy Sprague Mitchell, *Two Lives: The Story of Wesley Clair Mitchell and Myself* (New York: Simon and Schuster, 1953); Kim McQuaid, "Henry S. Dennison and the 'Science' of Industrial Reform, 1900–1950," *American Journal of Economics and Sociology* 36 (1977): 79–98; James T. Dennison, *Henry S. Dennison (1877–1950): New England Industrialist Who Served America!* (New York: Newcomen Society in North America, 1955); Alva Johnston, "The National Idea Man—I, II, and III," *The New Yorker*, 10, 17, and 24 February 1945, 28–32 ff., 26–30 ff., and 30–34 ff.; C. Hartley Grattan, "Beardsley Ruml and His Ideas," *Harper's Magazine* 204 (May 1952): 78–86.

7. Delano, "The Chicago Plan with Particular Reference to the Railway Terminal Problem," *Journal of Political Economy* 21 (1913): 819–31; Charles W. Eliot, "A Study of the New Plan of Chicago," *The Century Magazine* 79 (January 1910): 417–31; Michael P. McCarthy, "Chicago Businessmen and the Burnham Plan," *Journal of the Illinois State Historical Society* 63 (Autumn 1970): 228–56; Mel Scott, *American City Planning Since 1890* (Berkeley and Los Angeles: University of California Press, 1971), 100–109; Thomas Hines Page, *Burnham of Chicago: Architect and Planner* (Chicago: University of Chicago Press, 1974), 312–45.

8. Commission on Industrial Relations folder, Box 2, Series 1, Delano Papers; Federal Reserve Board folder, Box 3, Series 1, and Delano, "Memories of the Great War: Its Problems and Its Triumphs," typescript volume, World War I Papers File, Box 7, Series 1, Delano Papers.

9. Russell Sage Foundation folder, Box 6, Series 1, Delano Papers; John M. Glenn, Lilian Brandt, and F. Emerson Andrews, *Russell Sage Foundation: 1907–1946* (New York: Russell Sage Foundation, 1947), 2: 438–51; Harvey A. Kantor, "Charles Dyer Norton and the Origins of the Regional Plan of New York," *Journal of the American Institute of Planners* 39 (1973): 35–42; Scott, *American City Planning*, 198–204, 223–27, 261–65, and 289–94; Frederick Gutheim for the Commission, *Worthy of the Nation: The History of Planning for the National Capital* (Washington, D.C.: Smithsonian Institution Press, 1977), 139–233.

10. Karl, *Charles E. Merriam*, 42–83; Merriam, "Investigations as a Means of Securing Administrative Efficiency," *Annals* 41 (May 1912): 281–303; Merriam, "Budget Making in Chicago," ibid. 62 (November 1915): 270–76; Steven J. Diner, *A City and Its Universities: Public Policy in Chicago, 1892–1919* (Chapel Hill: University of North Carolina Press, 1980). The importance of efficiency ideology to reformers is discussed in Samuel Haber, *Efficiency and Uplift: Scientific Management in the Progressive Era* (Chicago: University of Chicago Press, 1964); and

Martin J. Schiesl, *The Politics of Efficiency: Municipal Administration in America, 1880–1920* (Berkeley and Los Angeles: University of California Press, 1977).

11. Merriam, "American Publicity in Italy," *American Political Science Review* 13 (1919): 541–55; Karl, *Charles E. Merriam*, 84–168; Merriam, *New Aspects of Politics* (1925; reprint, Chicago: University of Chicago Press, 1970); A. F. Kuhlman, "The Social Science Research Council: Its Origins and Objects," *Social Forces* 6 (June 1928): 583–88; SSRC, *Decennial Report: 1923–1933* (New York: SSRC, 1934), 1–18, 104–5; *Final Report of the Laura Spelman Rockefeller Memorial* (New York: LSRM, 1933), 10–16. On the 1921 Unemployment Conference see Carolyn Grin, "The Unemployment Conference of 1921: An Experiment in National Cooperative Planning," *Mid-America* 55 (April 1973): 83–107; Evan Metcalf, "Secretary Hoover and the Emergence of Macroeconomic Management," *Business History Review* 49 (1975): 60–80; Ellis W. Hawley, "Herbert Hoover and Economic Stabilization, 1921–22," in *Herbert Hoover as Secretary of Commerce*, ed. Ellis W. Hawley (Iowa City: University of Iowa Press, 1979), 43–77; Alchon, *The Invisible Hand of Planning*, 71–151; Reagan, "From Depression to Depression."

12. Correspondence between Charles and John Merriam in Box 194, John C. Merriam Papers, Library of Congress, and Box 35, Charles E. Merriam Papers, University of Chicago Library; George E. Vincent to Merriam, 14 March 1929, Box 39, and "Notes on Development of Spelman Fund Policy and Program" typescript (n.d.), Box 157, all in Charles E. Merriam Papers; *Spelman Fund of New York: Final Report* (New York: Spelman Fund, 1949); Karl, "Presidential Planning and Social Science Research."

13. Alvin Hansen, "Wesley Mitchell: Social Scientist and Social Counselor," *Review of Economics and Statistics* 31 (1949): 245–55; Robert L. Church, "Economists as Experts: The Rise of an Academic Profession in the United States, 1870–1920," in *The University in Society*, ed. Lawrence Stone (Princeton: Princeton University Press, 1974), 2: 571–609; David M. Grossman, "American Foundations and the Support of Economic Research, 1913–29," *Minerva* 20 (Spring–Summer 1982): 59–82; Wesley C. Mitchell, "Statistics and Government," *Quarterly Publications of the American Statistical Association* 16 (March 1919): 223–36.

14. Arthur F. Burns, "Wesley Mitchell and the National Bureau," NBER, *Twenty-Ninth Annual Report* (New York: NBER, 1949), 3–55; President's Conference on Unemployment folders, Box 86, Subseries 7, Series III, Laura Spelman Rockefeller Memorial Collection, Rockefeller Archive Center, Pocantico Hills, New York; President's Conference on Unemployment, Committee on Unemployment and Business Cycles, *Business Cycles and Unemployment* (New York: McGraw-Hill, 1923); Committee on Recent Economic Changes of the President's Conference on Unemployment, *Recent Economic Changes in the United States* (New York: McGraw-Hill, 1929), 2 vols.; President's Research Committee on Social Trends, *Recent Social Trends in the United States* (New York: McGraw-Hill, 1933), 2 vols.

15. E. P. Hayes, "History of the Dennison Manufacturing Company," *Journal of Economic and Business History* 1 (August 1929): 467–502; Charlotte Heath, "History of the Dennison Manufacturing Company—II," ibid. 2 (November 1929): 163–202; 1900–1915 folder, Henry S. Dennison Papers, Archives of the Harvard Graduate School of Business Administration, Cambridge, Mass.; Henry S. Dennison, "The Principles of Industrial Efficiency Applied to the Form of Corporate Organization," *Annals* 61 (September 1915): 183–86; Philip J. Reilly, "Work of the Em-

ployment Department at the Dennison Manufacturing Company, Framingham, Massachusetts," ibid. 65 (May 1916): 87–94.

16. "The Reminiscences of George Rublee (1951)," 149–52, Columbia Oral History Collection; Herbert Heaton, *A Scholar in Action: Edwin F. Gay* (Cambridge: Harvard University Press, 1952), 98–138; Henry S. Dennison and Ida Tarbell, "The President's Industrial Conference of October, 1919," *Bulletin of the Taylor Society* 5 (April 1920): 79–92; David Brody, *Labor in Crisis: The Steel Strike of 1919* (Philadelphia: J. B. Lippincott, 1965), 105, 115–28; Haggai Hurvitz, "Ideology and Industrial Conflict: President Wilson's First Industrial Conference of October 1919," *Labor History* 18 (1977): 509–24.

17. Kim McQuaid, "An American Owenite: Edward A. Filene and the Parameters of Industrial Reform, 1890–1937," *American Journal of Economics and Sociology* 35 (1976): 77–94; Adolf A. Berle, *Leaning Against the Dawn: An Appreciation of the Twentieth Century Fund* (New York: Twentieth Century Fund, 1969), 3–24; L. Urwick and E. F. L. Brech, *The Making of Scientific Management* (London: Management Publications Trust, 1949), 1: 116–19; David W. Eakins, "The Development of Corporate Liberal Policy Research, 1885–1965" (Ph.D. diss., University of Wisconsin, 1966), 141–42, 179, 225–67.

18. Dennison, "Methods and Results of the Unemployment Conference," typescript and memo, 24 October 1921, Dennison Papers; Kim McQuaid, "Corporate Liberalism in the American Business Community, 1920–1940," *Business History Review* 52 (1978): 342–68; Dennison, "Management," *Recent Economic Changes*, 2: 495–546.

19. Business Research Council, 1929–1934 folder and Dennison, "A Five Year Plan for Planning," typescript, August 1932, Dennison Papers; Dennison, "Suggestions for a Popular Presentation of Planning," probably written in June 1934, Ralph E. Flanders Papers, Syracuse University Archives; Dennison, "Business and Government," *Michigan Alumnus Quarterly Review* 41 (Summer 1935): 295–305; Kim McQuaid, "The Business Advisory Council of the Department of Commerce, 1933–1961: A Study in Corporate/Government Relations," in *Research in Economic History* 1 (1976), ed. Paul Uselding (Greenwich, Conn.: JAI Press, 1976), 171–97; Robert M. Collins, "Positive Business Responses to the New Deal: The Roots of the Committee for Economic Development, 1933–1942," *Business History Review* 52 (1978): 369–91; Kim McQuaid, "The Frustration of Corporate Revival During the Early New Deal," *The Historian* 41 (1979): 682–704.

20. Edmund C. Lynch, "Walter Dill Scott: Pioneer Industrial Psychologist," *Business History Review* 42 (1968): 149–70; Daniel Kevles, "Testing the Army's Intelligence: Psychologists and the Military in World War I," *Journal of American History* 55 (December 1968): 565–81; Ruml, "The Extension of Selective Tests to Industry," *Annals* 181 (January 1919): 38–46; Robert C. Clothier to Ruml, 31 May 1923, Beardsley Ruml Papers, University of Chicago Library; Loren Baritz, *The Servants of Power* (Middletown, Conn.: Wesleyan University Press, 1960), 51–52; Personnel Research Federation files in Box 44, Civic Interests File, Record Group 2, The Records of John D. Rockefeller, Jr., The Private Archives of the Messrs. Rockefeller, New York City.

21. "The Reminiscences of Robert M. Lester (1968)," 24–41, and "The Reminiscences of Samuel S. Hall, Jr. (1968)," 27–34 in Carnegie Corporation Project, Columbia Oral History Collection; letters in Raymond B. Fosdick file, Box 62,

Friends and Services File, RG 2, Records of John D. Rockefeller, Jr.; selections from Ruml's October 1922 memorandum to the Board of Trustees of the LSRM, Series II, Ruml Papers; LSRM, *Annual Report* (New York: LSRM, 1922–1933); Martin Bulmer and Joan Bulmer, "Philanthropy and Social Science in the 1920s: Beardsley Ruml and the Laura Spelman Rockefeller Memorial, 1922–29," *Minerva* 19 (Autumn 1981): 347–407; the percentage figures for the University of Chicago and the SSRC are calculated from "Appropriations for Social Science and Social Technology Made by the Laura Spelman Rockefeller Memorial Up to December 1, 1927," Box 63, Subseries 6, Series III, LSRM Collection. On the more general issue of philanthropic support for social science research, see Barry D. Karl and Stanley Katz, "The American Private Philanthropic Foundation and the Public Sphere, 1890–1930," *Minerva* 19 (Summer 1981): 236–70.

22. Economic Foundation folders, Box 51, National Research Council–Human Migration folders, Boxes 58–59, Social Science Research Council folders, Boxes 64–68, Hanover Conference folders, Boxes 52–53, all in Subseries 6, Series III, LSRM Collection; President's Conference on Unemployment folders, Box 86, Subseries 7, ibid.; Karl, *Charles E. Merriam*, 134–36.

23. Raymond B. Fosdick, *The Story of the Rockefeller Foundation* (New York: Harper & Brothers, 1952), 135–48, 192–209; Abraham Flexner, *Funds and Foundations: Their Policies Past and Present* (New York: Harper & Brothers, 1952), 77–83; LSRM, Inc. folders, Boxes 57–58, Rockefeller Boards File, RG 2, Records of John D. Rockefeller, Jr.; the records of the Spelman Fund of New York, Rockefeller Archive Center, Pocantico, New York, detail the work of that philanthropy; Ruml, "The Chicago Plan," *Educational Record* 12 (1931): 359–68; Ruml's work at Macy's noted in folder 21, Box 1, Series 2, Ruml Papers.

24. *Recent Social Trends* 1: xi–lxxv, was unsigned but clearly based on Merriam, "Tentative Draft of Committee Report," submitted 15 June 1932, folder 3879, Box 326, Series 200S, Record Group 1.1, Rockefeller Foundation Records, Rockefeller Archives Center. Recent historians of Hooverian associationalism have muted differences between Hooverian and early New Deal programs as seen in such key works as Herbert Stein, *The Fiscal Revolution in America* (Chicago: University of Chicago Press, 1969); Murray N. Rothbard, "The Hoover Myth," in *For A New America*, ed. James A. Weinstein and David W. Eakins (New York: Random House, 1970), 162–79; Peri Ethan Arnold, "Herbert Hoover and the Continuity of American Public Policy," *Public Policy* 20 (1972): 525–44; Ellis W. Hawley, Murray N. Rothbard, Robert F. Himmelberg, and Gerald D. Nash, *Herbert Hoover and the Crisis of American Capitalism* (Cambridge, Mass.: Schenkman, 1972); Ellis W. Hawley, *The Great War*, esp. 213–29; Frank Freidel, "Hoover and Roosevelt and Historical Continuity," U.S. Congress, Senate, *Herbert Hoover Reassessed*, S. Doc. 96–63, 96th Cong., 2nd sess., 1981, 275–91. Among the best recent studies along these lines are William J. Barber, *From New Era to New Deal: Herbert Hoover, the Economists, and American Economic Policy, 1921–1933* (Cambridge and New York: Cambridge University Press, 1985); Udo Sautter, "Government and Unemployment: The Use of Public Works Before the New Deal," *Journal of American History* 73 (June 1986): 59–86; James Stuart Olson, *Herbert Hoover and the Reconstruction Finance Corporation, 1931–1933* (Ames: Iowa State University Press, 1977); Bonnie Fox Schwartz, *The Civil Works Administration, 1933–1934: The*

Business of Emergency Employment in the New Deal (Princeton: Princeton University Press, 1984).

25. Alchon, *The Invisible Hand of Planning*; and Ellis W. Hawley, "The Corporate Ideal As Liberal Philosophy in the New Deal," in *The Roosevelt New Deal: A Program Assessment Fifty Years After*, ed. Wilbur J. Cohen (Austin, Tex.: Lyndon B. Johnson School of Public Affairs, 1986), 85–103, are the most perceptive works on this theme. That the planners saw planning as conservative in nature can be seen in representative documents such as Delano to Harold A. Osgood, 27 November 1937, Banking Reform, Gold Standard, Economics folder, Series 1, Delano Papers; Merriam, "Government and Society," *Recent Social Changes*, 2: 1489–1541 and "Government and Business," *Journal of Business* 6 (1933): 181–190; materials in Lucy Sprague Mitchell, *Two Lives*, 366–72; Dennison, "Planning," memorandum for Business Advisory and Planning Council meeting of 4 March 1934, 153.3B, Central Office Correspondence, Record Group 187, Records of the National Resources Planning Board, National Archives; Ruml, "Pulling Together for Social Service," *Social Service Review* 4 (March 1930): 1–10.

26. Byrd L. Jones, "A Plan for Planning in the New Deal," *Social Science Quarterly* 50 (1969): 525–34; Albert Lepawsky, "The Planning Apparatus: A Vignette of the New Deal," *Journal of the American Institute of Planners* 42 (January 1976): 16–32; Lepawsky, "Style and Substance in Contemporary Planning: The American New Deal's National Resources Planning Board as a Model," *Plan Canada* 18 (September–December 1978): 153–87; Robert L. Seifert, "A History of the National Resources Planning Board, 1939–1943" (M.A. thesis, Ohio State University, 1959).

27. Hawley, *The Great War*, 226–29; Stephen Kemp Bailey, *Congress Makes a Law: The Story Behind the Employment Act of 1946* (New York: Columbia University Press, 1950); Edward S. Flash, *Economic Advice and Presidential Leadership: The Council of Economic Advisers* (New York: Columbia University Press, 1965); David Naveh, "The Political Role of Academic Advisers: The Case of the U.S. President's Council of Economic Advisers, 1946–1976," *Presidential Studies Quarterly* 11 (1981): 492–510.

28. Arthur S. Miller, *The Modern Corporate State: Private Governments and the American Constitution* (Westport, Conn.: Greenwood, 1976); Robert Griffith, "Dwight D. Eisenhower and the Corporate Commonwealth," *American Historical Review* 87 (1982): 87–122; Kim McQuaid, *Big Business and Presidential Power: From FDR to Reagan* (New York: William Morrow, 1982); Robert M. Collins, *The Business Response to Keynes, 1929–1964* (New York: Columbia University Press, 1981); Collins, "The Persistence of Neo-Corporatism in Postwar Business-Government Relations" (Paper delivered at the Organization of American Historians Convention, Detroit, Mich., April 1981); Collins, "American Corporatism: The Committee for Economic Development, 1942–1964," *The Historian* 44 (1982): 151–73. Cf. William E. Leuchtenburg, "The Pertinence of Political History: Reflections on the Significance of the State in America," *Journal of American History* 73 (December 1986): 585–600.

6

NRA and the Planning Impulse

Francis Perna

> The cat is out of the Bag. There is no invisible hand. There never was. We must now supply a real and visible guiding hand to do the task which that mythical, non-existent invisible agency was supposed to perform, but never did.
>
> Rexford Tugwell, *The Battle for Democracy* (1935)

THE FIRST NEW DEAL: INSTITUTIONAL ECONOMICS AND THE RESPONSE TO DEPRESSION

As exemplified in the opening remarks of Rexford Tugwell, the weight of opinion within the original "Brains Trust" of Franklin Roosevelt was downright hostile to the philosophy of laissez-faire. The economic regulatory policies of the first administration of Franklin Roosevelt were strongly influenced by the academic and intellectual inclinations of FDR's earliest policy advisors—Raymond Moley, Rexford Tugwell, Hugh Johnson, and Adolph Berle.[1] These men were not intent upon overturning capitalism, rather they hoped the economic system could be salvaged and reformed. The structural-institutional changes contemplated by the "Brains Trust," however, diverged sharply from the ideals of competitive capitalism. FDR's early policy advisors above all else sought to develop administrative instruments of control which would facilitate government intervention and stabilization of the market economy along a number of diverse fronts.

In scrutinizing the political and economic origins of the early New Deal and the National Recovery Administration (NRA), we should always keep in mind that the Great Depression provided the immediate impetus for recovery and reconstruction of the American economy in the 1930s. It was a time of genuine national emergency because the collapse of the economy from 1929 to 1933 was unprecedented in terms of both its severity and duration. The American stock market crash in October 1929 marked the opening phase of a worldwide process of economic deflation and liquidation.

In a 1936 study entitled *The Recovery Problem in the United States*, Brookings Institution economists divided the Depression into two separable phases: the first extending from October 1929 to the spring of 1931 and the second from 1931 to the early months of 1933. The Brookings Institution study described the differential impact of these two phases of the Depression in the following terms:

> The first phase was comparatively moderate in character, resembling in many respects an ordinary business recession. While the extent of the business decline was extremely severe, there was no acute breakdown of the economic structure, and it seemed to many observers that the processes of normal recovery would shortly manifest themselves. The second, and acute, stage of the recession was marked by a collapse of international credit and monetary systems, and by a profound disruption of the internal banking and financial structure of many countries.[2]

The group of countries showing the greatest degree of economic decline included Germany, the United States, and Poland. Industrial production declined in Germany by 46.6 percent, in the United States by 46.2 percent, and in Poland by 46.1 percent.[3]

As international economic relations deteriorated, the governments of the industrialized, capitalist nations adopted a strikingly similar pattern of public policies to deal with the crisis. Each of the industrial nations sought to protect its domestic markets; however, each sought to stabilize or, if possible, increase its export trade. The high tariff rates embodied in the U.S. Hawley-Smoot Act of 1930, for instance, triggered reciprocal economic measures in Europe. But import restrictions—such as tariffs or quotas—represented only one manifestation of the drift toward economic autarky in the international economic system. National governments in the industrial nations were forced to adopt protectionist measures as a matter of self-preservation. No national government could commit itself to free trade in the face of intense, internal pressures to protect domestic social and economic interests from impending ruin. After experiencing years of deflation, the latter interests were fighting for their economic survival. The pressure of domestic constituency needs proved to be inexorable as economic nationalism emerged as the guiding principle of public economic policies in the 1930s.[4] Economic nationalism encouraged heavy deficit spending by central governments to meet domestic interest group demands for relief and protection from the operation of the "invisible" hand of the market.

The basic tenor of the early New Deal was typified by the economic assumptions of FDR's original "Brains Trust." The so-called First New Deal focused on sectoral economic planning and structural-institutional reforms. In short, the precepts of economic planning were not bantered about surreptitiously within FDR's first administration. During the 1933–1935 period, Roosevelt and his policy advisors were confident that the economy could be manipulated through two planning agencies—one in industry, the National Recovery Administration (NRA), and the other in agriculture, the Agricultural Adjustment Administration (AAA).

Drawing upon the intellectual and epistemological premises of institutional economics, FDR's Brains Trust approached the American economy as a highly integrated, functionally interdependent system. Consequently, the recovery and rehabilitation efforts exemplified in the NRA and the AAA focused on economic regulatory policies reflecting the Brains Trusters' faith in national regulation of industrial and agricultural markets. In *The Crisis of the Old Order*, Arthur M. Schlesinger, Jr. characterized the institutionalist policy orientation of the early New Dealers in the following terms:

> Moley, Tugwell, and Berle agreed on the nature of the economic problem. For them all, bigness was inevitable in economic life; "competition, as such," as Moley put it, "was not inherently virtuous . . . [but] created as many abuses as it prevented." They all dismissed the Wilson-Brandeis program of breaking up big business as futile. The problem was not to atomize bigness but to place it under control—to end what Moley vividly called "the anarchy of concentrated economic power which, like a cannon loose on a frigate's deck, tore from one side to another, crushing those in its path." "We are no longer afraid of bigness," said Tugwell, ". . . we are resolved to recognize openly that competition in most of its forms is wasteful and costly; that larger combinations must in any modern society prevail. . . . Unrestricted individual competition is the death, not the life, of trade."[5]

In most respects, the views of the Brains Trust toward the problem of monopoly and corporate reorganization echoed the sentiments and inclinations of Theodore Roosevelt's New Nationalism and the corporate liberals of the Progressive Era.

In facing the Great Depression of the early 1930s, Roosevelt, the Brains Trust, and elite decision makers in the Congress and in the peak organizations of business, labor, and agriculture confronted a social situation with ironic, indeed, tragic implications. Although continuing to pursue their own self-interests *and* maximizing profit margins, individual firms and corporations were generating cumulative macroeconomic movements in prices and wages completely at odds with those interests. In short, the prevailing conditions in competitive markets were not facilitating the revelation of the true preferences of individuals. In the midst of the deflationary spiral of the early 1930s, the manager or owner of a firm in a competitive industry might say something like this: "Yes, I would prefer to maintain the existing levels of production, employment, and price of my product, but—given market structure and conditions—I have no alternative but to cut my price, production, and employment." The NRA and the AAA were essentially compulsory-cooperative arrangements for dampening competition within functional economic interest groups in the economy. These economic planning programs were specifically formulated to curb competitive "maximizing" behavior among individuals and firms in the industrial and agricultural sectors. From this perspective, the NRA and the AAA were enacted to prevent the inexorable logic of the deflationary cycle and its concomitant supracompetitive market conditions from destroying the social and economic fabric of American society. The NRA and the AAA were specifically intended to construct minimum wage and price floors in industry and agriculture, thereby socializing market risks for various classes of entrepreneurs and producers in the economy. In contrast to the neoclassical economists and the Keynesians as well, members of the Brains Trust and other early New Deal policymakers recognized the paramount importance of the institutional-organizational structures governing the choices of individual producers.

NRA AND ECONOMIC PLANNING: EMERGENCE OF THE FRANCHISE STATE

Each nation's experience with economic planning is in a sense uniquely determined by past economic and political practices, and we should not be surprised by the institutional-organizational forms of early New Deal planning programs. These programs may not have conformed to many of our preconceived notions or models of economic planning, but describing and analyzing the goals and accomplishments of the NRA should help delineate the general contours of the modern economic regulatory state in the United States.

For the purposes of conceptualizing the scope and breadth of the NRA's administrative coverage of American business, trade, and industrial activities, it would be advantageous to review the several distinct approaches to national economic planning of the market economy. In *Central Planning for the Market Economy* (1969), Vera Lutz delineated three distinguishable conceptions of economic planning:

> a. a system of *integral* planning from the centre, implying that all economic operations are centrally "guided," "coordinated," or "directed" by a "National Plan";
>
> b. a system of *partial* planning from the centre, entailing measures of government intervention for purposes of modifying specific aspects of the pattern of production, consumption, or distribution;
>
> c. the government's programme for the public sector of the economy or what M. Masse calls the "Plan of the State" as distinct from the "National Plan" of which it would constitute only a part.[6]

From the outset, the NRA was a partial, sectoral economic planning program. Title I of the National Industrial Recovery Act (NIRA) represented the primary industrial and reemployment effort of FDR's first New Deal administration. NRA codes of fair competition directly influenced specific aspects of consumption, production, and distribution. NRA codes of fair competition directly influenced specific aspects of consumption, production, and distribution. NRA codes of fair competition were intended specifically to increase aggregate purchasing power in the economy by forcing private employers to reabsorb unemployed industrial workers at minimum wage standards. Business firms in turn were exempted from Sherman Antitrust Act (1890) anticartel provisions and allowed to cooperate in fixing industrial prices and production. The operation of the National Recovery Administration was contingent on the basis of cooperation between the federal government and business trade associations. Despite the collective bargaining provisions and guarantee of Section 7(a) of the NIRA, organized labor was expected to function as a junior partner in the institutional-organizational arrangements between the federal government and private sector business and labor trade groups.

As an administrative agency, the NRA emerged as an institutional bargaining arena for competing economic interest groups. The principle of industrial self-government evinced in NRA policy and administrative processes, however, weighted the industrial recovery program as a whole toward noncompeting hierarchical-oligarchical control of U.S. manufacturing and industrial sectors of the economy. Although several bureaus within the NRA parent organization (most notably the Code Analysis Division, Research and Planning, and the Legal Division) lobbied for rational-deductive approaches toward the problem of industrial recovery and rehabilitation, there was no coordinated, systematic effort on the part of the NRA to balance sectoral shortages and surpluses in the economy. For instance, minimum wage and minimum price schedules were established with only perfunctory analysis of their potential economic consequences and impacts on the national economy. A partial, piecemeal approach to national economic planning emerged under the auspices of the NRA. On the basis of the organizational development, policies, and administrative processes of the NRA, we surmise that any agency delegated responsibilities to resolve many economic problems at the same time and in the face of grave, emergency conditions is likely to rely upon comparable incrementalist, interest-group techniques for regulating and controlling the national economy.

Many political scientists, economists, and historians have criticized the economic approach to the Depression embodied in the NRA, especially in the wake of the *Schechter* decision. Most social scientists who have written about the NRA have used the classical model of the competitive market as the standard for evaluating its economic regulation of business and labor interests. But as historian William Leuchtenburg emphasized in *Franklin D. Roosevelt and the New Deal*, NRA price policies and the issue of monopolization under the codes of fair competition have prevented a balanced appraisal of this organization. The substantive accomplishments of the NRA consistently have been overlooked by economists and social theorists. Leuchtenberg indicated that

> too great fault has been found with the NRA's price policies; the Recovery Administration has been blamed unfairly for the acceleration of industry toward concentration; and commentators have exaggerated the degree to which the NRA hurt small business. The main grievance of small businessmen against the Recovery Administration lay not in the fact that they were oppressed by monopoly but that the government would not permit them to continue to exploit labor. Finally, the NRA could boast some considerable achievements: it gave jobs to some two million workers; it helped stop a renewal of the deflationary spiral that had almost wrecked the nation; it did something to improve business ethics and civilize competition; it established a national pattern of maximum hours and minimum wages; and it all but wiped out child labor and the sweat shop.[7]

Only if we examine the NRA from the perspective of substantive changes in federal economic regulatory policies can the full scope and breadth of its impact on the U.S. economy properly be assessed and evaluated.

The NIRA was intended primarily to stabilize wages and prices by creating minimum wage and price floors in the industrial sectors of the economy. Several diverse viewpoints which went into the formulation of NIRA intellectual currents contributed to the administrative ambiguities associated with NRA economic policies. Ellis Hawley emphasized that the NRA typified the ambivalent and diverse approaches to industrial organization in the early New Deal:

> That New Deal policy was inconsistent, then, should occasion little surprise. Such inconsistency, in fact, was readily apparent in the National Industrial Recovery Act, the first major effort to deal with the problems of industrial organization. When Roosevelt took office in 1933, the depression had reached its most acute stage. Almost every economic group was crying for salvation through political means, for some sort of rationalization and planning, although they might differ as to just who was to do the planning and the type and amount of it that would be required. Probusiness planners, drawing upon the trade association ideology of the 1920's and the precedent of the War Industries Board, envisioned a semi-cartelized business commonwealth in which industrial leaders would plan and the state would enforce the decisions. Other men, convinced that there was already too much planning by businessmen, hoped to create an order in which other economic groups would participate in the policy-making process. Even under these circumstances, however, the resulting legislation had to be clothed in competitive symbols. Proponents of the NRA advanced the theory that it would help small businessmen and industrial laborers by protecting them from predatory practices and monopolistic abuses. The devices used to erect monopolistic controls became "codes of fair competition." And each such device contained the proper incantation against monopoly.[8]

The NIRA was couched in terminology intended to provide maximum flexibility in its administration. It was not a single-purpose statute; and it should therefore be no surprise that an intense clash over NRA economic regulatory policies emerged among the interest groups involved in its administration. The NRA was exemplary of the compromise political economy that emerged on an ad hoc basis in the 1930s. In the process of interest group planning that emerged under the NRA, public policy-making was dominated by the most cohesive and well-organized constituencies.

The NRA to a great extent protected vested economic interests with the authority of the state. NRA regulations were often proportional to the strength of the interest groups involved in the economic regulatory process as Murray Edelman pointed out: "Because NRA policy formulation involved the pitting of private economic groups against each other, the outcome could never be too different from the parties' estimate of their chances of winning in a direct conflict in the economic area. Unions won important gains in NRA codes only where they were economically strong."[9] We do not dispute the view generally accepted among historians that the NRA code-making process was dominated by organized business interests. Indeed, the owners of productive facilities were well-organized, knowledgeable, and aggressive in pressing for their own economic advantage under NRA. Organized business interests were strongly attracted to government-sanctioned price fixing arrangements and production controls, especially in the deflationary marketplace of the early 1930s. Organized business interests conceived of cartelization (with public controls) as the only avenue to stabilize markets and guarantee reasonable profit margins. So historian William Leuchtenburg qualified his assessment of NRA achievements in the following terms:

> The NRA could maintain a sense of national interest against private interests only so long as the spirit of national crisis prevailed. As it faded, restriction-minded businessmen moved into a decisive position of authority. By delegating power over price and production to trade associations, the NRA created a series of private economic governments. The codes, as Walter Lippman observed, were, in effect, charters like those granted the East India Company. The large corporations which dominated the code authorities used their power to stifle competition, cut back production, and reap profits from price-raising rather than business expansion. Since Roosevelt, Johnson, and Richberg hesitated to use punitive powers, and had little intention of undertaking extensive national planning, the private interest of business corporations overwhelmed the public interest.[10]

The NRA emerged as a series of fragmented and uncoordinated policy initiatives; nonetheless, the cumulative effect of the NRA code-making process was to bestow formidable powers on the code authorities and, in effect, on the business trade associations. The NRA delegated wide powers over price and production to these private agencies—powers which Congress had wanted the federal government to exercise itself. NRA effectuated (for the most part, but not entirely) the conceptions of the "Business-Commonwealth" because the federal government and FDR were actively soliciting business cooperation in the early years (1933–1935) of the New Deal. Roosevelt would in time shift the center of gravity of his political coalition, but in the early years of his presidency, he was still very much concerned with maintaining the confidence and support of the organized business community.

But economic planners, including Rexford Tugwell of the Brains Trust and Leon Henderson of the NRA, would have preferred to strengthen government, labor, and consumer representation in the process of code-making and code administration. This approach envisaged the democratic adjustment of functional interest groups with each group participating in making the decisions significant to it. In a research article on the public policy-making process of the 1930s, Ernest Griffith described how a system of functional interest group representation in industry could serve as a surrogate for a competitive economic order:

> If corporatism rather than government regulation is the path chosen, the obvious answer is so to constitute the governing body or functional authority for each industry that a majority of its members will have their primary stake in what has been defined as the "public interest" or the "national objective." If this be maximum production at low unit profits and prices, then a majority of the membership must come from groups such as producers of raw materials, consumers (including other businesses), the government, and perhaps even the unemployed who would find employment under a program of increased production. The majority would presumably also be composed of those committed to the survival of private enterprise and the capitalist system, so as to avoid confiscatory tendencies. An ancillary device is to give the governing body a secretariat with full right of access to the books of the business affected. The resultant publicity, in and of itself, would be a mighty force in the direction of compelling groups to justify their conduct in the light of the over-all objectives, the attainment of which constitutes the public interest.[11]

The corporatist solution would have gone beyond merely vesting government power in business trade associations or private cartels. It would have involved instead the judicious choice and weighting of the functional economic interests to be represented on the industrial boards or code authorities. Majority representation would be given to those groups with a stake in maximum production and low marginal costs. The need for overall, administrative integration could be minimized; but, in all likelihood, a central planning agency or board would be needed to regulate the relationship across diverse sectors of the economy. Some rules and procedures would have to be developed to control conflict among sectors. If the various sectors of the economy failed to work out voluntary mechanisms of cooperation, then the state would necessarily intervene to mediate conflicts.

The dominant role of organized business in the code-making process of the NRA did not go unchallenged; trade unions, consumers, and NRA planners continually pressured for broader representation and stricter federal controls over the code authorities. In *The Limits of Legitimacy: Political Contradictions of Contemporary Capitalism* (1977), Alan Wolfe described the resistance of organized business to the creation of countervailing power within the NRA:

> Thus it becomes clear that industrialists were more interested in a flirtation with corporatism than in an embrace of the real thing. They preferred a kind of truncated version that applied only to the self-organization of business, and not to anyone else. They found out, however, that the self-organization of business through the state leads directly to demands from other groups for the same thing, and once the principle is admitted, there is no way, logically or practically, to prevent such an extension. Further, when corporatism is put into practice, the problem of the state reasserts itself. While in theory the role of the state should be minimal, in actuality that can only come about when the state itself defines the reality, when it permits corporatism to take place. Hence, no matter what is said, the state has the final authority, since it can remove the corporatist arrangements any time it pleases.[12]

The *Schechter* decision may have put an end to interest group and intraorganizational conflict within the NRA, but the principle of delegated state power would be drawn upon repeatedly in the post–*Schechter* era to promote interest group objectives.

In the post–*Schechter* era neither the economic planners nor the Keynesians proved capable of imposing a rational, consistent approach to the economic problems of the Depression decade. A federal economic regulatory program would emerge in the 1930s, but it lacked overall direction. It was partial, piecemeal, pressure-group planning—responsive to the claims of specific economic groups and industrial sectors. The state would admit all organized interest groups to a share of power, and the federal government would limit itself to managerial or broker functions within the confines of what enfranchised groups would accept. A system of "countervailing powers" would emerge—a system in which strategic economic interests sought government sanctions and controls to maximize their own group objectives and organizational goals. Ellis Hawley offered a graphic description of the fragmented, functionally-specialized economic regulatory process which emerged in the 1930s:

> The programs of the early New Deal, however, had generated a new organization consciousness among previously weak and relatively unorganized groups. For the farmer and the laborer, the independent grocer or druggist, the coal mine operator, used car dealer, and crude oil producer, the trucker, barber, and beauty shop operator, and for others that lacked market power in an economic world where price and production control had become increasingly characteristic, the NRA and AAA had been eye openers. Public power, they learned, could be used to reinforce private power and control markets.[13]

Most of the new federal economic regulatory legislation which emerged in the post–*Schechter* era was along the guidelines of the NRA. Interest group or "partial" planning was designed to restrict production and control competition. Because consumer organizations were weak and ineffective, economic benefits were allowed to accrue to producer groups intent upon promoting restrictionist market policies.

NRA LAWMAKING AND INTEREST GROUP ORGANIZATION

Since the inception of the American republic, federal government policies have influenced the patterns of economic growth and industrial organization and development in the private sector. Most notably, in the nineteenth century, federal tariff policies and tax subsidies represented highly particularized economic regulatory statutes which impacted differentially on private industrial and trade organizations. Private economic interests, business firms, and corporations have in turn endeavored to influence, individually as well as collectively, the formulation and implementation of federal economic regulatory statutes. In this respect, the historic precedents for the NRA, the legislative origins of the NIRA, and subsequent NRA administrative law-making help delineate generally the subtle and complex sets of interdependent institutional-organizational relations between the federal government and business and labor groups that have emerged in the modern industrial economy of the United States. Toward this end, I shall make five distinguishable, but by no means mutually exclusive, arguments in evaluating the historical, political, and economic significance of the NRA.

(1) First, three social movements—progressivism, the business trade association movement, and the industrial mobilization effort of the War Industries Board (WIB) in World War I—set the stage for the NRA economic planning movement and program in the 1930s. Progressive economic regulatory statutes in the late nineteenth and early twentieth centuries contributed generally to the expansion in the scope and magnitude of the federal government's regulatory authority over private market operations. Further, many of the NRA's substantive policies with respect to minimum wages, maximum hours, child labor, collective bargaining, and business trade practices emerged earlier as Progressive measures enacted at either the state or federal level.

Business trade association organizational development prior to the 1930s also influenced early New Deal industrial recovery and rehabilitation programming. The concept of industrial self-government, which trade associationists preferred as a solution to the Depression, strongly affected the implementation goals and strategies of the NRA parent organization and its code authorities in the years 1933–1935. NRA's "procedure by scheme" in many respects represented the formal administrative law technique for operationalizing business trade associationist demands for group autonomy and a business commonwealth.

The administrative experience of the War Industries Board (WIB) in World War I also provided early New Deal policymakers with a workable model for national mobilization of the economy in the face of severe macroeconomic disequilibria and sectoral imbalances in business, trade, and manufacture. Notwithstanding the liberal Democratic predilections of Woodrow Wilson and Franklin Roosevelt, both presidents reached out for the support of the organized business community in time of economic crisis. The NRA planning experience suggests a most remarkable paradox: that even in the midst of the most severe depression in the nation's economic history, organized business groups played a strategic role in the formulation and implementation of economic regulatory policies. The NRA parent organization essentially bargained with the industrial groups, delegating administrative discretion over minimum prices and business trade practices to the code authorities in exchange for the minimum wage, maximum hours, child labor, and collective bargaining provisions. In short, the pattern of business-government relations manifested in the administration of the WIB reemerged under the NRA; and, in both cases, private sector business entrepreneurs organized their respective industries and trades, supplanting competitive markets with price-fixing, production quotas, and cooperative-collusive arrangements. In the process of administrative regulation, both the WIB and the NRA industrial mobilization programs counted heavily upon the support of organized business; and the planning agencies themselves (largely because they lacked specialized competencies for managing private sector industries) necessarily entered into symbiotic relations with the regulated business groups.

(2) Second, although many of the component substantive and procedural parts of the NRA policy package emerged earlier historically, the National Industrial Recovery program itself represented a qualitative and quantitative surge in the economic regulatory powers of the federal government. Notably, in this respect the NRA constituted the most comprehensive peacetime economic planning effort ever undertaken by the U.S. federal government until the Economic Stabilization Program of the Nixon administration in the 1971–1974 period. The NRA, for that matter, was the only federal government agency ever to rely upon industrial codes of fair competition as administrative instruments of control over the national economy. Although the WIB and Federal Trade Commission administrative procedures and substantive policies anticipated NRA administrative techniques of control, neither of these agencies approached the scope and breadth of coverage of the national economy attained under the NIRA and the National Recovery Administration.

The administrative experience of the War Industries Board in 1917–1918 stimulated dramatically the formation of business trade associations during the war years. Largely as a consequence of WIB recommendations and White House pressures, the federal Departments of War and Navy eschewed negotiations and contracts with individual business firms. Instead, business firms in the various sectors of the economy were more or less compelled to organize themselves into industrial and trade groups. In addition to the practical necessity of organizing for potential benefits, business trade associations were expected to help implement WIB rationing and priorities regulations. The War Service committees of the Chamber of Commerce, representing the functional economic interests of the industrial and business trade organizations, participated with the WIB Commodity sections in coordinating war contracts, price-fixing arrangements, production quotas, and conservation measures. But the WIB business-government institutional patterns were never legitimized by federal statute; so, in this respect, the NRA codes of fair competition and industrial code authorities represented a more thorough and far-reaching formalization of the system of government-sponsored cartelism.

In addition to the administrative experience of the WIB, Federal Trade Commission (FTC) procedures and policies anticipated the NRA economic regulatory "procedure by scheme" in which the affected business and trade groups participated in the formulation and implementation of administrative regulations. The FTC's trade practice conference procedure enlisted business trade associations in the formulation of "codes of ethics" for various industries during the 1920s. The Commission relied upon prevailing opinion in the trade groups for ascertaining and proscribing several categories of "unfair competition." The FTC went considerably beyond the common law conception of "unfair competition." Although the Supreme Court insisted on broad review of FTC definitions of "unfair competition" in the *Gratz* case, the Commission's trade practice submittals, conferences, cease and desist orders, and administrative stipulations altered dramatically the meaning and application of the law of "unfair" business competition. In this respect, FTC administrative procedures and substantive policies toward business competition in the 1920s developed concurrently with the cartel movement in the American business community. Both the FTC and Secretary of Commerce Herbert Hoover worked strenuously in the 1920s to alter sub rosa application of Section 1 of the Sherman Act to trade associations via open-price, statistical exchange, and uniform cost accounting programs. However, the NRA went considerably beyond these efforts toward the end of institutionalizing industrial self-government and legitimizing the cartel plans of established business trade associations. In contrast to the FTC's voluntary codes of ethics, the NRA codes of fair competition were subject to stringent informal administrative sanctions as well as the formal penalties of criminal law specified in the National Industrial Recovery Act.

(3) Third, in delineating the particular impetuses for the NRA, I want to

stress the saliency of the internal organizational needs of both business trade associations and American Federation of Labor (AFL) craft union affiliates in the early 1930s. Elite leaders in the business and labor communities recognized that their voluntary cooperative efforts to stem the cycle of deflation and liquidation were proving fruitless. Although counseling price maintenance and restricted production within their particular industries, trade associationists in the business community could not dampen the supracompetition engendered by depressed market conditions in the 1930s. Individual competitors in a particular industry could not accede to fix minimum prices and restrict production unless all members of the trade agreed to abide by the terms of the restrictive agreements. So on the one hand, trade associations programs to fix minimum prices and to apportion market shares faced the deterrent of the anticartel provisions of the Sherman Act because Section 1 of Sherman proscribed collusive-cooperative behavior among individual trade competitors. On the other hand, the dynamics of competitive market conditions in the midst of a severe, general deflation of economic values militated against cooperative trade agreements of any form. Firms in a particular industry which either refused to participate in the cartel plan or "cheated" on the terms of the restrictive agreement by shading prices and maximizing production could redistribute potential monopoly gains from the price-fixers to themselves. Trade association leaders in the business community supported NIRA and NRA for essentially two sets of reasons: (1) to suspend the anticartel provisions of the Sherman Act and circumvent its per se application by the courts; and (2) to enlist the support of federal government administrative and criminal sanctions toward the end of disciplining minority factions within their respective industrial constituencies. Trade associations, in order to operationalize cartel plans, had to deter individual firms from maximizing their institutional self-interests at the expense of group interests.

Business trade organizations were therefore seeking to accomplish two fundamental objectives under NRA: removal of the external constraint on group organization posed by Sherman *and* the imposition of negative sanctions on "free-riding" behavior within particular industrial and business trade groups.[14] Business trade organizations were intent upon using public law to reinforce their schemes for market control or, more precisely, establish nonmarket institutional-organizational arrangements for the elimination of "free-riding" within their respective constituencies and maximize aggregate industrial-group profits.

Similarly, trade union leaders within the American labor movement recognized the need for a federal economic regulatory statute which would enable them to arrest the massive disaffections of industrial workers in the early 1930s from the AFL affiliates. Historically the AFL had been as committed to laissez-faire economics as the National Association of Manufacturers (NAM) and the United States Chamber of Commerce and had eschewed federal government intervention into industrial labor disputes and collective bargaining between workers' groups and employers.

But the Great Depression altered dramatically and permanently the objectives and strategies of organized labor in the United States. The period saw an unparalleled decline in wage rates, escalation of mass unemployment, wholesale repudiation of collective bargaining contracts with employers, and mounting membership losses from AFL affiliates. Trade union leaders recognized the need for federal government protection and promotion of workers' rights to organize and bargain collectively with employers. During White House and congressional deliberations on the industrial recovery bill, representatives of the AFL insisted on the incorporation of Section 7(a) union and collective bargaining provisions as a basic precondition for their support of the NIRA.

Organized labor's demand for Section 7(a) and federal statutory rights to organize and bargain collectively split the business community with the U.S. Chamber of Commerce acceding to the demand and the NAM resisting any challenge to the open shop in American industry and trade sectors. During the formulation of the NRA codes of fair competition and subsequent administrative interpretations of Section 7(a), the code authorities and business trade associations staunchly opposed full recognition and exclusive monopsony powers over labor markets to AFL craft internationals and federal unions. In this regard, organized business achieved notable success with the NRA parent organization. Both the NRA Administrator and his institutional successor, the National Industrial Recovery Board (NIRB), favored a "pluralist" interpretation of Section 7(a)—a pro-business interpretation which would have legitimized company unions and guaranteed individually-bargained contracts between workers and employers.

(4) Fourth, the strategic historical significance and policy implications of Section 7(a) of the National Industrial Recovery Act cannot be understated. The collective bargaining provisions of the NIRA had unintended policy consequences for the American Federation of Labor as well as business corporations and trade groups. On the one hand, Section 7(a) of the Recovery Act and federal statutory guarantees of workers' rights to organize and bargain collectively with employers challenged the hegemony of management and ownership groups in the national economy's major business corporations, introducing the principle of bilateralism in labor-capital relations in these institutions. On the other hand, federal government support for workers' rights to organize and to bargain collectively with employers proved to be a mixed blessing for the American Federation of Labor in particular and the American labor movement in general. The statutory guarantees of Section 7(a) of the NIRA, which were incorporated in all NRA codes of fair competition, altered dramatically the balance of institutional authority within America's business corporations. AFL craft international

and federal unions recouped their 1930s membership losses and surpassed the peak membership years of 1919–1920. In the decades prior to the New Deal, the American business community (except for the hiatus of the war years in 1917–1918) had met the challenge of independent trade unionism with an implacable resistance. Ownership and management groups in the mass production industries successfully maintained open shop conditions by resorting to a diverse range of fair and foul techniques such as yellow-dog contracts and Sherman Act injunctions as well as private police and unrestricted violence against workers and union organizers. Before the New Deal, American business corporations and trade associations managed to confine independent trade unionism to the institutional and technological backwaters of the economy—namely, small-scale and medium-size firms relying upon skilled labor and craftsmen. Despite the periodic resurgence of indigenous American labor radicalism—exemplified in the original Knights of Labor, the Industrial Workers of the World, and the Socialist Party—the American Federal of Labor represented the most durable, successful peak organization in the labor movement.

In the years from its inception until the first New Deal administration of Franklin Roosevelt, leaders of the American Federation of Labor's Executive Council and their craft international affiliates eschewed federal government intervention with respect to the employment conditions of adult male workers—minimum wage rates, maximum hours, unemployment compensation, and collective bargaining. The AFL, in all essential respects, shared the commitment of the business community to laissez-faire and voluntarism. The American Federation of Labor retained exclusive jurisdiction over its craft internationals, but the Federation sacrificed potential membership gains among unskilled industrial workers in the mass production sectors of the economy.

American Federation of Labor support for the NIRA, including federal intervention in the determination of minimum wage rates, maximum hours, and industrial-labor relations therefore represented a decisive shift in the basic policy premises of the Federation. In the initial stages of NRA code formulation, AFL affiliate unions attempted to participate directly in negotiations over the terms and provisions of the various codes of fair competition, but, except in rare instances, NRA's substantive and administrative policies emerged from negotiations exclusively between the federal government and the business trade associations. The staff of the NRA Labor Advisory Board participated as surrogate representatives of American Federation of Labor craft internationals and federal labor unions in the negotiations over minimum wages, maximum hours, and general employment conditions for the codified industries.

From a theoretical perspective, labor unions faced essentially the same institutional and behavioral constraints in their organizing strategies as the business trade associations. Any institution, for that matter, which seeks to exercise control over either the supply or demand side of a particular market must utilize sanctions as well as incentives to eliminate "free-riding." The NRA system of compulsory cartels provided the business associations with the essential nonmarket institutions for maximizing collective benefits and eliminating the "free-rider" problem within their respective constituencies. But neither the NRA parent organization nor its satellite code authorities were prepared to interpret Section 7(a) of the Recovery Act so as to provide American Federation of Labor craft internationals and federal unions with monopsony powers over their respective labor markets. In short, NRA administrative interpretations of Section 7(a) would have emasculated the collective bargaining provisions of the recovery statute. But organized labor recognized the antipathy of the NRA leadership and the trade associations toward independent unionism as early as summer 1933, and consequently, the American Federation of Labor and its institutional successor, the National Labor Relations Board (NLRB), clashed openly with the NRA parent organization and its code authorities over the meaning and application of the collective bargaining provisions of the industrial recovery statute.

For the first time in industrial-labor relations, the National Labor Board-NLRB common law interpretation of Section 7(a) introduced a set of administrative procedures for resolving jurisdictional disputes between employers' company union organizations and independent trade affiliates. The NLB's "Reading Formula" provided for representational elections and majority rule in jurisdictional disputes. The NLRB elaborated upon these principles in the *Houde* case by providing for exclusivity in collective bargaining for the agent of the majority. In contrast to NRA support for pluralist collective bargaining privileges and proportional representation, the NLB-NLRB interpretation and application of Section 7(a) proved to be one of the most enduring, significant legacies of NIRA statutory provisions because NLB-NLRB policies and procedures were incorporated in the National Labor Relations Act of 1935.

American Federation of Labor political support for NLB-NLRB policies had unintended consequences for the Federation. Government-sponsored representational elections and the principles of majority rule and exclusivity for the agent of the majority unquestionably strengthened the competitive position of AFL affiliates vis-a-vis the company unions of the employers, but these NLB-NLRB policies also provided dissident industrial unions within the AFL opportunities to compete against established craft internationals. In short, federal government intervention in labor-management relations under the NIRA strengthened and reinvigorated independent trade unionism in the economy. But in the process of promoting trade unionism, NLB-NLRB representational elections and majority rule favored neither horizontal (craft) nor vertical (industrial) labor organizations. Consequently, Section 7(a) and particularly NLB-NLRB policies toward union organization and collective bargaining set the stage for the fratricidal jurisdictional disputes in the late 1930s between AFL craft internationals and CIO industrial unions.

(5) Fifth, the administrative history of the NRA helps to illuminate the institutional and behavioral constraints confronting a national economic planning agency in the United States. It should be emphasized at this point that the NRA was a partial sectoral economic planning program of the federal government. From one perspective, it exerted an enormous centripetal influence over the American economy—as representatives of business trade associations reported dutifully to Washington in summer 1933 to participate in public hearings and to bargain with NRA deputy administrators on their proposed codes of fair competition. But from another point of view, the system of industrial codes anticipated during the legislative origins of the NIRA and the NRA's application of the principle of industrial self-government ensured that authority for management of the recovery program would be highly dispersed. The relationship between the NRA parent organization and the industrial code authorities, at various points in time, manifested elements of both competition and cooperation, depending on the particular substantive and procedural policies at stake.

Generally, study of the NRA demonstrates the saliency of this early New Deal recovery program in the formation of the modern economic regime in the United States. Specifically, NRA's substantive labor policies including national minimum wage and hours standards, the abolition of child labor, and collective bargaining guarantees for individual workers were permanently institutionalized in the National Labor Relations Act of 1935 and the Fair Labor Standards Act of 1938. These latter statutes continue to constitute the cornerstones of federal government regulation of labor markets in interstate commerce. Although the NRA administrative approach embodied in "procedure by scheme" expired with the *Schechter* decision in 1935, the principle of delegation of legislative authority to administrative agencies has advanced sub rosa and has permeated the modern economic regulatory process in the United States. Paradoxically, the judicial activism of the courts with respect to economic regulation so clearly in evidence in the constitutional law cases of the early New Deal has given way to judicial restraint in this field.[15] New Deal politics and policy initiatives (as well as the overt threat to the institutional autonomy of the Supreme Court posed by FDR's "court-packing" plan) forced the courts to adopt a posture of judicial passivity with respect to federal and state economic regulatory agencies and administrative law regulations governing various sectors of the American economy. Between the 1935 *Schechter* decision and the 1937 *NLRB v. Jones and Laughlin Steel Corp.* decision, the justices of the Supreme Court reversed judicial doctrine 180 degrees. In the latter case, the Court eschewed broad judicial review of congressional and administrative economic regulatory standards, and in doing so, it reversed *Schechter* sub rosa. In short, it vacated its institutional responsibilities with respect to the determination of the "reasonableness" of federal economic regulatory standards. The Court abandoned its distinction between interstate and intrastate commerce as well as its discrimination between legitimate and illegitimate delegations of legislative authority. As a consequence, it ceded all substantive policy-making powers in the field of economic regulation to the Congress *and*, perhaps even more significantly, to the bureaucratic estate. The National Recovery Administration set the stage for a rapid expansion in administrative law regulation of the economy, once New Deal ideology and the new state paternalism became permanently entrenched in the late 1930s.

The administrative life history of the NRA—including code formulation, code compliance and enforcement activities, and various procedural and substantive problems in constitutional, statutory, and administrative law—illustrates how the centrifugal forces at work in a pluralist, industrial democracy like the United States can impede national economic growth policies. Any comprehensive wage, price, and income stabilization program of the federal government must adapt itself to established private sector organizations and coalitions of organizations, as well as public sector agencies, congressional committees, the White House, and the courts.

The National Recovery Administration suggests generally the broad range of formal institutions and interest group coalitions facing a national economic planning agency in the United States. Our description and analysis of the NRA confirm the diverse social and political forces shaping the recovery program in the spring of 1933, including White House and congressional policy groups and elite representatives of the peak organizations in business and labor. In terms of scope and coverage of the economy, the NRA surpassed by far the War Industries Board of World War I and, for that matter, represented the most comprehensive *peacetime* national economic planning effort until the Economic Stabilization Program of the Nixon presidency in the 1970s.

From the earliest stages in the formulation of the economic policies of the NIRA, the industrial recovery program of the New Deal was strongly influenced by the organizational needs and demands of private interest groups. In the Depression of the 1930s, New Deal intervention was a pragmatic response to market failure through government accommodation to the demands of economic interest groups for nonmarket institutions and group optimization plans. As Walton Hamilton of the NRA Consumers Division suggested: "The larger issue bears a faint taint of immortality; its current expression presents a novelty and a variety. The laborers demand the buffer of a minimum wage, the managers of industry want the protection of a floor through which prices may not fall; the farmers will be content if agriculture can be restored to the parity with industrial prices which prevailed for a little while in the good days just before the World War. But these schemes, and all of their kind, are only themes for policy which invite endless variation."[16] Although NRA represented a dramatic expansion in the economic regulatory powers of the federal government, the administrative development of the organization reflected the strong, centrifugal forces at work in the American political economy.

On the one hand, the strong executive form of the parent NRA organization, particularly the administrative style of Hugh Johnson as administrator for industrial recovery in 1933–1934, imbued the program with a direct action orientation and a singular concern with immediate results, namely, the reemployment of industrial workers and the stabilization and reflation of commodity price levels and money wage rates. But on the other hand, the NRA codes of fair competition were adopted in great haste in the summer and fall of 1933, and in the process of code formulation the NRA conceded far too much policy and administrative discretion to the industrial code authorities and the business trade associations. Roosevelt, the Brains Trust, and the early New Deal Congress, although anti-laissez-faire, were not antibusiness. Policymakers in the federal government recognized that no program of industrial recovery and rehabilitation could succeed without the cooperation and support of the American business community.

In one sense, the NRA administrative experience demonstrated clearly that America's business elites ownership and management groups, even in the midst of the Depression, remained politically efficacious and continued to exert influence over the federal government's industrial growth policies. In this respect, the NRA provided a forum and framework for the collective optimizing plans of various industrial and trade groups in the economy. NRA and the federal government could neither subordinate nor command the organized business community; instead, NRA negotiated, cajoled, and in every way conceivable sought to persuade business corporations and industrial group coalitions to participate in the program and to comply with the economic objectives of the New Deal.

Business trade associations played a strategic role in the administrative systems of both the War Industries Board and the National Recovery Administration, respectively the first and second industrial mobilization programs of this century. Both of these economic planning efforts highlight the subtle and complex institutional-organizational interdependencies between the federal government and organized business. The experiences of the WIB and the NRA suggest that any comprehensive economic mobilization program in the United States must secure the cooperation of organized business groups. Business corporations and peak trade associations in the strategic sectors of the economy are likely to be in a strong bargaining posture vis-a-vis the federal government. Any effort to formulate synoptic-comprehensive economic growth policies must accommodate, substantively and procedurally, the group optimizing plans of these organizations.

NOTES

1. Raymond Moley, *After Seven Years* (New York: Harper, 1939) and *The First New Deal* (New York: Harcourt, Brace and World, 1966); Rexford Tugwell, *The Battle for Democracy* (New York: Columbia University Press, 1935); Tugwell, *The Brains Trust* (New York: Viking Press, 1968); Tugwell, *The Democratic Roosevelt* (Garden City, N.Y.: Doubleday, 1957); Tugwell, *The Industrial Discipline and the Government Arts* (New York: Columbia University Press, 1933); Hugh Johnson, *The Blue Eagle From Egg to Earth* (Garden City, N.Y.: Doubleday, 1935); Adolph Berle, *America's Recovery Program* (New York: Oxford University Press, 1934).

2. *The Recovery Problem in the United States* (Washington, D.C.: Brookings Institution, 1936), 28.

3. Ibid., 70. Arthur M. Schlesinger, Jr., *The Age of Roosevelt: Crisis of the Old Order* (Boston: Houghton Mifflin, 1957), 248, highlights other indices of the economic decline in the United States: "National income, which had been $87.4 billion in 1929, fell with the value of the dollar to $41.7 billion in 1932. Unemployment rose: 4 million in 1930, 8 million in 1931, 12 million in 1932—nearly one out of every four workers in the nation seeking a job. Net investment in 1931 was minus $358 million (in 1929 prices); the next year it fell to a disheartening minus $5.8 billion. The Federal Reserve Board index of manufacturing production went down from 110 in 1929 to 57 in 1932; wage payments from $50 billion to $30 billion. And, as prices and income fell, the burdens of indebtedness—farm mortgages, railroad bonds, municipal and state debts—became insupportable."

4. *Recovery Problem in the United States*, 49, notes that "The ultimate consequence of this series of national measures—the suspension of gold payments, exchange controls, increased tariffs, import quotas, monopolies, licensing systems, each of which was introduced with a view to maintaining the stability of a particular country —was to produce profound instability in the international economic system as a whole. However unavoidable or inescapable some of these policies may have been, once the breakdown of the international monetary system had begun, the net result was greatly to reduce production, increase employment, and impoverish the people of the world."

5. Cited in Schlesinger, *Crisis of the Old Order*, 400–401.

6. Vera Lutz, *Central Planning for the Market Economy* (London: Longmans, 1969), 17.

7. William E. Leuchtenburg, *Franklin D. Roosevelt and the New Deal, 1932–1940* (New York: Harper and Row, 1963), 69.

8. Ellis Hawley, "The New Deal and the Problem of Monopoly," in *The New Deal: Analysis and Interpretation*, ed. Alonzo Hamby (New York and London: Longman, Inc., 1969, 1981), 101.

9. Murray Edelman, "New Deal Sensitivity to Labor Interests," in *Labor and the New Deal*, ed. Milton Derber and Edwin Young (Madison: University of Wisconsin Press, 1957), 167.

10. Leuchtenburg, 69–70.

11. Ernest Griffith, "The Changing Pattern of Public Policy Formulation," *American Political Science Review* 38 (June 1944): 454–55.

12. Alan Wolfe, *The Limits of Legitimacy: Political Contradictions of Contemporary Capitalism* (New York: Free Press, 1977), 121.

13. Ellis Hawley, *The New Deal and the Problem of Monopoly* (Princeton: Princeton University Press, 1966), 189.

14. James Buchanan, *The Demand and Supply of Public Goods* (Chicago: Rand McNally, 1968); Mancur Olson, *The Logic of Collective Action* (Cambridge: Harvard University Press, 1971); William Loehr and Todd Sandler, *Public Goods and Public Policy* (Beverly Hills, Calif.: Sage Publications, 1978).

15. *National Labor Relations Board v. Jones and Laughlin Steel Corp.* 301 U.S. 1, 57 (1937) and *West Coast Hotel Co. v. Parrish*, 300 U.S. 379 (1936).

16. Walton W. Hamilton, *NRA Work Materials 1 (A Prologue to Prices)*, Washington, D.C., 1935, 73–74.

7

The "Death of OPA" and the Postwar Reaction against Economic Planning

Gordon P. Henderson

> If [the Office of Price Administration] is a foretaste of the planned economy, heaven save us from the planners.[1]

The interwar years witnessed numerous attempts, and failures, at economic and military planning. But these efforts during the interwar period occurred under conditions of relative peace and thus remained bound in their scope by the traditionally minimalist constraints of the American liberal creed. Even the New Deal constantly had to be defended and trimmed so as to fit the creed's niggardly perimeters. Without an actual war or comparable crisis to press the liberal boundaries outward, planning would remain experimental, piecemeal, and incomplete.

The conditions of relative peace which had prevailed to limit the zeal for planning were shattered by American entry into World War II. Memories of the economic experiences of World War I led to the creation of a vast array of wartime economic management agencies. The Office of Price Administration (OPA) was the leading and most visible of these.[2] Granted formal authority to fix "fair and equitable" prices by the Emergency Price Control Act of 1942, the OPA was responsible for price and rent control, as well as rationing from time to time. Throughout the war, the OPA's authority to control the minutiae of the crisis economy went largely, though not entirely, unchallenged, despite annual attacks during congressional reauthorization debates on its competence, integrity, and practices. The Japanese surrender in August 1945, however, brought tremendous pressure on the relatively new President, Harry Truman, to dismantle many of the economic control mechanisms which had helped the OPA continue to "hold-the-line" on prices.

By spring 1946 when the OPA came under its annual congressional review, Truman had removed many of the wartime wage, resource allocation, rationing, and agricultural subsidy policies which had served to support the

OPA's price ceilings. In addition, Truman was forced to yield to wage hikes in steel and other major industries which, tacitly supported by management, led to demands for increased price ceilings to cover the additional labor costs. While the program naturally remained popular with the general public, the loss of the patriotic incentive led coalitions of large and small businesses and farm groups to urge further decontrol, while organized public support dissipated as private concerns became paramount.

In June 1946, Truman vetoed the reauthorization bill passed by the Congress arguing, on the OPA's suggestion, that it contained too many "crippling amendments" for the OPA successfully to prevent inflation. Its authority to command price ceilings expired on 30 June 1946, and a price hike of nearly 6 percent followed in July. Under public pressure to reimpose controls, Truman "reluctantly" signed another bill in late July authorizing the agency through June 1947. But continued criticism saw the agency pass into history that November, five months before its legislatively manadated end.

The public rhetoric of most of the OPA's critics focused not so much on self-serving calculations of the profits to be made, but rather on the idea that the American public interest, both economic and otherwise, would be served best if all persons possessed the liberty to pursue those profits. They condemned the OPA as an obstruction to that liberty and, rightly or wrongly, regarded and portrayed the agency as the epitome of planning. It is this perspective on the OPA—that it was the epitome of collectivist economic planning—with which we are concerned most. For if in the thinking and rhetoric of its opponents the OPA represented planning, then it becomes possible to regard arguments made against the OPA as typical of those which would be made against planning in general at this crucial juncture in American history. Our focus will be on the lack of enthusiasm for planning as a historical phenomenon.

The search for indicators of antiplanning thought during the immediate postwar period was accomplished through an analysis of the aforementioned attacks on the OPA as they appeared in the editorial columns of the *New York Times* and the *Wall Street Journal* during the period from January 1945 through December 1946.[3] The arguments are grouped according to one of three "problems" regarded by its critics as sound justification for the OPA's complete dissolution. These groupings are more nearly "ideal types" than exact empirical constituents of the attack on the OPA and planning. But they have the added significance that each "problem" area addresses a different element crucial to the formulation of an ideology: a world view—the Knowledge Problem; a conception of human nature—the Cooperation Problem; and the values constituting the ideal state—the Political Problem. The result is an ideological map of mainstream American opposition to planning as it emerged from nearly three decades of theorizing, debate, and experiment. This account is intended not only to further clarify the status of planning in the immediate postwar period, but also to serve as a benchmark for studies of the evolution of planning discourse since the end of World War II.[4]

Analytically, rather than chronologically, the opening salvos in the attack on the OPA as a planning institution focused on the empirical elements of the universe—the economy—which was the principal object of the OPA's activities. In formulating their justification for the dissolution of the OPA and planning in general, critics sought to show that what the OPA and planning advocates proposed to do was contrary to the reality of the object of their efforts. Consistent with ideological construction, they began by defining a world view, though limited to the United States, which differed substantially from that held, at least implicitly, by the OPA. Planning, in short, was impossible. The "knowledge problem" was that the processes for acquiring the necessary information were beyond even the most competent and well-staffed of human institutions. "These Washington gentlemen," as one *Wall Street Journal* editorial put it on 4 February 1946, "seem to live in a world of their own."

A profoundly complex economy lay at the core of this contrary world view. Simply a technical and practical matter, it is here labeled the "knowledge problem" because its entire focus is on the abject inaccessibility of the knowledge the OPA would require to be even moderately successful.[5] Ideologists must always assert the existence of a reality which nonbelievers have either failed or refused to accept. In this case, where the ideologists concentrated on the acquisition of knowledge itself, they humbly asserted their own limitations and, with that, established a threshold beyond which not even they could advance. In other words, the absence rather than misuse of information was at the heart of OPA's problem.

Illustrative of the fundamental knowledge problem argument is the following comment in an 18 February 1946 *Wall Street Journal* editorial: "in a great country with complex economy, with activities greatly diversified, with conditions that vary greatly between one locality and its neighboring locality, with custom and tradition which are accepted in one place and rejected in another—that in such circumstances some central authority can make rigid rules which will have any effect except to paralyze is an assumption which must pile one absurdity upon another absurdity."

Perhaps in anticipation of the sensational advances in computer technology to come, the *New York Times* expressed its own skepticism about price control during the pre–computer age in a 30 October 1945 editorial. Commenting on the upcoming policy address concerning the future of price control by President Truman, the *Times* inveighed: "it is impossible for government to decide what the relationships of thousands of prices should be to each other, what the relation of thousands of wage rates should be to each other, and what the relation of thousands of wage rates should be to thousands of prices. Such a problem cannot be solved by any human mind or any small group of government experts. It can be solved only by the operation of a free competitive market."

Although at first glance this statement in the *Times* appears fully to agree with the position of the *Wall Street Journal*, it leaves open to the *Times* the option of advocating a more moderate price control alternative which would nonetheless remain unacceptable to the *Journal's* stridently anticontrol position. This alternative, commonly referred to as "selective control," would allow certain prices (and wages) to remain free of control while other, presumably more troublesome, ones remained subject to OPA ceilings. While the *Times* could continue to insist that "thousands" of prices and wages could not possibly be controlled by any authority, it could also maintain that some nevertheless should be.[6] The government, therefore, avoided the "enormous proportions" of total control while preventing "needless price rises in those cases in which a shortage cannot be made up for a long time, and in which a price increase could do little to speed the process." In particular, the *Times* referred to "rents on existing housing" and to "luxury, semi-luxury, or unessential items."[7]

As far as the *Wall Street Journal* was concerned, however, there could be no halfway approach to a policy of price control. This was so because "every single price has a cause-and-effect connection with every other price." While it might appear to advocates of selective control that such a policy reduced the "enormous proportions" of total control, the *Journal* insisted that "the national economy cannot prosper, cannot work effectively, while two-thirds free and one-third controlled."[8]

Selective control advocates overlooked the fact, according to the *Journal*, that the profound complexity of the economy, which lies at the heart of the "knowledge problem," extends beyond its sheer size into its tightly-woven inner dynamic. The task of price control is an impossible one argued the *Journal*, no matter how it is done. To make itself perfectly clear, it absolved postwar OPA Administrator Chester Bowles of principal responsibility for the agency's various "failures" with the argument that "the real culprit [in those failures] is the attempt at fixing prices. Unless there is control of the entire economy, the thing is doomed to failure." But since the knowledge required for such a comprehensive program was unattainable, the *Journal* concluded its comments on the proposed amendments to the OPA's 1946 reauthorization bill with the following: "We remain convinced that immediate abolition of all price control... would do more for the long-term general welfare than extension of OPA rule in any form."[9]

As a foundation for their respective positions on the "knowledge problem," both the *New York Times* and the *Wall Street Journal* expressed the view that price control, as a means of holding down inflation, was merely a palliative incapable of getting to the roots of the postwar inflation problem. According to the *Journal*, controls dealt with only the surface while "avoiding any serious attempt to grapple with price making factors that lie below."

According to the *Times*, "price control deals only with the symptoms and consequences of inflation; it does not deal at all with its . . . causes."[10]

The negative consequences of this control of "symptoms" rather than "causes" stemmed from the fact of the economy's complex inner dynamic. Since each price, indeed each economic activity, affected and was affected by all others, the result was to "multiply absurdities." Goods in short supply remained so because the official price served as an inadequate incentive to production. Consumers, armed with excess cash and desperate for those goods, either bid up the price in the black market or, as one *Wall Street Journal* editorial argued, became so discouraged at the unavailability of goods that they simply opted for more leisure, less work, and, consequently, less production. "Effective price control for non-existent items," argued the *Times*, "does little to help the consumer," and little also to stimulate production.[11]

As the foregoing discussion of the knowledge problem indicates, its essential quality as a category of argument in opposition to price control and to planning in general is that the object of control and planning, the economy, is far too complex to admit of central direction. But it is also the case that OPA's opponents are not speaking of a mechanical universe. Indeed, it might be possible to control an economy which, true to its conceptual image, is simply a machine with interacting, and impersonal, parts. Setting aside for the moment the magnitude of the problems which a dynamic and complex economy presents to such efforts, another significant problem is that an economy's "parts" consist of human beings who choose on the basis of signals and who cannot really be compelled, without very good reason, to produce more or consume less. But according to its critics, that was precisely what the OPA was attempting to do. In that effort, they argued, the agency was also doomed to failure. To its critics, the OPA's fatal flaw as regards the "knowledge problem," was the inability of any central governmental agency to acquire and integrate all the information necessary to place the economy on a stable and prosperous path. Were information gathering capabilities to improve beyond these limits, it would nonetheless remain to the actions and judgments of each economic actor to make the application and integration of that information effective. Such is the basic character of the arguments opposing the OPA and planning that are grouped under the "cooperation problem." The appropriate cliché concerns the independence of choice possessed by a four-legged beast when it is led to water.

In late 1945, the *Wall Street Journal* was especially incensed by the Truman administration's stated policy of increasing production through enhanced consumer purchasing power. Government, it argued, cannot expect that the supply of goods will increase when consumers, through liberalized wage and credit policies, have greater purchasing power, while producers are forbidden to increase prices to meet greater demand. The problem was that "wages and prices must be adjusted to production." Even "if Washington were a hundred times as wise as it is," regarding its fixing of wage and price levels, "it could not make the adjustment by fiat." In other words, producers would increase production only when, in their own judgment, circumstances warranted it.[12]

Turning its attention to the consumer, the *Journal* reiterated its opinion that economic actors would do as their own judgment told them and that no government policy would be acted upon unless it conformed favorably with that judgment. After control authorization had expired on President Truman's veto in July 1946, the *Journal* offered the following assessment of consumer behavior:

> Over the long run, the consumer will act according to his own individual wants, his ability to satisfy them, and his judgment as to the price he should pay. At this time a . . . number of people . . . are attempting to tell the consumer what to do and what they want him to do is to organize a "buyers' strike."
>
> Buyer strikes are not organized. The high prices that followed the first world war were not broken because someone got on a soapbox and made a speech . . . people just refused to pay such prices. When people stop buying it is similarly difficult to get them to resume.[13]

The *New York Times* tended to agree with the *Journal* on Truman's purchasing power policy and the conclusion regarding the likely response of producers to increased demand accompanied by increased costs left unmet by price ceilings: "Prices that are too high discourage buyers . . . wage rates that are too high discourage employment, and actually reduce the total income of labor. To increase wage rates is to increase production costs. It is useless to talk of labor's purchasing power encouraging business if business is asked to produce goods at a loss. We cannot have full employment if people are discouraged from becoming employers." The *Times* also found itself defending the behavior of various economic groups against charges by OPA and administration officials that they were aggravating the inflation problem through selfish disregard for the public interest. Business, for instance, could not really be held responsible for the inflationary pressures with which the OPA was intended to deal. Those price increases were made possible and encouraged by a government policy of easy credit and overstimulation through deficit spending. Even support for controls by workers and businesses, the *Times* argued, was understandable in these terms: "Vested interests have grown up even among the groups that are controlled. Some businessmen have succeeded in getting the prices of the goods they make themselves up to a satisfactory level . . . but are not so confident they could do so well under free competition . . . Many factory workers who have doubled their incomes since 1939 while the costs of living have gone up only about a third believe the continuation of controls can either improve their situation further or at least safely freeze the improvement."[14]

According to its critics, the effectiveness of OPA policies depended in large part on the cooperativeness of the independent persons at whom those policies were aimed. That meant that OPA's officials could not legitimately take credit for its successes without acknowledging the role played by public cooperation in those successes. The *New York Times* said as much in a 9 April 1946 editorial responding to the claims of the OPA that its record of accomplishment in stemming inflation was a demonstration of the great strides it had made in its technical ability to do so. Such self-confident praise, the *Times* argued, not only overlooked the important supportive role played by the other war agencies in restraining inflationary pressures but also overlooked the fact that "cooperation by the public, stimulated by wartime patriotic fervor, helped immeasurably." From a slightly different perspective, the *Wall Street Journal* argued on 11 September 1946 that various economic groups "are quick to invoke the government's intervention when it looks promising to them but are quick to resist it when it cramps their style."

Opponents of the OPA were not only confident that the agency's success had always depended on public cooperation, but also that as the war became increasingly a thing of the past, so too would public cooperation. Controls are wartime measures, the necessary cooperation for which, as the *Times* put it, is "stimulated by wartime patriotic fervor." In early 1945, the *Wall Street Journal* sought to warn its readers of the increasing difficulty that would arise in efforts to "hold the line" on prices: "The trouble with 'holding the line' as it is practiced is that it works imperfectly under the constraints of war and is certain to be less effective when the war is over." Controls had achieved a measure of success during the war despite their often "wavering" and "whimsical" administration, the *Journal* reiterated in March 1945, "[b]ut as the end of the war approaches, group pressures against 'the line' are increasing, threatening to break it altogether."[15]

In the absence of patriotic cooperation, there would be increasing evasion. "People will make allowances and put up with absurdities in times of war; they will not do so when the war is ended." In January 1946, the *Wall Street Journal* reported the results of a nationwide survey it had conducted of evasion and black-marketeering and concluded that while manufacturers and consumers were perhaps less able to circumvent OPA regulations, "hosts of middlemen . . . have no respect for wartime regulations now that the shooting war is over." Disregard for OPA regulations was becoming increasingly rampant, not only complicating the job OPA was attempting but also feeding on itself and spawning even more evasion. As its failure to "hold the line" became increasingly apparent, the public reacted accordingly: "The people are well-aware of the OPA failures; they are the ones who are disregarding its rules."[16]

The lack of patriotic fervor was not the only complicating factor in the decreasing post-war effectiveness of OPA. According to the *New York*

Times, "OPA officials . . . continue their wartime approach to the price problem despite the fact that the underlying situation has changed markedly." With its special demand for certain resources and supplies, the war had necessitated controls and made them somewhat successful. With the war's passing, those special demands would disappear and in combination with the withdrawal of "patriotic fervor," that circumstance would alter the economic landscape altogether. After controls had accidentally expired in July of 1946, the *Times* pleaded with the Congress that in framing new control legislation it "should recognize the profound change brought about not only by the ten months that have elapsed since the end of the war but by the existing 'price holiday'." A free market economy, along with the rational individual behavior associated with it, would return with a vengeance and would not be as easy to manage as before. Attempts to manage it nevertheless would "tie up the business of the United States . . . chiefly because we refuse to admit that the war is over and act accordingly."[17]

What worried each newspaper about this was that control advocates, especially those in official positions, might have other reasons for their advocacy beyond controlling inflation. How else, they wondered, could proponents advocate controls in the face of such overwhelming evidence? They feared that enforcement would become stricter and more highly political as peacetime eroded what might be called self-enforcement. That prospect threatened to usurp the free political economy which they believed both necessary and desirable. They began to ascribe sinister motives to those who stubbornly continued to advocate controls.

The distinction between conditions of war and conditions of peace was central to arguments opposing the OPA. The task of administering the program had been easier during the war when accompanied by public "patriotic fervor" and by other war agencies and policies, such as rationing, which dampened inflationary pressure. Opponents also agreed that controls constituted a necessary, albeit regrettable, element in the effort toward final victory. But when hostilities ended in fall 1945, those supports and justifications diminished significantly. It then became much more difficult to successfully administer the controls program and that much more difficult to provide normative justification for the OPA and its mission.

Opponents of the OPA believed they had presented enough evidence of the difficulties the agency would face during peacetime to persuade anyone that its complete dissolution in the near future was the only rational course. Since their underlying assumption was that controls were inconsistent, in peace or in war, with the traditional American adherence to a free market economy, they grew suspicious of those who advocated the continuation of controls. In order to explain this apparent disregard for the empirical and normative cases against OPA, opponents turned to an assessment of the motives of control advocates. We group those assessments under the heading of the "political problem," because advocates were accused of desiring the political advantages which would accrue to the controllers. In other words, they accused advocates of placing political opportunity above the public interest.

The editorial staffs at the *New York Times* and the *Wall Street Journal* regarded controls, especially in peace, as patently un-American from a normative point of view. Such policies, they believed, tended toward the totalitarian. For instance, the *New York Times* bemoaned the fact that "many persons who are relatively disinterested [had no vested interest in seeing controls continued] have come to take for granted the exercise by the government of economic controls which, prior to the war, they would have considered totalitarian." In 1946, the *Wall Street Journal*, true to its more strident opposition, commented that the "exercise of federal authority over a naturally competitive private enterprise—based on the legal fiction that World War Two is still going on—is a bit of fascist syndicalism, a near approach to totalitarianism." The stated goal of each newspaper was to reconvert to a market economy. The *Times* advocated selective decontrol as a "secondary and transitional weapon against inflation," while the *Journal* advocated immediate and unconditional decontrol.[18]

If the outbreak of peace ended the "emergency which excused" controls, the element of postwar, as well as wartime, controls which most needed excusing was the tendency toward a degree of unfairness which opponents felt was not typical of the free market. In March 1945, the *Wall Street Journal* took note of the growing number of veterans seeking to open new businesses and highlighted the difficult questions the government faced in balancing the interests of deserving new market entrants ("considering their service") and those established businesses operating under OPA price constraints. The *New York Times* found unfair the Truman administration's executive order in late 1945 requiring that price hikes permitted "upstream" at the manufacturing level not reappear "downstream" at the retail level. The result, the *Times* argued, was to force the retailer to subsidize either the producer or the consumer.[19]

According to arguments in both newspapers, the principal victim of the inherent unfairness of controls, was the business community. Both newspapers continually accused the OPA and its political leadership of favoring organized labor with permissive wage hikes while preventing the price increases necessitated by those wage hikes. Price control had become "profit control," wrote the *New York Times*, "and 'fair' profits were left to the discretion of OPA." In another complaint, the *Times* objected to permitting price hikes in industries where wages had been increased on the ground that this was unfair to those consumers not benefitting from those wage hikes because they did not work in those industries.[20]

According to the *Wall Street Journal*, price control was undeniably "profit control" under which "the ordinary civilian business enterprise does not tread a path of roses." OPA price ceilings, it argued, were insensitive to the varied abilities of different firms to absorb losses, thereby forcing everyone "to take a beating." At one point, the *Journal* claimed that the imbalance between price control and wage levels implied an "unnatural, illogical, and obstructive liaison between OPA and the major CIO unions."[21]

These arguments concerning the unfairness of OPA regulations did not imply that opponents believed the market to be eminently fair. In fact, both newspapers sought to clarify on numerous occasions that economic life under a free market system would not necessarily be "a path of roses" for everyone either. Rather, opponents worried that controls would too easily lend themselves to political opportunism. The *Times* regarded "treating wages and prices in different ways" as an attempt to solve the inflation problem "politically." Since opponents viewed the wage-price balance under the OPA as profit control, they regarded it also as "the arbitrary power of a governmental agency . . . to say whether a given firm or industry will live, grow, or die."[22]

To the *Wall Street Journal*, the problem of unfairness went farther than mere arbitrary injustice. Given its objections to proposals for selective control in regard to the "knowledge problem," it is not surprising to find the same arguments appearing here. As complaints of unfairness from various politically significant sectors reached the political authority, the OPA would have to reach farther and more comprehensively into the economy to rectify those imbalances which its policies, inadvertently or not, had created initially. "Government intervention in the economy, once started," wrote the *Journal's* editors, "cannot stop until it takes control of even the smallest business." While the *Times* complained of the OPA reauthorization process that "[t]his special interest approach is highly undesirable, though perhaps inevitable once prices are thrown into politics," the *Journal* complained that to try and manage new home construction, OPA director "[Chester] Bowles would use his dictatorship . . . in every big and little community between the Atlantic and the Pacific, as bureaucrats invariably do." The political problem inherent in unfairness, then, was not only the possibility of an arbitrary pandering to one interest over another, but also that as more interests cried foul, control would have to become more extensive.[23]

Opposition arguments in both newspapers also indicated that their authors saw several similarities between the policies and behavior of the American price control authority and the governments against which the entire war effort had been directed. One of these observations, largely peculiar to editorials in the *Wall Street Journal*, was that the OPA tended, as in totalitarian systems, toward the paternalistic. If the OPA were not soon eliminated, wrote the *Journal*, "we shall be struggling for years under their obsession that a government bureau always knows what is good for us." Another complaint found in both newspapers was that the OPA and the Truman administration sought to evade their responsibility to the parliamentary form of government. An agency like the OPA could not carry out its task if it were restrained by the legislative process. It must possess discretion. The *Journal* argued that "parliaments dig their own graves when they vote a managed economy." Along the same lines, in January 1945 the *Journal* characterized as "the Junior Gestapo" a New York regional OPA plan to have schoolchildren compare OPA ceiling prices with those paid by their parents. In the midst of the heated war of words over OPA reauthorization during 1946, the *Journal* again could not resist the Nazi Germany comparison, this time focusing on the OPA's "monstrous propaganda": "Adolf Hitler pronounced the theory that if one will lie largely, assiduously, and vehemently, he will find many people ready to believe his lies and a great many others too weak to call the lies what they are. The fear to combat the official propaganda in behalf of OPA is certainly evidence in support of that proposition."[24]

Finally, we turn to the most sinister of the motives acribed by its opponents to advocates of the OPA. For the *New York Times*, it was simply that "[o]n political grounds... the case for extension of OPA is extremely alluring." It hinted at other more sinister motives in comments that the OPA continually had failed to comply with congressional wishes or to keep its promises to facilitate decontrol. The OPA's policy of waiting "for supply to meet demand" may have been consciously manipulated in order to perpetuate a need for the agency. But the *Wall Street Journal* was far more creative and blunt in claiming at different points that the OPA sought to "sabotage capitalism" with its chaotic policies, to establish a system of "socio-economic planning," to continue controls as a means of income redistribution, and generally to perpetuate "controls for controls' sake" until such a time as it had a firm grip on the economy.[25]

All of the arguments under the "political problem" heading stemmed from the problem of enforcement as well as from the "knowledge problem." For opponents, the practical obstacles to controls would inevitably lead to the need for increasingly totalitarian methods of administration in the absence of public "patriotic fervor." Control authorities increasingly would have to rely on political means of control, arbitrarily favoring those most willing and able to tolerate and/or frustrate it. The resulting unfairness would drive the agency toward deeper intervention until economic and political power had become identical.

Analysis of the arguments opposing the Office of Price Administration during the immediate postwar period was primarily intended as an examination of arguments typical of the opposition to planning in general at this historical juncture. We began with the assumption that arguments against the OPA would be typical antiplanning arguments of the period because their authors had themselves characterized the OPA as the epitome of planning. Given the vast difficulties one confronts when attempting to define planning, we could suspect that the characterization of the OPA as the epitome of planning was perhaps itself the product of the American liberal creed.

The elements of that liberal creed centered around three "problems" with which ideologies must deal. The "knowledge problem" consisted of various arguments that the human capacity for economic planning was restricted by limited means for the collection and processing of requisite information. The "cooperation problem" centered on the idea that planning could not occur in a society where so much depended on the cooperation and judgment of the human beings constituting it. The "political problem" was the tendency of planners with limited access to information and limited control over implementation to turn toward greater politicization of their tasks at the expense of both justice and liberty. In that the arguments fit these "problems" so well, the arguments against the OPA also shaped the antiplanning ideology.

At the time the editorials we have examined were published, Americans were given the rare opportunity to make decisions about their national future in the wake of their immediate past. World War II was a watershed in American history which changed the American international and domestic landscape forever. The antiplanning ideology evidenced in arguments against the Office of Price Administration revealed how Americans stood on planning at the time. The important thing is whether the way they address the three problems changes. If the means for gathering and integrating information improves, it might be possible to deemphasize the "knowledge problem" as an objection to planning. The "super-computer" technology of the 1980s might be construed as doing that. If people and their economic judgments become more manageable, perhaps the "cooperation problem" would be less important. The vocational direction in education and the growing faith in "rational choice" economic models might also deemphasize this objection. Turning to the "political problem" however, we find its resolution so dependent on the outcome of the previous two, that it is difficult to discern what relevant change it could produce. The elements that would constitute the ideal state are so dependent on a world view and a theory of human nature, that they cannot be identified without them. And that gets to the heart of the problem of ideology in the modern world.

NOTES

1. Title and headnote quotations are from *Wall Street Journal*, 1 July 1946; and 18 December 1945.

2. Among the more useful primary acounts of the OPA are U.S. Bureau of the Budget, *The United States at War* (Washington, D.C.: Government Printing Office, 1946); and Harvey C. Mansfield, *A Short History of OPA* (Washington, D.C.: Office of Temporary Controls, 1947). See also Andrew H. Bartels, "The Politics of

Price Control: The Office of Price Administration and the Dilemmas of Economic Stabilization, 1940–1946" (Ph.D. diss., Johns Hopkins University, 1980), summarized in "The Office of Price Administration and the Legacy of the New Deal, 1939–1946," *The Public Historian* 5 (Summer 1983): 5–29; Allen F. Matusow, *Farm Policies and Politics in the Truman Years* (Cambridge: Harvard University Press, 1967); Richard Polenberg, *War and Society: The United States, 1941–1945* (Philadelphia: J. B. Lippincott Co., 1972); Hugh L. Rockoff, *Drastic Measures: A History of Wage and Price Controls in the United States* (New York: Cambridge University Press, 1984); Roland Young, *Congressional Politics in the Second World War* (New York: Columbia University Press, 1956).

3. All material from the *Wall Street Journal* was gathered by a screening of its editorial pages for the entire two-year period due to the lack of a suitable index. Such an index is available for the *New York Times* and was utilized. In all there were 312 editorials, 136 of which came from the *New York Times* and the remainder from the *Wall Street Journal*. Specific editorials are used in the text to evoke the sense of the arguments there being discussed. They are illustrative and the reader should assume that many others like them could have been used. Methodological sources include Barbara Hobbie, *Oil Company Divestiture and the Press* (New York: Praeger Publishers, 1977); Klaus Krippendorf, *Content Analysis: An Introduction to Its Methodology* (Beverly Hills, Calif.: Sage Publications, 1980); Ole R. Holsti, *Content Analysis for the Social Sciences and Humanities* (Reading, Mass.: Addison-Wesley, 1969); and Ithiel de Sola Pool et al., *The Prestige Press: A Comparative Study of Political Symbols* (Cambridge: MIT Press, 1970).

4. The great sociologist Karl Mannheim wrote in *Ideology and Utopia*, trans. Louis Wirth and Edward Shils (New York: Harcourt, Brace & Jovanovich, 1936), 83, that "nowhere else in the realm of culture is the interdependence in the shifts in meaning and emphasis so clearly evident and precisely determinable as in thought itself. For thought is a particularly sensitive index of change." This is what we are attempting in the discussion of the antiplanning ideology. Gordon P. Henderson, "Editorial Page Perspectives on American Political Economy: The Case of Wage and Price Controls Immediately Following World War Two and During the Nixon Years" (Paper delivered at the American Political Science Association Convention, New Orleans, 1985) compares the debates over price control during the 1940s with those of the early 1970s. For a similar study of the 1946 debate over the OPA based on a different data set, see Gordon P. Henderson, "Planning's Opponents: An Ideological Analysis of the Post World War Two Price Control Debate," *Northern Social Science Review* 11 (1986): 71–86.

5. The two most forceful and articulate proponents of the "knowledge problem" in economic planning are Friedrich A. Hayek, *The Road to Serfdom* (Chicago: University of Chicago Press, 1944); and Milton Friedman, *Capitalism and Freedom* (Chicago: University of Chicago Press, 1962). Excellent recent discussions of the problem may be found in Charles E. Lindblom, *Politics and Markets: The World's Political-Economic Systems* (New York: Basic Books, 1977); and Don Lavoie, *National Economic Planning: What is Left?* (Cambridge, Mass.: Ballinger Publishing and the Cato Institute, 1985).

6. Henderson, "Editorial Page Perspectives," notes a significant difference in proportions in the rhetoric of the 1940s and that of the 1970s. During the latter, it is "millions" rather than "thousands" of prices needing to be related.

7. *New York Times*, 30 July 1945; 6 April 1946; 30 September 1945.
8. *Wall Street Journal*, 21 March 1945; and 22 May 1946.
9. *Wall Street Journal*, 6 December 1945; and 22 May 1946.
10. *Wall Street Journal*, 2 January 1946; and *New York Times*, 6 April 1946.
11. *Wall Street Journal*, 14 June and 11 October 1945; *New York Times*, 12 September 1945.
12. *Wall Street Journal*, 26 October 1945.
13. *Wall Street Journal*, 22 July 1946.
14. *New York Times*, 30 October, 8 December, 30 November 1945.
15. *New York Times*, 9 April 1946; *Wall Street Journal*, 31 January and 21 March 1945.
16. *Wall Street Journal* 14 June 1945, 11 January and 11 June 1946.
17. *New York Times*, 15 October 1945 and 9 July 1946; *Wall Street Journal*, 11 September 1946.
18. The "totalitarian" problem is part of the classical attack on the idea of economic planning as seen in the works cited in note 5; *New York Times*, 30 October 1945; *Wall Street Journal*, 21 March 1946; *New York Times*, 9 April 1946.
19. *Wall Street Journal*, 26 February 1946, 23 March 1945; and *New York Times*, 10 September 1945.
20. *New York Times*, 12 March 1946; and 6 October 1945.
21. *Wall Street Journal*, 17 July, 23 April, 20 November 1945.
22. *New York Times*, 10 October 1945.
23. *Wall Street Journal*, 17 September 1945; *New York Times*, 7 June 1946; *Wall Street Journal*, 21 September 1945.
24. *Wall Street Journal*, 17 April and 8 April 1946, 26 January 1945, 11 June 1946.
25. *New York Times*, 30 May, 1 July, 19 April 1946; and *Wall Street Journal*, 19 October and 23 March 1945, 19 February 1946, 21 June 1945.

American Planning: A Bibliographical Essay

Patrick D. Reagan

OVERVIEWS

Scholars have begun to pay close attention to the subject of planning from a variety of disciplinary perspectives. While traditionally the preserve of political scientists, specialists in public administration, and actual planners, the subject has come under closer scrutiny in regard to historical evolution and cross-national perspectives. The best places to start with overviews of American national planning are Otis L. Graham, Jr., *Toward a Planned Society: From Roosevelt to Nixon* (New York: Oxford University Press, 1976); David E. Wilson, *National Planning in the United States: An Annotated Bibliography* (Boulder, Colo.: Westview Press, 1979); David E. Wilson, *The National Planning Idea in U.S. Public Policy: Five Alternative Approaches* (Boulder, Colo.: Westview Press, 1980).

The essays included here draw heavily on the historiographical insights of the "organizational school" of modern American history summarized in Alfred D. Chandler, Jr. and Louis Galambos, "The Development of Large-Scale Economic Organizations in Modern America," *Journal of Economic History* 30 (1970): 201–17; Louis Galambos, "The Emerging Organizational Synthesis of Modern American History," *Business History Review* 44 (1970): 279–90; Louis Galambos, "Technology, Political Economy, and Professionalization: Central Themes of the Organizational Synthesis," *Business History Review* 57 (1983): 471–93; James H. Soltow, "American Institutional Studies: Present Knowledge and Past Trends," *Journal of Economic History* 31 (1971): 87–105; and Robert F. Berkhofer, Jr., "The Organizational Interpretation of American History: A New Synthesis," *Prospects* 4 (1979): 611–29. Major works of this school of interpretation include Samuel Hays, *The Response to Industrialism, 1885–1914* (Chicago: University of Chicago Press, 1957); Robert Wiebe, *The Search for Order, 1877–1920* (New York: Hill and Wang, 1967); Jerry Israel, ed., *Building the Organizational Society: Essays on Associational Activities in Modern*

America (New York: Free Press, 1972); Alfred D. Chandler, Jr., *The Visible Hand: The Managerial Revolution in American Business* (Cambridge: Harvard University Press, 1977); Thomas K. McCraw, "The Challenge of Alfred D. Chandler, Jr.: Retrospect and Prospect," *Reviews in American History* 15 (1987): 160–78; Ellis W. Hawley, *The Great War and the Search for a Modern Order* (New York: St. Martin's Press, 1979); Gerald D. Nash, *The Great Depression and World War II: Organizing America, 1933–1945* (New York: St. Martin's Press, 1979); Louis Galambos, *America at Middle Age: A New History of the U.S. in the Twentieth Century* (New York: McCraw-Hill, 1982); Barry D. Karl, *The Uneasy State: The United States From 1915 to 1945* (Chicago: University of Chicago Press, 1983); and Louis Galambos, ed., *The New American State: Bureaucracies and Policies Since World War II* (Baltimore: Johns Hopkins University Press, 1987). For several informed cautionary views of the approach, see Robert D. Cuff, "American Historians and the 'Organizational Factor'," *Canadian Review of American Studies* 4 (1973): 19–31; Richard B. Du Boff and Edward S. Herman, "Alfred Chandler's New Business History: A Review," *Politics and Society* 10 (1980): 87–110; and James Livingston, "The Social Analysis of Economic History and Theory: Conjectures on Late Nineteenth-Century American Development," *American Historical Review* 92 (1987): 69–95. Good overviews of American economic growth over the period are in Anthony S. Campagna, *U.S. National Economic Policy, 1917–1985* (Westport, Conn.: Greenwood Press, 1987); and Peter Fearon, *War, Prosperity and Depression: The U.S. Economy, 1917–45* (Lawrence: University Press of Kansas, 1987).

In the last twenty-five years, other competing schools of interpretation centered on the radical "corporate liberal" view have emerged beginning with William Appleman Williams, *The Contours of American History* (1961; reprint, Chicago: Quadrangle, 1966); Gabriel Kolko, *The Triumph of Conservatism: A Reinterpretation of American History, 1900–1916* (1963; reprint, Chicago: Quadrangle, 1967); James Weinstein, *The Corporate Ideal in the Liberal State, 1900–1918* (Boston: Beacon Press, 1968); James Weinstein and David W. Eakins, eds., *A New History of Leviathan: Essays on the Rise of the American Corporate State* (New York: E. P. Dutton, 1972); and Daniel Fusfeld, "Rise of the Corporate State in America," *Journal of Economic Issues* 6 (1972): 1–22. More recent and sophisticated examples of the "corporate liberal" interpretation include David F. Noble, *America By Design: Science, Technology, and the Rise of Corporate Capitalism* (New York: Alfred A. Knopf, 1977) and R. Jeffrey Lustig, *Corporate Liberalism: The Origins of Modern American Political Theory, 1890–1920* (Berkeley and Los Angeles: University of California Press, 1982). Ellis W. Hawley, "The Discovery and Study of a Corporate Liberalism'," *Business History Review* 52 (Autumn 1978): 309–20, summarizes recent work, while the same issue has case studies on corporate liberalism. See Robert M. Collins, "American Corporatism: The Committee for Economic Development, 1942–1964," *The Historian* 44 (1982): 151–73 for an especially well done case study. Other reviews of this school with an emphasis on foreign policy include Thomas J. McCormick, "Drift or Mastery? A Corporatist Synthesis for American Diplomatic History," *Reviews in American History* 10 (1982): 318–30; and John Lewis Gaddis, "The Corporatist Synthesis: A Skeptical View," and Michael J. Hogan, "Corporatism: A Positive Appraisal," both in *Diplomatic History* 10 (1986): 357–72. Comparative perspectives on corporatism include Phillipe C. Schmitter, "Still the Century of Corporatism?" *Review of Politics* 36 (1974): 85–131; and Gerhard Lehmbruch and Phillipe C. Schmitter, eds., *Patterns of Corporatist Policy-Making* (Beverly Hills, Calif.: Sage Publications, 1982).

Even more recently, scholars have begun pointing to the importance of reassessing the role of the state in comparative historical contexts as a way of understanding national differences between administrative capacities to plan. Pioneering efforts are found in Theda Skocpol and Kenneth Finegold, "State Capacity and Economic Intervention in the Early New Deal," *Political Science Quarterly* 97 (1982): 255–78; Stephen Skowronek, *Building a New American State: The Expansion of National Administrative Capacities, 1877–1920* (Cambridge and New York: Cambridge University Press, 1982); Theda Skocpol, "Bringing the State Back In: Strategies of Analysis in Current Research," in *Bringing the State Back In*, ed. Peter B. Evans, Dietrich Rueschemeyer, Theda Skocpol (Cambridge and New York: Cambridge University Press, 1985); Peter Gourevitch, *Politics in Hard Times: Comparative Responses to International Economic Crises* (Ithaca: Cornell University Press, 1986); William E. Leuchtenburg, "The Pertinence of Political History: Reflections on the Significance of the State in America," *Journal of American History* 73 (December 1986): 585–600.

Recent Marxist interpretations are considered in Theda Skocpol, "Political Response to Capitalist Crisis: Neo-Marxist Theories of the State and the Case of the New Deal," *Politics and Society* 10 (1980): 155–201. Recent examples of radical interpretations include Donald Stabile, *Prophets of Order: The Rise of the New Class, Technocracy and Socialism in America* (Boston. Mass.: South End Press, 1984); and John Friedmann, *Planning in the Public Domain: From Knowledge to Action* (Princeton: Princeton University Press, 1987). Libertarians challenge the Marxist view in Don LaVoie, *National Economic Planning: What is Left?* (Cambridge, Mass.: Ballinger Publishing Company, 1985); and Robert Higgs, *Crisis and Leviathan: Critical Episodes in the Growth of American Government* (New York: Oxford University Press, 1987).

Scholars of American planning could benefit from a consideration of the role of voluntarism in American life noted in Alexis de Toqueville's classic, *Democracy in America* (1835–1840, many editions); Michael Rogin, "Voluntarism: The Political Functions of an Antipolitical Doctrine," *Industrial and Labor Relations Review* 15 (1962): 521–35; Grant McConnell, *The*

Decline of Agrarian Democracy (Berkeley and Los Angeles: University of California Press, 1953); Grant McConnell, *Private Power and American Democracy* (New York: Alfred A. Knopf, 1966); Bruce L. R. Smith, ed., *The New Political Economy: The Public Use of the Private Sector* (New York: Wiley, 1975); and essays in J. David Greenstone, ed., *Public Values and Private Power in American Politics* (Chicago: University of Chicago Press, 1982).

UNEMPLOYMENT PLANNING

For the study of unemployment planning, one must begin with the history of the problem of unemployment as detailed in John A. Garraty, *Unemployment in History: Economic Thought and Public Policy* (New York: Harper and Row, 1978) and a brilliant case study approach in Alexander Keyssar, *Out of Work: The First Century of Unemployment in Massachusetts* (Cambridge and New York: Cambridge University Press, 1986). To place the issue in context, see Sanford M. Jacoby, *Employing Bureaucracy: Managers, Unions, and the Transformation of Work in American Industry, 1900–1945* (New York: Columbia University Press, 1985).

For the reformers' response, especially that of the American Association for Labor Legislation, see Clarke A. Chambers, *Seedtime of Reform: American Social Service and Social Action, 1918–1933* (Minneapolis: University of Minnesota Press, 1963); Irwin Yellowitz, *Labor and the Progressive Movement in New York State, 1897–1916* (Ithaca: Cornell University Press, 1965); Irwin Yellowitz, "The Origins of Unemployment Reform in the United States," *Labor History* 9 (1968): 338–60; Roy Lubove, *The Struggle for Social Security, 1900–1935* (Cambridge: Harvard University Press, 1968); Daniel Nelson, *Unemployment Insurance: The American Experience, 1915–1935* (Madison: University of Wisconsin Press, 1969); and Hace Sorel Tishler, *Self-Reliance and Social Security, 1870–1917* (Port Washington, N.Y.: Kennikat Press, 1971).

The AALL's program was published in John B. Andrews, "A Practical Program for the Prevention of Unemployment in America," *American Labor Legislation Review* 5 (June 1915): 171–92. On the statist component of the AALL's program, see J. Lee Kreader, "Isaac Max Rubinow: Pioneering Specialist in Social Insurance," *Social Service Review* 50 (1976): 402–25; Isaac M. Rubinow, *Social Insurance with Special Reference to American Conditions* (New York: Henry Holt, 1913); and I. M. Rubinow, *The Quest for Security* (New York: Henry Holt, 1934). For insight into the AALL's reform ideology, see John R. Commons, *Myself: The Autobiography of John R. Commons* (New York: Macmillan, 1934); *John B. Andrews Memorial Symposium on Labor Legislation and Social Security, November 4 and 5, 1949* (Madison: University of Wisconsin Press, 1949); and Henry

Rogers Seager, *Social Insurance: A Program of Social Reform* (New York: Macmillan, 1910). The most important sources for examination of the AALL's efforts are the American Association for Labor Legislation Papers, Cornell University, Ithaca, New York, and the AALL's journal, the *American Labor Legislation Review*. The Herbert Hoover Presidential Library in West Branch, Iowa has a microfilm edition of the AALL Papers, while the Microfilming Corporation of America (Glen Rock, New Jersey) released the *Microfilm Edition of the Papers of the American Association for Labor Legislation, 1905–1943*, edited by Mary S. Arluck, in 1973.

On the influence of the Wisconsin reforms for Commons and Andrews, see Gerd Korman, *Industrialization, Immigrants, and Americanizers: The View from Milwaukee, 1866–1921* (Madison: State Historical Society of Wisconsin, 1967); and Robert Asher, "The 1911 Wisconsin Workmen's Compensation Law: A Study in Conservative Labor Reform," *Wisconsin Magazine of History* 57 (1973): 123–40. For a comparative work focusing on the pre–World War I years, see Udo Sautter, "North American Labor Agencies Before World War I: A Cure for Unemployment?" *Labor History* 24 (1983): 366–93.

For the acceleration of reform efforts during the Great War, see Sidney Kaplan, "Social Engineers as Saviors: Effects of World War I on Some American Liberals," *Journal of the History of Ideas* 17 (1956): 347–69; Allen F. Davis, "Welfare, Reform, and World War I," *American Quarterly* 19 (1967): 516–33; Stanley Shapiro, "The Great War and Reform: Liberals and Labor, 1917–19," *Labor History* 12 (1971): 323–44; John F. McClymer, *War and Welfare: Social Engineering in America, 1890–1925* (Westport, Conn.: Greenwood Press, 1980); David M. Kennedy, *Over Here: The First World War and American Society* (New York: Oxford University Press, 1980); and the important unpublished 1984 paper by Ellis W. Hawley, "The Great War and Organizational Innovation: The American Case."

For the transition from wartime to the 1920s, see Hawley, *The Great War and the Search for a Modern Order*; Carolyn Grin, "The Unemployment Conference of 1921: An Experiment in National Cooperative Planning," *Mid-America* 55 (1973): 83–107; Guy Alchon, *The Invisible Hand of Planning: Capitalism, Social Science, and the State in the 1920s* (Princeton: Princeton University Press, 1985); and Patrick D. Reagan, "From Depression to Depression: Hooverian National Planning, 1921–1933," *Mid-America* 70 (1988).

On the importance of the voluntary associational emphasis of the 1920s, see Ellis W. Hawley, "Herbert Hoover, the Commerce Secretariat, and the Vision of an 'Associative State', 1921–28," *Journal of American History* 61 (June 1974): 116–40. On New Era efforts at unemployment and social welfare planning, see Vaughn Davis Bornet, "Herbert Hoover's Planning for Unemployment and Old Age Insurance Coverage, 1921–1933," in *The Quest for Security: Papers on the Origins and the Future of the American*

Social Insurance System, ed. John N. Schacht (Iowa City: The Center for the Study of the Recent History of the United States, 1982), 35–71; Edward D. Berkowitz and Kim McQuaid, "Bureaucrats as 'Social Engineers': Federal Welfare Programs in Herbert Hoover's America," *American Journal of Economics and Sociology* 39 (1980): 321–35; the especially thought-provoking ideas in Edward Berkowitz and Kim McQuaid, *Creating the Welfare State: The Political Economy of Twentieth-Century Reform* (New York: Praeger Publishers, 1980); Udo Sautter, "Unemployment and Government: American Labor Exchanges Before the New Deal," *Histoire sociale/ Social History* 18 (1986): 335–58; and Udo Sautter, "Government and Unemployment: The Use of Public Works Before the New Deal," *Journal of American History* 73 (June 1986): 59–86. Representative examples of works dealing with voluntarist efforts include Herman Feldman, *The Regularization of Employment: A Study in the Prevention of Unemployment*(New York: Harper & Bros., 1925); Sam A. Lewisohn et al., *Can Business Prevent Unemployment?* (New York: Harper & Bros., 1925); and Bryce M. Stewart et al., *Unemployment Benefits in the United States: The Plans and Their Settings* (New York: Industrial Relations Counselors, Inc., 1930).

For works covering developments in the 1930s and 1940s, see Lubove, *The Struggle for Social Security*; Nelson, *Unemployment Insurance*; Robert H. Bremner, "The New Deal and Social Welfare," in *Fifty Years Later: The New Deal Evaluated*, ed. Harvard Sitkoff (New York: Alfred A. Knopf, 1985), 69–92; and James T. Patterson, "Comparative Welfare History: Britain and the United States, 1930–1945," and Clarke A. Chambers, "Social Security: The Welfare Consensus of the New Deal," in *The Roosevelt New Deal: A Program Assessment Fifty Years After*, ed. Wilbur J. Cohen (Austin, Tex.: Lyndon B. Johnson School of Public Affairs, Lyndon B. Johnson Library, 1986), 125–59.

LABOR RELATIONS PLANNING IN THE POST–WORLD WAR I YEARS

To place the industrial conferences of 1919–1920 in perspective, one should begin with a reading of David M. Kennedy's *Over Here*; Robert K. Murray, *Red Scare: A Study in National Hysteria, 1919–1920* (Minneapolis: University of Minnesota Press, 1955); William Preston, Jr., *Aliens and Dissenters: Federal Suppression of Radicals, 1903–1933* (Cambridge: Harvard University Press, 1963); David Brody, *Labor in Crisis: The Steel Strike of 1919* (Philadelphia: J. B. Lippincott, 1965); and Burl Noggle, *Into the Twenties: The United States from Armistice to Normalcy* (Urbana: University of Illinois Press, 1974). The standard accounts of the industrial conferences are Brody, *Labor in Crisis*; Haggai Hurvitz, "Ideology and Industrial Conflict: President Wilson's First Industrial Conference of October, 1919," *Labor History* 18 (1977): 509–24; and Gary Dean Best, "President Wilson's Second Industrial Conference, 1919–1920," *Labor History* 16 (1975): 505–20. For the international context, see Arno J. Mayer, *Politics and Diplomacy of Peacemaking: Containment and Counterrevolution at Versailles, 1918–1919* (New York: Alfred A. Knopf, 1967); John M. Thompson, *Russia, Bolshevism, and the Versailles Peace* (Princeton: Princeton University Press, 1966); and Charles S. Maier, *Recasting Bourgeois Europe: Stabilization in France, Germany, and Italy in the Decade After World War I* (Princeton: Princeton University Press, 1975).

Much of the information and interpretation presented in the text is based on Charles E. Harvey, "Religion and Industrial Relations: John D. Rockefeller, Jr. and the Interchurch World Movement of 1919–1920," *Research in Political Economy* 4 (1981): 199–227; Charles E. Harvey, "John D. Rockefeller, Jr., and the Interchurch World Movement," *Church History* 51 (June 1982): 189–209; Charles E. Harvey, "John D. Rockefeller, Jr. and the Social Sciences: An Introduction," *Journal of the History of Sociology* 2 (Fall 1982): 1–31; and Charles E. Harvey, "Speer Versus Rockefeller and Mott," *Journal of Presbyterian History* 60 (Winter 1982): 282–300. Sources consulted for these works included materials in personal and philanthropic organizational papers at the Rockefeller Archives Center, Pocantico Hills, New York.

For information on Hoover's activities during this period, see Murray Rothbard, "Herbert Hoover and the Myth of Laissez-Faire," in *A New History of Leviathan*, 111–45; Joan Hoff Wilson, *Herbert Hoover: Forgotten Progressive* (Boston: Little, Brown, 1975); David Burner, *Herbert Hoover: A Public Life* (New York: Alfred A. Knopf, 1978); Lawrence E. Gelfand, ed., *Herbert Hoover: The Great War and Its Aftermath, 1914–23* (Iowa City: University of Iowa Press, 1979); Gary Dean Best, *The Politics of American Individualism: Herbert Hoover in Transition, 1918–1921* (Westport, Conn.: Greenwood, 1975); and Ellis W. Hawley, ed., *Herbert Hoover as Secretary of Commerce, 1921–1928: Studies in New Era Thought and Practice* (Iowa City: University of Iowa Press, 1981). On Rockefeller, Jr., see Raymond B. Fosdick, *John D. Rockefeller, Jr., A Portrait*; John D. Rockefeller, Jr., *The Personal Relation in Industry* (New York: privately printed, 1923); Allan Nevins, *A Study in Power: John D. Rockefeller, Industrialist and Philanthropist* (New York: Charles Scribners' Sons, 1953), 2 vols. On the question of wealthy families' influence, see G. William Domhoff, *Who Rules America Now?* (Englewood Cliffs, N.J.: Prentice Hall, 1983), while the issue of philanthropic influences is dealt with in Robert F. Arnove, ed., *Philanthropy and Cultural Imperialism* (Boston: G. K. Hall, 1980). Economic and cultural influences of the United States abroad are dealt with in Emily S. Rosenberg, *Spreading the American Dream: American Economic and Cultural Expansion, 1890–1945* (New York: Hill and Wang,

1982), and Michael J. Hogan, "Revival and Reform: America's 20th Century Search for a New Economic Order Abroad," *Diplomatic History* 8 (1984): 287–310.

For information dealing with corporate labor policy during this period, see Stephen J. Scheinberg, "The Development of Corporate Labor Policy, 1880–1940" (Ph.D. diss., University of Wisconsin, 1966), published as *Employers and Reformers: The Development of Corporation Labor Policies,1900–1940* (New York: Garland Publishing, 1986); Robert Ozanne, *A Century of Labor-Management Relations at McCormick and International Harvester* (Madison: University of Wisconsin Press, 1967); Kim McQuaid, "A Response to Industrialism: Liberal Businessmen and the Evolving Spectrum of Capitalist Reform, 1886–1960" (Ph.D. diss., Northwestern University, 1975), published under the same title (New York: Garland Publishing, 1987); Daniel Nelson, *Managers and Workers: Origins of the New Factory System in the United States, 1880–1920* (Madison: University of Wisconsin Press, 1975); Stuart Brandes, *American Welfare Capitalism, 1880–1940* (Chicago: University of Chicago Press, 1976); David F. Noble, *America By Design*; Richard Edwards, *Contested Terrain: The Transformation of the Workplace in the Twentieth Century* (New York: Basic Books, 1979); Dan Clawson, *Bureaucracy and the Labor Process: The Transformation of U.S. Industry, 1860–1920* (New York and London: Monthly Review Press, 1980); David M. Gordon, Richard Edwards, Michael Reich, *Segmented Work, Divided Workers: The Historical Transformation of Labor in the United States* (Cambridge and New York: Cambridge University Press, 1982); Sanford M. Jacoby, *Employing Bureaucracy.*

For overviews on the place of workers and organized labor in the American political economy of the early twentieth century, see Daniel T. Rodgers, *The Work Ethic in Industrial America, 1850–1920* (Chicago: University of Chicago Press, 1978); James R. Green, *The World of the Worker: Labor in Twentieth-Century America* (New York: Hill and Wang, 1980); David Montgomery, *Workers' Control in America: Studies in the History of Work, Technology, and Labor Struggles* (Cambridge and New York: Cambridge University Press, 1979); Robert H. Zieger, *American Workers, American Unions, 1920–1985* (Baltimore: Johns Hopkins University Press, 1986); and David Montgomery, *The Fall of the House of Labor: The Workplace, the State, and American Labor Activism, 1865–1925* (Cambridge and New York: Cambridge University Press, 1987).

On Rockefeller's early labor policies stemming from the Colorado Fuel and Iron Company conflict, see George S. McGovern and Leonard F. Guttridge, *The Great Coalfield War* (Boston: Houghton Mifflin, 1972); Graham Adams, Jr., *Age of Industrial Violence, 1910–15: The Activities and Findings of the United States Commission on Industrial Relations* (New York: Columbia University Press, 1966); and Stephen J. Scheinberg, "Rockefeller and King: The Capitalist and the Reformer," in *Mackenzie King: Twelve*

Essays, ed. John English and J. O. Stubbs (Toronto: Macmillan, 1978), 89–104.

For the wartime context of labor relations, see Ellis W. Hawley, "The Great War and Organizational Innovation: The American Case"; Robert D. Cuff, *The War Industries Board: Business-Government Relations During World War I* (Baltimore: Johns Hopkins University Press, 1973); Robert D. Cuff, "Herbert Hoover, the Ideology of Voluntarism, and War Organization During the Great War," *Journal of American History* 64 (September 1977): 358–72, reprinted in *Herbert Hoover: The Great War and Its Aftermath*; Robert D. Cuff, "The Politics of Labor Administration During World War I," *Labor History* 21 (1980): 546–69; Melvin I. Urofsky, *Big Steel and the Wilson Administration* (Columbus: Ohio State University Press, 1969); and Valerie Jean Conner, *The National War Labor Board: Stability, Social Justice, and the Voluntary State in World War I* (Chapel Hill: University of North Carolina Press, 1983). For Rockefeller's work during the war, see the anonymous *War Work of John D. Rockefeller, Jr.*, commissioned and published by his wife in the early 1920s. For information on Raymond Fosdick, see Raymond B. Fosdick, *Chronicle of a Generation: An Autobiography* (New York: Harper, 1958); Darryl L. Revoldt, "Raymond B. Fosdick: Reform, Internationalism, and the Rockefeller Foundation" (Ph.D. diss., University of Akron, 1982); and Raymond B. Fosdick, *The Old Savage and the New Civilization* (Garden City, N.Y.: Doubleday-Doran, 1929), a collection of his speeches from the 1920s.

For changes in working-class life and labor relations in the 1920s, the standard work is Irving Bernstein, *The Lean Years: A History of the American Worker, 1920–1933* (Boston: Houghton Mifflin, 1960). More recent evaluations include, David Brody, "The Rise and Decline of Welfare Capitalism," in *Change and Continuity in Twentieth-Century America: The 1920's*, ed. John Braeman, Robert H. Bremner, David Brody (Columbus: Ohio State University Press, 1968), 147–78, reprinted in slightly revised form in David Brody, *Workers in Industrial America: Essays on the Twentieth Century Struggle* (New York: Oxford University Press, 1980), 48–81; Charles Holt, "Who Benefitted from the Prosperity of the 1920s?" *Explorations in Economic History* 14 (July 1977): 277–89; Frank Stricker, "Affluence for Whom?—Another Look at Prosperity and the Working Classes in the 1920s," *Labor History* 24 (1983): 5–33; and David Montgomery, "Thinking About American Workers in the 1920s," *International Labor and Working-Class History* 32 (Fall 1987): 4–24, with responses by Charles Maier and Susan Porter Benson, ibid., 25–38.

For the Republican administrations' labor policies of the 1920s, see Robert H. Zieger, *Republicans and Labor, 1919–1929* (Lexington: University of Kentucky Press, 1969); and Robert H. Zieger, "Herbert Hoover, the Wage-Earner, and the 'New Economic System,' 1919–29," *Business History Review* 51 (1977): 161–89, reprinted in *Herbert Hoover as Secretary of*

Commerce, 82–112. Information on Hoover's labor policies is scattered in the Pre-Commerce and Secretary of Commerce Papers, Herbert Hoover Papers, Herbert Hoover Presidential Library, West Branch, Iowa; and in Hoover, *American Individualism* (Garden City, N.Y.: Doubleday, 1923). For the failure of Rockefeller's labor policy in the coal industry, see Ellis W. Hawley, "Secretary Hoover and the Bituminous Coal Problem, 1921–1928," *Business History Review* 42 (1968): 247–70; Mary Van Kleeck and Ben Selekman, *Miners and Management* (New York: Russell Sage Foundation, 1934); James P. Johnson, *The Politics of Soft Coal: The Bituminous Industry from World War I Through the New Deal* (Urbana: University of Illinois Press, 1979); and Melvyn Dubofsky and Warren Van Tine, *John L. Lewis: A Biography* (New York: Quadrangle/New York Times, 1977).

INTERWAR MILITARY PLANNING

For recent developments in the field of military history in relation to the organizational synthesis, see Daniel R. Beaver, "The American Military and the 'New' Institutional History" (Paper delivered at the Organization of American Historians Convention, Minneapolis, Minnesota, April 1985). Students of military planning have wrestled with the issue of the existence, extent, and influence of the military-industrial complex as seen in Paul A. C. Koistinen, "The 'Industrial-Military Complex' in Historical Perspective: World War I," *Business History Review* 41 (1967): 378–403; Koistinen, "The 'Industrial-Military Complex' in Historical Perspective: The Interwar Years," *Journal of American History* 56 (March 1970): 819–39; and Koistinen, "Mobilizing the World War II Economy: Labor and the Industrial-Military Alliance," *Pacific Historical Review* 42 (November 1973): 443–78, all reprinted in Koistinen, *The Military-Industrial Complex: A Historical Perspective* (New York: Praeger Publishers, 1980); Sidney Lens, *The Military-Industrial Complex* (Philadelphia: Pilgrim Press, 1970); Seymour Melman, ed., *The War Economy of the United States: Readings in Military Industry and Economy* (New York: St. Martin's Press, 1971); Carroll W. Pursell, Jr., ed., *The Military-Industrial Complex* (New York: Harper & Row, 1972); Sam C. Sarkesian, ed., *The Military-Industrial Complex: A Reassessment* (Beverly Hills, Calif.: Sage Publications, 1972); Steven Rosen, ed., *Testing the Theory of the Military-Industrial Complex* (Lexington, Mass.: D. C. Heath, 1973); Benjamin Franklin Cooling, ed., *War, Business, and American Society: Historical Perspectives on the Military-Industrial Complex* (Port Washington, N.Y.: Kennikat Press, 1977); and Robert D. Cuff, "An Organizational Perspective on the Military-Industrial Complex," *Business History Review* 52 (1978): 250–67. More recent case studies include Benjamin Franklin Cooling, *Gray Steel and Blue Water Navy: The Formative Years of America's Military-Industrial Complex, 1881–1917* (Hamden, Conn.: Archon Books, 1979); and essays in Merritt Roe Smith, ed., *Military Enterprise and Technological Change: Perspectives on the American Experience* (Cambridge: MIT Press, 1985). For a review of the recent developments in military history in the interwar years, see Russell F. Weigley, "The Interwar Army, 1919–1941," in *Against All Enemies: Interpretations of American Military History from Colonial Times to the Present*, ed. Kenneth J. Hagan and William R. Roberts (Westport, Conn.: Greenwood Press, 1986), 257–77; and John Major, "The Navy Plans for War, 1937–1941," in *In Peace and War: Interpretations of American Naval History, 1775–1984*, 2nd ed., ed. Kenneth J. Hagan (Westport, Conn.: Greenwood Press, 1984), 237–62.

On the issue of an independent air force, see Carroll V. Glines, Jr., *The Compact History of the United States Air Force*, new and rev. ed. (New York: Hawthorne Books, 1980); Herbert M. Mason, Jr., *The United States Air Force: A Turbulent History* (New York: Charter Press, 1976); and R. Earl McClendon, *The Question of Autonomy for the United States Air Arm* (Montgomery, Ala.: Air University Library, 1950). A thought-provoking work which places the issue of air power planning in a broader perspective is Michael S. Sherry, *The Rise of American Air Power: The Creation of Armageddon* (New Haven: Yale University Press, 1987).

Much of the interwar planning controversy centered on Billy Mitchell, for which see Alfred F. Hurley, *Billy Mitchell: Crusader for Air Power*, new ed. (1964; Bloomington: Indiana University Press, 1975) and Burke Davis, *The Billy Mitchell Affair* (New York: Random House, 1967). Mitchell's papers are available for use in the Library of Congress in Washington, D.C.

Developments in interwar air planning by the military should be compared with parallels in the civilian economy, for which see Ellis W. Hawley, "Three Facets of Hooverian Associationalism: Lumber, Aviation, and Movies, 1921–1930," in *Regulation in Perspective: Historical Essays*, ed. Thomas K. McCraw (Cambridge: Harvard University Press, 1981), 95–123; David D. Lee, "Herbert Hoover and the Development of Commercial Aviation, 1921–1926," *Business History Review* 58 (1984): 78–102, reprinted with other important essays in *Herbert Hoover and the Republican Era: A Reconsideration*, ed. Carl E. Krog and William R. Tanner (Lanham, Md.: University Press of America, 1984).

For military aviation planning in the 1919–1926 period, see U.S. Congress, House, *United Air Service, Hearings before the Committee on Military Affairs*, 66th Cong., 2nd sess., 1919–1920; *Report of a Committee of Officers....* (Lassiter Board Report) 27 March 1923 (Washington, D.C.: Government Printing Office, 1923); U.S. Congress, House, *Investigation of the Air Service, Hearings before the Committee on Rules*, 68th Cong., 1st sess., 1924; the recommendations of the 1924–1925 special committee appointed by the House of Representatives chaired by Florian Lampert in U.S. Congress, House, *Inquiry into Operations of the United States Air Services, Hearings before the Select Committee of Inquiry into Operations of the*

United States Air Service, 68th Cong., 1st sess., 1925; U.S. Congress, House, *Air Service Unification, Hearings before the Committee on Military Affairs*, 68th Cong., 2nd sess., 1925; and U.S. Congress, House, *Department of Defense and Unification of Air Service, Hearings before the Committee on Military Affairs*, 69th Cong., 1st sess., 1926. On the President's Aircraft Board (Morrow Board), see Harold Nicholson, *Dwight Morrow* (New York: Harcourt, Brace & Co., 1935); materials in the Dwight Morrow Papers, Amherst College, Amherst, Massachusetts; *Hearings Before the President's Aircraft Board* (Washington, D.C.: Government Printing Office, 1925); and *Report of the President's Aircraft Board* (Washington, D.C.: Government Printing Office, 1925).

For developments following the report of the Morrow Board, see Edwin H. Rutkowski, *The Politics of Military Aviation Procurement, 1926–1934: A Study in the Political Assertion of Consensual Values* (Columbus: Ohio State University Press, 1966). On the Air Corps Act of 1926, see 44 Stat. 780–90 (1926) for the exact language; and Alfred Goldberg, ed., *A History of the United States Air Force, 1907–1957* (Princeton: D. Van Nostrand Company, 1957) for an early evaluation of the act. For information dealing with implementation of the planning provisions of the Air Corps Act, see *Reports of the Secretary of War to the President, 1926–1932*; Chief of the Air Corps, *Annual Report, 1926–1931*; materials in 145.91, Albert F. Simpson Historical Research Center, Maxwell AFB, Alabama; U.S. Congress, House and Senate, *Sale of Surplus Real Estate by the War Department, Joint Hearings before the Committees on Military Affairs*, 68th Cong., 2nd sess., 1924–1925; U.S. Congress, House and Senate, *War Department Appropriation Bill for 1930, 1931, 1932, 1933, Hearings before the Committee on Appropriations*, 70th–72nd Cong., 1928, 1929, 1930, 1932; various House and Senate Reports (1928–1931); U.S. Congress, House, *Construction at Army Air Corps Posts, Hearings before the Committee on Military Affairs*, 70th Cong., 2nd sess., 1929; U.S. Congress, House, *Various Bills for Construction and Acquisition of Land, Hearings before the Committee on Military Affairs*, 71st Cong., 2nd sess., 1931; U.S. Congress, House, *1932 Increment Army Housing Program and Technical Air Corps Construction, Hearings before the Committee on Military Affairs*, 71st Cong., 2nd sess., 1930.

For information on individual air facility construction projects from 1927 through 1932, see U.S. Congress, House, *H. Rept. 1511*, 72nd Cong., 1st sess., 1932, 2–26. For more detailed information on separate fields, see *Randolph Field Dedication, June 20–21, 1930*, dedication program, in the Albert F. Simpson Historical Research Center collection for the field near San Antonio, Texas; "World's Largest Airport Reservation," *Manufacturers Record* 103 (June 1934): 25, for Barksdale Field in Louisiana; and Jerold E. Brown, "Army-Navy 'Cooperation' in the Interwar Years: The Case of

North Island," *Periodical*, forthcoming, for the field near San Diego, California.

The topic of military planning is still a relatively unstudied one, though for a pioneering effort, see Irving Brinton Holley, Jr., *Buying Aircraft: Materiel Procurement for the Army Air Forces* (Washington, D.C.: Office of the Chief of Military History, 1964). Recent efforts with a comparative dimension are noted in Lt. Col. Harry R. Borowski, ed., *Military Planning in the Twentieth Century: Proceedings of the Eleventh Military History Symposium, 10–12 October 1984, U.S. Air Force Academy* (Washington, D.C.: Office of Air Force History, 1986), which can be compared with the broadening of military historians' focus noted in Peter Karsten, "The 'New' American Military History: A Map of the Territory, Explored and Unexplored," *American Quarterly* 36 (1984): 389–418, reprinted in revised form as "Introduction," in *The Military in America From the Colonial Era to the Present*, new and rev. ed., ed. Peter Karsten (New York: Free Press, 1986), 1–24; and the essays included in James Titus, ed., *The Home Front and War in the Twentieth Century: Proceedings of the Tenth Military History Symposium, October 20–22, 1982* (Colorado Springs, Colo.: United States Air Force Academy and Office of Air Force History, 1984). For source materials to use in study of military planning, one can consult the chapter bibliographies in Allan R. Millett and Peter Maslowski, *For the Common Defense: A Military History of the United States of America* (New York: Free Press, 1984) and specific sections in Robin Higham, ed., *A Guide to the Sources of United States Military History* and Robin Higham and Donald J. Mrozek, eds., *Supplement I and II* (Hamden, Conn.: Archon Books, 1975, 1981, 1986).

NEW DEAL NATIONAL PLANNING

For the best overviews of New Deal national planning, see Otis L. Graham, Jr., "The Planning Ideal and American Reality: The 1930s," in *The Hofstadter Aegis: A Memorial*, ed. Stanley Elkins and Eric McKitrick (New York: Alfred A. Knopf, 1974), 257–99; and Otis L. Graham, Jr., *Toward a Planned Society: From Roosevelt to Nixon* (New York: Oxford University Press, 1976). Published histories of the New Deal planning agency include Philip W. Warken, *A History of the National Resources Planning Board, 1933–1943* (New York: Garland Publishing, 1979); and Marion Clawson, *New Deal Planning: The National Resources Planning Board* (Baltimore: Johns Hopkins University Press, 1981) which are based on study of the Records of the National Resources Planning Board, Record Group 187, National Archives, Washington, D.C. For the pre–1933 roots of national planning, see Clifford J. Hynning, "Administrative Evolution of National Planning in the Pre–New Deal Era," *Plan Age* 5 (June 1939): 157–89;

Robert D. Cuff, *The War Industries Board* (Baltimore: Johns Hopkins University Press, 1973); Cuff, "We Band of Brothers—Woodrow Wilson's War Managers," *Canadian Review of American Studies* 5 (Fall 1974): 135–48; Cuff, "Herbert Hoover, the Ideology of Voluntarism and War Organization During the Great War," *Journal of American History* 64 (September 1977): 358–72; Ellis W. Hawley, "The Great War and Organizational Innovation: The American Case"; Hawley, *The Great War and the Search for a Modern Order*; Hawley, "Herbert Hoover, the Commerce Secretariat, and the Vision of an 'Associative State,' 1921–1928," *Journal of American History* 61 (June 1974): 116–40; and Hawley, " 'Industrial Policy' in the 1920s and 1930s," in *The Politics of Industrial Policy*, ed. Claude E. Barfield and William A. Schambra (Washington, D.C.: American Enterprise Institute for Public Policy Research, 1986), 63–86.

On the importance of the President's Conference on Unemployment of 1921 as part of a Hooverian planning process carried over into the New Era decade, see Ellis W. Hawley, "Herbert Hoover and Economic Stabilization, 1921–22," in *Herbert Hoover as Secretary of Commerce*, 43–77; Carolyn Grin, "The Unemployment Conference of 1921: An Experiment in National Cooperative Planning," *Mid-America* 55 (1973): 83–107; Evan B. Metcalf, "Secretary Hoover and the Emergence of Macroeconomic Management," *Business History Review* 49 (1975): 60–80; Guy Alchon, *The Invisible Hand of Planning: Capitalism, Social Science, and the State in the 1920s* (Princeton: Princeton University Press, 1985); and Patrick D. Reagan, "From Depression to Depression: Hooverian National Planning, 1921–1933," *Mid-America* 70 (1988).

New Deal planners provided accounts of their ideas, institutional networks, and work in Charles E. Merriam, "Planning Agencies in America," *American Political Science Review* 29 (1935): 197–211; Charles E. Merriam, "The National Resources Planning Board: A Chapter in American Planning Experience," *American Political Science Review* 38 (1944): 1075–88; and Wesley Clair Mitchell, *The Backward Art of Spending Money* (New York: McGraw-Hill, 1937). Biographical information on the individual planners has been gathered from a variety of sources. For Delano, see David Cushman Coyle, "Frederic A. Delano: Catalyst," *Survey Graphic* 35 (July 1946): 252–54; the Delano Family Papers and the Frederic A. Delano Papers at the Franklin D. Roosevelt Library, Hyde Park, New York. On Merriam, see Barry D. Karl, *Charles E. Merriam and the Study of Politics* (Chicago: University of Chicago Press, 1974) and the Charles E. Merriam Papers, University of Chicago Library. On Mitchell, see Joseph Dorfman, "Wesley Clair Mitchell (1874–1948)," *Economic Journal* 59 (September 1949): 448–58; Alvin Hansen, "Wesley Mitchell: Social Scientist and Social Counselor," *Review of Economics and Statistics* 31 (1949): 245–55; Arthur F. Burns, "Wesley Mitchell and the National Bureau," National Bureau of Economic

Research, *Twenty-Ninth Annual Report* (New York: NBER, 1949), 1–55; Lucy Sprague Mitchell, *Two Lives: The Story of Wesley Clair Mitchell and Myself* (New York: Simon and Schuster, 1953); and the Welsey Clair Mitchell Papers, Columbia University Library, New York City. On Dennison, see Kim McQuaid, "Henry S. Dennison and the 'Science' of Industrial Reform, 1900–1950," *American Journal of Economics and Sociology* 36 (1977): 79–98; James T. Dennison, *Henry S. Dennison (1877–1950): New England Industrialist Who Served America!* (New York: Newcomen Society in North America, 1955); and the Henry S. Dennison Papers, Harvard Graduate School of Business Administration Archives, Cambridge, Massachusetts. For Ruml, see Alva Johnston, "The National Idea Man—I, II, and III," *The New Yorker*, 10, 17, and 24 February 1945, respectively 28–32 ff., 26–30 ff., 30–34 ff.; C. Hartley Grattan, "Beardsley Ruml and His Ideas," *Harper's Magazine*, May 1952, 78–86; and the Beardsley Ruml Papers, University of Chicago Library.

To fully understand New Deal planning, the scholar must understand the institutional context in which planners had to work both before and during the New Deal. On city and regional planning, see John L. Hancock, "Planners in the Changing American City, 1900–1940," *Journal of the American Institute of Planners* 33 (1967): 290–304; Mel Scott, *American City Planning Since 1890* (Berkeley and Los Angeles: University of California Press, 1969); and Eugenie Ladner Birch, "Urban Planning and Technological Development: Responses to the Modern City, 1909–1945," in *Energy and Transport: Historical Perspectives on Policy Issues*, ed. George H. Daniels and Mark H. Rose (Beverly Hills, Calif.: Sage Publications, 1982), 179–200. For city and regional planning efforts in which Delano and Merriam were involved, see Michael P. McCarthy, "Chicago Businessmen and the Burnham Plan," *Journal of the Illinois State Historical Society* 63 (Autumn 1970): 228–56; Steven J. Diner, *A City and Its Universities: Public Policy in Chicago, 1892–1919* (Chapel Hill: University of North Carolina Press, 1980); Harvey A. Kantor, "Charles Dyer Norton and the Origins of the Regional Plan of New York," *Journal of the American Institute of Planners* 39 (1973): 35–42; Frederick Gutheim for the Commission, *Worthy of the Nation: The History of Planning for the National Capital* (Washington, D.C.: Smithsonian Institution Press, 1977).

On the emergence of American social science research, see David W. Eakins, "The Development of Corporate Liberal Policy Research in the United States, 1885–1965" (Ph.D. diss., University of Wisconsin, 1966); Gene M. Lyons, *The Uneasy Partnership: Social Science and the Federal Government in the Twentieth Century* (New York: Russell Sage Foundation, 1969); Dorothy Ross, "The Development of the Social Sciences," in *The Organization of Knowledge in Modern America, 1860–1920*, ed. Alexandra Oleson and John Voss (Baltimore: Johns Hopkins University Press, 1979),

107–38; Robert L. Church, "Economists as Experts: The Rise of an Academic Profession in the United States, 1870–1920," in *The University in Society*, ed. Lawrence Stone (Princeton: Princeton University Press, 1974), 2: 571–609. For the founding of the Social Science Research Council, one should consult A. F. Kuhlman, "The Social Science Research Council: Its Origins and Objects," *Social Forces* 6 (June 1928): 583–88; the Charles E. Merriam Papers; the John C. Merriam Papers at the Library of Congress, Washington, D.C.; and the Laura Spelman Rockefeller Memorial Collection, Rockefeller Archives Center, Pocantico Hills, New York.

On the role of philanthropic foundation support for social science research as part of the planning networks in the 1920s, see David M. Grossman, "American Foundations and the Support of Economic Research, 1913–29," *Minerva* 20 (Spring–Summer 1982): 59–82; Martin Bulmer and Joan Bulmer, "Philanthropy and Social Science in the 1920s: Beardsley Ruml and the Laura Spelman Rockefeller Memorial, 1922–29," *Minerva* 19 (Autumn 1981): 347–407; Barry D. Karl and Stanley Katz, "The American Private Philanthropic Foundation and the Public Sphere, 1890–1930," *Minerva* 19 (Summer 1981): 236–70; Barry D. Karl and Stanley Katz, "Foundations and Ruling Class Elites," *Daedulus* 116 (Winter 1987): 1–40. Landmark studies of the Hooverian networks of the 1920s that led into New Deal planning include President's Conference on Unemployment, *Report of the President's Conference on Unemployment* (Washington, D.C.: Government Printing Office, 1921); President's Conference on Unemployment, Committee on Business Cycles and Unemployment, *Business Cycles and Unemployment* (New York: McGraw-Hill, 1923); Committee on Recent Economic Changes of the President's Conference on Unemployment, *Recent Economic Changes in the United States* (New York: McGraw-Hill, 1929), 2 vols.; President's Research Committee on Social Trends, *Recent Social Trends in the United States* (New York: McGraw-Hill, 1933), 2 vols.

For recent works dealing with the Hooverian precedents for the early New Deal which have implications for the study of New Deal planning, see Barry D. Karl, "Presidential Planning and Social Science Research: Mr. Hoover's Experts," *Perspectives in American History* 3 (1969): 347–409; Herbert Stein, *The Fiscal Revolution in America* (Chicago: University of Chicago Press, 1969); Peri Ethan Arnold, "Herbert Hoover and the Continuity of American Public Policy," *Public Policy* 20 (1972): 525–44; Ellis W. Hawley, *The Great War and the Search for a Modern Order*; Frank Freidel, "Hoover and Roosevelt and Historical Continuity"; U.S. Congress, Senate, *Herbert Hoover Reassessed*, S. Doc. 96–63, 96th Cong., 2nd sess., 1981, 275–91; William J. Barber, *From New Era to New Deal: Herbert Hoover, the Economists, and American Economic Policy, 1921–1933* (Cambridge and New York: Cambridge University Press, 1985); Udo Sautter, "Government and Unemployment: The Use of Public Works Before the New Deal," *Journal of American History* 73 (June 1986): 59–86; James Stuart Olson, *Herbert Hoover and the Reconstruction Finance Corporation,*

1931–1933 (Ames: Iowa State University Press, 1977); Bonnie Fox Schwartz, *The Civil Works Administration, 1933–1934: The Business of Emergency Employment in the New Deal* (Princeton: Princeton University Press, 1984); and Ellis W. Hawley, "The Corporate Ideal As Liberal Philosophy in the New Deal," in *The Roosevelt New Deal: A Program Assessment Fifty Years After*, ed. Wilbur J. Cohen (Austin, Tex.: Lyndon B. Johnson School of Public Affairs, 1986), 85–103.

On the implementation of the New Deal planners' ideas, see Byrd L. Jones, "A Plan for Planning in the New Deal," *Social Science Quarterly* 50 (1969): 525–34; Albert Lepawsky, "Style and Substance in Contemporary Planning: The American New Deal's National Resources Planning Board as a Model," *Plan Canada* 18 (September–December 1978): 153–87; Arlene Inouye and Charles Susskind, " 'Technological Trends and National Policy,' 1937: The First Modern Technology Assessment," *Technology and Culture* 18 (1977): 593–621; Albert Lepawsky, "The Planning Apparatus: A Vignette of the New Deal," *Journal of the American Institute of Planners* 42 (January 1976): 16–32; Barry D. Karl, *Executive Reorganization and Reform in the New Deal* (Cambridge: Harvard University Press, 1963); Richard Polenberg, *Reorganizing Roosevelt's Government: The Controversy Over Executive Reorganization, 1936–1939* (Cambridge: Harvard University Press, 1966); Peri E. Arnold, *Making the Managerial Presidency: Comprehensive Reorganization Planning, 1905–1980* (Princeton: Princeton University Press, 1986); and Robert M. Collins, *The Business Response to Keynes, 1929–1964* (New York: Columbia University Press, 1981). On the abolition of the planning board in 1943, see Robert L. Seifert, "A History of the National Resources Planning Board, 1939–1943" (M.A. thesis, Ohio State University, 1959). An assessment of planning since the New Deal is in Otis L. Graham, Jr., "The Planning Idea From Roosevelt to Post-Reagan," in *The New Deal: Viewed From Fifty Years*, ed. Lawrence E. Gelfand and Robert J. Neymeyer (Iowa City, Iowa: The Center for the Study of the Recent History of the United States, 1983), 1–19.

NEW DEAL INDUSTRIAL AND LABOR RELATIONS PLANNING: THE NRA AND NLRB

New Deal reformers not only attempted to implement national planning, they also sought to experiment with sectoral, or piecemeal, planning for industrial and agricultural recovery. The classic model for agricultural planning history is Richard S. Kirkendall, *Social Scientists and Farm Politics in the Age of Roosevelt* (1966; reprint, Ames: Iowa State University Press, 1982). Standard histories of New Deal reform which deal with industrial and agricultural planning include Arthur M. Schlesinger, Jr., *The Age of Roosevelt* (Boston: Houghton Mifflin, 1957–1960), 3 vols.; William E. Leuchtenburg, *Franklin D. Roosevelt and the New Deal, 1932–1940* (New York: Harper and Row, 1963); Paul K. Conkin, *The New Deal* (1967;

Arlington Heights, Ill.: AHM Publishing, 1975) 2nd ed.; Albert U. Romasco, *The Politics of Recovery: Roosevelt's New Deal* (New York: Oxford University Press, 1983); and Robert S. McElvaine, *The Great Depression: America, 1929–1941.* (New York: Times Books, 1984).

Recent evaluations of the New Deal include John Braeman, Robert H. Bremner, and David Brody, eds., *The New Deal* (Columbus: Ohio State University, 1975), 2 vols.; articles by Alan Brinkley, Bradford A. Lee, and William E. Leuchtenburg in "The New Deal," *The Wilson Quarterly* 6 (Spring 1982): 51–97; Theda Skocpol, "Legacies of New Deal Liberalism," *Dissent* 30 (Winter 1983): 33–44; Wilbur J. Cohen, ed., *The New Deal: Fifty Years After, A Historical Assessment* (Austin, Tex.: Lyndon B. Johnson School of Public Affairs, 1984); Harvard Sitkoff, ed., *Fifty Years Later: The New Deal Evaluated* (New York: Alfred A. Knopf, 1985); and Wilbur J. Cohen, ed., *The Roosevelt New Deal: A Program Assessment Fifty Years After.* Several reference works on the New Deal provide additional help, for which see Otis L. Graham, Jr. and Meghan Robinson Wander, eds., *Franklin D. Roosevelt: His Life and Times, An Encyclopedic View* (Boston: G. K. Hall, 1985); and James S. Olson, ed., *Historical Dictionary of the New Deal: From Inauguration to Preparation for War* (Westport, Conn.: Greenwood Press, 1985).

To understand industrial and labor relations planning under the New Deal, one should consult recent works on the political economy of the period, for which see Ellis W. Hawley, *The New Deal and the Problem of Monopoly* (Princeton: Princeton University Press, 1966); Hawley, "The New Deal and Business," in *The New Deal*, ed. John Braeman et al., 50–82; Hawley, "A Partnership Formed, Dissolved, and in Renegotiation: Business and Government in the Franklin D. Roosevelt Era," in *Business and Government: Essays in 20th-Century Cooperation and Confrontation*, ed. Joseph R. Frese and Jacob Judd (Tarrytown, N.Y.: Sleepy Hollow Press, 1985), 187–219; Herbert Stein, *The Fiscal Revolution in America*; Robert Lekachman, *The Age of Keynes* (New York: Random House, 1966); Theodore Rosenhof, *Dogma, Depression, and the New Deal: The Debate of Political Leaders Over Economic Recovery* (Port Washington, N.Y.: Kennikat Press, 1975); Theodore Rosenhof, "New Deal 'Pragmatism' and Economic 'Systems': Concepts and Meanings," *The Historian* 49 (1987): 368–82; Kim McQuaid, *Big Business and Presidential Power: From FDR to Reagan* (New York: William Morrow, 1982); and Robert M. Collins, *The Business Response to Keynes.* For the scholarly debate between pluralists and Marxists, see David Vogel, "Why Businessmen Distrust Their State: The Political Consciousness of American Corporate Executives," *British Journal of Political Science* 8 (1978): 45–78; Theda Skocpol, "Political Response to Capitalist Crisis: Neo-Marxist Theories of the State and the Case of the New Deal," *Politics and Society* 10 (1980): 155–201; Robert F. Himmelberg, "Government and Business, 1917–1932: The Triumph of

'Corporate Liberalism'?" and Louis Galambos, "Foundation Stones for a New History of Business-Government Relations in Modern America," both in *Business and Government*, ed. Frese and Judd, 1–52; and Louis Galambos, *America at Middle Age.*

Theoretical works which informed the analysis of the National Recovery Administration and the National Labor Board/National Labor Relations Board in the text include Theodore J. Lowi, *The End of Liberalism: The Second Republic of the United States* (New York: W. W. Norton, 1969, 1979); Vera Lutz, *Central Planning for the Market Economy* (London: Longmans, 1969); Alan Wolfe, *The Limits of Legitimacy: Political Contradictions of Contemporary Capitalism* (New York: Free Press, 1977); James Buchanan, *The Demand and Supply of Public Goods* (Chicago: Rand McNally, 1968); Mancur Olson, *The Logic of Collective Action* (Cambridge: Harvard University Press, 1971); and William Loehr and Todd Sandler, *Public Goods and Public Policy* (Beverly Hills, Calif.: Sage Publications, 1978).

On the origins of the National Recovery Administration, one should begin with the debate over the Brains Trust discussed in Elliot A. Rosen, "Roosevelt and the Brains Trust: An Historiographical Overview," *Political Science Quarterly* 87 (1972): 531–63; Elliot A. Rosen, *Hoover, Roosevelt, and the Brains Trust: From Depression to New Deal* (New York: Columbia University Press, 1977); Bernard Sternsher, *Rexford Tugwell and the New Deal* (New Brunswick, N.J.: Rutgers University Press, 1964); Jordan A. Schwarz, *Liberal: Adolph A. Berle and the Vision of an American Era* (New York: Free Press, 1987). For the Brains Trusters' own evaluations, see Adolph Berle, *America's Recovery Program* (New York: Oxford University Press, 1934); Raymond Moley, *After Seven Years* (New York: Harper & Brothers, 1939); Raymond Moley, *The First New Deal* (New York: Harcourt, Brace and World, 1966); Rexford G. Tugwell, *The Industrial Discipline and the Government Arts* (New York: Columbia University Press, 1933); Rexford G. Tugwell, *The Battle for Democracy* (New York: Columbia University Press, 1935); Tugwell, *The Democratic Roosevelt* (Garden City, N.Y.: Doubleday, 1957); Tugwell, *The Brains Trust* (New York: Viking Press, 1968); Tugwell, *Roosevelt's Revolution: The First Year—A Personal Perspective* (New York: Macmillan, 1977). For Roosevelt's role, see Frank Freidel, *FDR: Launching the New Deal* (Boston: Little, Brown, 1973).

Studies of the NRA and the role of businessmen in it include Robert F. Himmelberg, *The Origins of the National Recovery Administration: Business, Government, and the Trade Association Issue, 1921–1933* (New York: Fordham University Press, 1976); Kim McQuaid, "Corporate Liberalism in the American Business Community, 1920–1940," *Business History Review* 52 (1978): 342–68; McQuaid, "The Business Advisory Council of the Department of Commerce, 1933–1961: A Study in Corporate/Government

Relations," *Research in Economic History* 1 (1976), ed. Paul Uselding (Greenwich, Conn.: JAI Press, 1976), 171–97; McQuaid, "The Frustration of Corporate Revival During the Early New Deal," *The Historian* 41 (1979): 682–704; John Kennedy Ohl, *Hugh S. Johnson and the New Deal* (DeKalb: Northern Illinois University Press, 1985); Hugh Johnson, *The Blue Eagle: From Egg to Earth* (Garden City, N.Y.: Doubleday, 1935); Leverett S. Lyon et al., *The National Recovery Administration* (Washington, D.C.: Brookings Institution, 1935); Michael M. Weinstein, *Recovery and Redistribution Under the NIRA* (New York: North-Holland Publishing Co., 1980); and Bernard Bellush, *The Failure of the NRA* (New York: W. W. Norton, 1975). For libertarian analyses of the NRA, see Jonathan R. T. Hughes, *The Governmental Habit: Economic Controls from Colonial Times to the Present* (New York: Basic Books, 1977), chap. 5; and Robert Higgs, *Crisis and Leviathan: Critical Episodes in the Growth of American Government* (New York: Oxford University Press, 1987), chap. 8.

Scholars rarely see the labor law reforms of the New Deal from the perspective of planning, though more recent scholarship has implications in this area. Standard works on the subject include Irving Bernstein, *The New Deal Collective Bargaining Policy* (Berkeley and Los Angeles: University of California Press, 1950); Irving Bernstein, *Turbulent Years: A History of the American Worker, 1933–1941* (Boston: Houghton Mifflin, 1969), esp. chap. 13; Milton Derber and Edwin Young, eds., *Labor and the New Deal* (Madison: University of Wisconsin Press, 1957); and Stanley Vittoz, *New Deal Labor Policy and the American Industrial Economy* (Chapel Hill: University of North Carolina Press, 1987). For the origins of New Deal labor policy, see J. Joseph Huthmacher, *Senator Robert F. Wagner and the Rise of Urban Liberalism* (New York: Atheneum, 1968); James A. Gross, *The Making of the National Labor Relations Board: A Study in Economics, Politics and the Law, 1933–1937* (Albany: State University of New York Press, 1974); James A. Gross, *The Reshaping of the National Labor Relations Board: National Labor Policy in Transition, 1937–1947* (Albany: State University of New York Press, 1981); Howell Harris, "The Snares of Liberalism? Politicians, Bureaucrats, and the Shaping of Federal Labor Relations Policy, 1915–47," in *Shop Floor Bargaining and the State: Historical and Comparative Perspectives*, ed. Steven Tolliday and Jonathan Zeitlin (Cambridge and New York: Cambridge University Press, 1985), 148–91.

More recently, Marxist scholars have revitalized the debate over the meaning of labor law and its institutional implementation as seen in Karl Klare, "Judicial Deradicalization of the Wagner Act and the Origins of Modern Legal Consciousness, 1937–1941," *Minnesota Law Review* 62 (1978): 265–339; Klare, "Labor Law as Ideology: Toward a New Historiography of Collective Bargaining Law," *Industrial Relations Law Journal* 4 (1981): 450–82; Klare, "Critical Theory and Labor Relations Law," in *The Politics of Law: A Progressive Critique*, ed. David Kairys (New York: Pantheon Books, 1982); a critique in Matthew Finkin, "Revisionism in Labor Law," *University of Maryland Law Review* 43 (1984): 23–92; and the important study, Christopher L. Tomlins, *The State and the Unions: Labor Relations, Law, and the Organized Labor Movement in America, 1880–1960* (Cambridge and New York: Cambridge University Press, 1985). On implementation of labor law, see Peter Irons, *The New Deal Lawyers* (Princeton: Princeton University Press, 1982).

Scholars of labor relations planning should pay close attention to the historical context as noted in the analysis of the interrelationships between labor law, leadership, rank and file militancy, and Democratic party politics in the rise of the CIO as discussed in Melvyn Dubofsky and Warren Van Tine, *John L. Lewis*. Works which deal with the extension of administrative law into the field of labor policy in the World War II years and beyond include Nelson Lichtenstein, *Labor's War At Home: The CIO in World War II* (Cambridge and New York: Cambridge University Press, 1982); Howell John Harris, *The Right to Manage: Industrial Relations Policies of American Business in the 1940s* (Madison: University of Wisconsin Press, 1982); David Brody, "The Uses of Power, I and II," *Workers in Industrial America*, 173–257; and David Montgomery, "American Workers and the New Deal Formula," in *Workers' Control in America*, 153–80.

ECONOMIC PLANNING IN WORLD WAR II

Economic mobilization and planning during World War II are discussed in Richard Polenberg, *War and Society: The United States, 1941–1945* (Philadelphia: J. B. Lippincott, 1972); Geoffrey Perrett, *Days of Sadness, Years of Triumph: The American People, 1939–1945* (1973; reprint, Baltimore: Penguin Books, 1974); John Morton Blum, *V Was for Victory: Politics and American Culture During World War II* (New York: Harcourt Brace Jovanovich, 1974); David Brody, "The New Deal and World War II," in *The New Deal: The National Level*, ed. John Braeman et al., 1: 267–309; and Harold G. Vatter, *The U.S. Economy in World War II* (New York: Columbia University Press, 1985). On the history of wage and price controls during the war, see U.S. Bureau of the Budget, *The United States at War* (Washington, D.C.: Government Printing Office, 1946); Harvey Mansfield, *A Short History of OPA* (Washington, D.C.: Office of Temporary Controls, 1947); and Hugh L. Rockoff, *Drastic Measures: A History of Wage and Price Controls in the United States* (Cambridge and New York: Cambridge University Press, 1984). For the political context in which the battle over controls was waged, see Roland Young, *Congressional Politics in the Second World War* (New York: Columbia University Press, 1956); Allen F. Matusow, *Farm Policies and Politics in the Truman Years* (Cambridge: Harvard University Press, 1967); and Andrew Hudson Bartels,

"The Politics of Price Control: The Office of Price Administration and the Dilemmas of Economic Stabilization, 1940–1946" (Ph.D. diss., Johns Hopkins University, 1980), summarized in Andrew H. Bartels, "The Office of Price Administration and the Legacy of the New Deal, 1939–1946," *The Public Historian* 5 (Summer 1983): 5–29.

Methodological sources for the editorial analysis in the text include Barbara Hobbie, *Oil Company Divestiture and the Press* (New York: Praeger Publishers, 1977); Klaus Krippendorf, *Content Analysis: An Introduction to Its Methodology* (Beverly Hills, Calif.: Sage Publications, 1980); Ole R. Holsti, *Content Analysis for the Social Sciences and Humanities* (Reading, Mass.: Addison-Wesley, 1969); and Ithiel de Sola Pool et al., *The Prestige Press: A Comparative Study of Political Symbols* (Cambridge: MIT Press, 1970). Editorials in the *New York Times* and the *Wall Street Journal* were consulted for the period from January 1945 through December 1946. For a similar study of the 1946 debate over the Office of Price Administration using a different data set, see Gordon P. Henderson, "Planning's Opponents: An Ideological Analysis of the Post World War Two Price Control Debate," *Northern Social Science Review* 11 (1986): 71–86.

Libertarian arguments regarding the "knowledge problem" are in Friedrich A. Hayek, *The Road to Serfdom* (Chicago: University of Chicago Press, 1944); and Milton Friedman, *Capitalism and Freedom* (Chicago: University of Chicago Press, 1962). Recent discussions of the problem include Charles E. Lindblom, *Politics and Markets: The World's Political-Economic Systems* (New York: Basic Books, 1977); Don Lavoie, *National Economic Planning*; and John Friedmann, *Planning in the Public Domain.*

OVERVIEWS OF POST–WORLD WAR II AMERICAN PLANNING

For planning since World War II—especially in regard to the contemporary debate—the interested reader can consult Samuel Bowles, David M. Gordon, and Thomas E. Weiskopf, *Beyond the Wasteland: A Democratic Alternative to Economic Decline* (Garden City, N.Y.: Anchor Press/Doubleday, 1983); Robert B. Reich, *The Next American Frontier* (New York: Times Books, 1983); Felix G. Rohatyn, *The Twenty-Year Century: Essays on Economics and Public Finance* (New York: Random House, 1983); Chalmers Johnson, ed., *The Industrial Policy Debate* (San Francisco: ICS Press, 1984); and essays in Claude E. Barfield and William A. Schambra, eds., *The Politics of Industrial Policy* (Washington, D.C.: American Enterprise Institute for Public Policy Research, 1986).

Index